Paramedic Licensing Exam

LearningExpress

NEW YORK

Library of Congress Cataloging-in-Publication Data
Paramedic licensing exam. -- *New York: Learning Express, 1998*

        p. cm.
    ISBN 1–57685–148–6
        1. Emergency medicine—Examinations, questions, etc.   2. Emergency
medical technicians—Licenses—United States.   I. LearningExpress (Organization)
    RC86.9.P34   1998
    616.02'5'076—dc21   98–26285
                                                                                                      CIP

Printed in the United States of America
9 8 7 6 5 4 3 2
First Edition

Regarding the Information in this Book

We attempt to verify the information presented in our books prior to publication. It is always a good idea, however, to double-check such important information as minimum requirements, application and testing procedures, and deadlines, as such information can change from time to time.

For Further Information

For information on LearningExpress, other LearningExpress products, or bulk sales, please call or write to us at:

    LearningExpress®
    900 Broadway
    Suite 604
    New York, NY 10003
    212-995-2566

ISBN 1–57685–148–6

7 85555 85148 1

FOREWORD

Licensing and certification examinations are inherently very stressful events. Proper preparation can ease the associated anxiety. This book is a valuable tool in preparing for both the written and practical portions of paramedic tests, including the National Registry of Emergency Medical Technicians Paramedic exam.

Steven C. Wood
EMS Specialist
San Diego, California

PRAISE FOR LEARNINGEXPRESS'S *EMT-Basic Exam*

As an EMT instructor, I want to do the best for my students that I can. I have found that I can allay their apprehensions and reinforce their knowledge by suggesting that each student review your book methodically, page by page, test by test, and answer by answer. It seems to be working well. My students are passing with an average well above the requirement and have the confidence they need to do well.

Catherine Bandy, R.N.
EMT Instructor
Los Angeles Unified School District

CONTENTS

C·H·A·P·T·E·R 1

ABOUT THE EMT-PARAMEDIC EXAM

CHAPTER SUMMARY

This chapter tells you how to become certified as an Emergency Medical Technician-Paramedic (EMT-Paramedic). It outlines the certification requirements of the National Registry of Emergency Medical Technicians and tells you how to use this book to study for the written exam.

T he National Registry of Emergency Medical Technicians (NR-EMT) was established in 1970 in response to a suggestion of the U.S. Committee on Highway Safety. Today, the NR-EMT is an independent, not-for-profit agency whose job is to certify that EMTs and paramedics have the knowledge and skills to do their jobs—to save lives and preserve health. By setting uniform national standards for training, testing, and continuing education, the NR-EMT helps ensure patient safety throughout the United States.

In some states, the NR-EMT certification process is the only licensure process for EMTs and paramedics. Other states have their own testing procedures. (A list of specific certification requirements for all fifty states is found in Chapter 8.) Both the NR-EMT and the state tests are based on the same curriculum, which is issued by the U.S. Department of Transportation. Therefore, whether you will be taking a state test or the NR-EMT test, you will be learning and studying the same material. This book is based on the NR-EMT written examination.

IMPORTANT ADDRESS & PHONE NUMBER

National Registry of Emergency Medical Technicians
P.O. Box 29233
Columbus, Ohio 43229
614-888-4484

MINIMUM REQUIREMENTS

To apply for national registration as an EMT-Paramedic with the NR-EMT, you must meet the following requirements:

- You must be at least 18 years old.
- You must hold current National Registry or state certification at the EMT-Basic level.
- You must have successfully completed a state-approved EMT-Paramedic program within the last two years.
- If your state does not mandate national EMT-Paramedic training, you must submit documentation of current state paramedic certification.
- You must truthfully complete the felony statement on the application and, if necessary, submit documentation.
- You must submit current CPR credentials.
- You must submit proof of your competence in EMT-Basic level skills, signed by the director of your training program or the service director of training and operations.

HOW TO APPLY

When you have met all the requirements outlined above and are ready to take the exam, contact the NR-EMT to obtain an application and find out where you can take the exam in your state. (See page 1 for address and phone number.)

When you contact the NR-EMT, you will find out whether the examination is administered through your state EMT office or whether you need to make individual arrangements to take the exam.

Finally, you must submit to the National Registry an application stating that you have met all the above requirements, accompanied by a $35 fee.

THE EMT-PARAMEDIC WRITTEN EXAM

The EMT-Paramedic written exam consists of 180 multiple-choice questions. The questions are divided into six major parts, each corresponding to a division or major section of the National Standard EMT-Paramedic Training Curriculum. The parts of the exam, which correspond exactly to the exams in this book, are given in the table below.

BREAKDOWN OF CONTENT AREAS OF THE EXAMS IN THIS BOOK

Content Area	Questions			
	Exam 1	**Exam 2**	**Exam 3**	**Exam 4**
Patient Assessment	1–29	1–34	1–34	1–30
Airway & Breathing	30–59	35–65	35–63	31–61
Circulation	60–92	66–98	64–97	62–96
Musculoskeletal, Behavioral, Neurological, Environmental	93–125	99–128	98–125	97–125
Children, OB/GYN	126–151	129–152	126–157	126–154
EMS Systems, Ethical, Legal, Communications, Documentation, Safety, Triage, and Transportation	152–180	153–180	158–180	155–180

To pass the exam, you must obtain a minimum score on each part of the exam, as well as an overall average score. Your exam results will indicate both your actual score, as well as the required minimum score for each part and the overall passing score for that particular examination. If you fail to obtain the overall passing score, or if you fail any part of the exam, you will fail the entire exam.

You are allowed three opportunities to pass the exam. If you fail on your third try, you must complete 48 hours of remedial training before you will be allowed to take the exam a fourth time.

THE EMT-PARAMEDIC PRACTICAL EXAMINATION

The practical exam consists of six stations, arranged as scenarios, that approximate the situations that the EMT-Paramedic will encounter in the prehospital setting. The stations match the National Standard EMT-Paramedic Training Curriculum, as well as current American Hospital Association standards.

To pass the practical exam, you must demonstrate competence in the following areas and sub-areas:

1. Patient Assessment/Management
   a. Primary survey/resuscitation
   b. Secondary survey

2. Ventilatory Management

3. Cardiac Arrest Skills
   a. Dynamic cardiology (managing a code)
   b. Static cardiology (interpreting ECG tracings)

4. IV and Medication Skills
   a. Intravenous therapy
   b. Intravenous bolus medications
   c. Intravenous piggyback medications

5. Spinal Immobilization (seated patient)

6. Random Basic Skills (includes two of the following):
   a. Bleeding-wounds-shock
   b. Long bone splinting
   c. Traction splinting
   d. Spinal immobilization (lying patient)

Chapter 7 contains the official NR-EMT Paramedic practical examination.

USING THIS BOOK TO PREPARE

In addition to the EMT-Paramedic practical exam, this book contains four complete written practice tests, each containing 180 items similar to those on the National Registry EMT-Paramedic written exam. The practice test items are grouped in content areas, just like the items on the EMT-Paramedic exam. The table on page 2 shows the breakdown of content areas in each of the practice tests in this book.

The first step in using this book to prepare for the EMT-Paramedic written examination is to read Chapter 2, which presents the nine-step EasySmart Test Preparation System. This chapter shows you essential test-taking strategies that you can practice as you take the exams in this book.

Next, take one complete practice exam and score your answers using the answer key. Complete explanations for the answers are included in the key. Remember, the passing score on the EMT-Paramedic exam varies, but in most cases it is approximately 75 percent of each section, and of the complete test, correct. If you score over 75 percent on your first practice test, and on each section of the test, congratulations! However, don't assume that you'll easily pass the actual test—the items on the test will be similar but not exactly like those on the practice test. You'll still need some test preparation. No matter what your initial score is, follow the suggestions in the next paragraphs.

If you score below 75 percent on the entire exam or on any part, don't panic, but do put in some concentrated study time. Begin by determining your major areas of weakness. For example, suppose you answered 60 items on the practice test incorrectly, giving you a score of 120, or approximately 67 percent. (To determine the percent correct, divide the number of correct answers by the total number of questions: $120 \div 180 = 0.667$.) On rereading the questions you missed, you find that they break down into the following content areas:

- Patient Assessment: missed 13 out of 30 questions
- Airway & Breathing: missed 7 out of 30 question
- Circulation: missed 14 out of 33 questions
- Musculoskeletal, Behavioral, Neurological, Environmental: missed 8 out of 33 questions
- Children & OB/GYN: missed 12 out of 26 questions
- EMS Systems, Ethical, Legal, Communications, Documentation, Safety, Triage and Transportion: missed 6 out of 28 questions

This analysis tells you that you did not achieve 75 percent correct in three areas: patient assessment, circulation, and children & OB/GYN. Try putting in one or two concentrated evenings of study on each of these areas. Review all materials on these topics in the textbook and printed materials from your paramedic training program. Then take a second practice test and check your total score and content area breakdown again. Chances are that both will have improved.

In the time leading up to the EMT-Paramedic written exam, use the remaining practice tests to further pinpoint areas of weakness and to find areas to review. For example, after several more study sessions, you take the third practice test. You now do well on all the questions in the circulation area except those that concern specific characteristics of dysrhythmias. That knowledge tells you what specific materials to review.

Once you have worked on and improved your areas of weakness, use the final days before the test to do some general "boning up." Devote a short period of time each day to reviewing several chapters of your textbook. Then use the fourth practice test to rehearse test-taking strategies and procedures.

After reading and studying this book, you'll be well on your way to obtaining certification as an EMT-Paramedic. Good luck as you advance in this rewarding and worthwhile career!

C·H·A·P·T·E·R

EASYSMART TEST PREPARATION SYSTEM

CHAPTER SUMMARY

Taking the EMT-Paramedic exam can be tough. It demands a lot of preparation if you want to achieve a top score, and your career in emergency medical services depends on your passing the exam. The EasySmart Test Preparation System, developed exclusively for LearningExpress by leading test experts, gives you the discipline and attitude you need to be a winner.

First, the bad news: Taking the EMT-Paramedic exam is no picnic, and neither is getting ready for it. Your future career as a paramedic depends on your getting a passing score, but there are all sorts of pitfalls that can keep you from doing your best on this all-important exam. Here are some of the obstacles that can stand in the way of your success:

- Being unfamiliar with the format of the exam
- Being paralyzed by test anxiety
- Leaving your preparation to the last minute
- Not preparing at all!

- Not knowing vital test-taking skills: how to pace yourself through the exam, how to use the process of elimination, and when to guess
- Not being in tip-top mental and physical shape
- Messing up on test day by arriving late at the test site, having to work on an empty stomach, or shivering through the exam because the room is cold

What's the common denominator in all these test-taking pitfalls? One word: *control.* Who's in control, you or the exam?

Now the good news: The EasySmart Test Preparation System puts *you* in control. In just nine easy-to-follow steps, you will learn everything you need to know to make sure that *you* are in charge of your preparation and your performance on the exam. *Other* test-takers may let the test get the better of them; *other* test-takers may be unprepared or out of shape, but not *you.* *You* will have taken all the steps you need to take to get a high score on the EMT-Paramedic exam.

Here's how the EasySmart Test Preparation System works: Nine easy steps lead you through everything you need to know and do to get ready to master your exam. Each of the steps listed below includes both reading about the step and one or more activities. It's important that you do the activities along with the reading, or you won't be getting the full benefit of the system. Each step tells you approximately how much time that step will take you to complete.

Step 1. Get Information	50 minutes
Step 2. Conquer Test Anxiety	20 minutes
Step 3. Make a Plan	30 minutes
Step 4. Learn to Manage Your Time	10 minutes
Step 5. Learn to Use the Process of Elimination	20 minutes
Step 6. Know When to Guess	20 minutes
Step 7. Reach Your Peak Performance Zone	10 minutes
Step 8. Get Your Act Together	10 minutes
Step 9. Do It!	10 minutes
Total	**3 hours**

We estimate that working through the entire system will take you approximately three hours, though it's perfectly OK if you work faster or slower than the time estimates assume. If you can take a whole afternoon or evening, you can work through the whole EasySmart Test Preparation System in one sitting. Otherwise, you can break it up, and do just one or two steps a day for the next several days. It's up to you—remember, *you're* in control.

STEP 1: GET INFORMATION

Time to complete: 50 minutes
Activities: Read Chapter 1, "The EMT-Paramedic Exam" and Chapter 8, "State Certification Requirements"
Knowledge is power. The first step in the EasySmart Test Preparation System is finding out everything you can about the EMT-Paramedic exam. Once you have your information, the next steps in the EasySmart Test Preparation System will show you what to do about it.

Part A: Straight Talk About the EMT-Paramedic Exam

Why do you have to take this exam, anyway? Simply put, because lives depend on your performance in the field. The EMT-Paramedic written exam is just one part of a whole series of evaluations you have to go through to show that you can be trusted with the health and safety of the people you serve. The written exam attempts to measure your knowledge of your trade. The practical skills exam attempts to measure your ability to apply what you know.

It's important for you to remember that your score on the EMT-Paramedic written exam does not determine how smart you are or even whether you will make a good paramedic. There are all kinds of things a written exam like this can't test: whether you are likely to show up late or call in sick a lot, whether you can keep your cool under the stress of trying to revive a victim of cardiac arrest, whether you can be trusted with confidential information about people's health. Those kinds of things are hard to evaluate, while whether you can fill in the right little circles on a bubble answer sheet is easy to evaluate.

This is not to say that filling in the right little circles is not important! The knowledge tested on the written exam is knowledge you will need to do your job. And your ability to enter the profession you've trained for depends on your passing this exam. And that's why you're here—using the EasySmart Test Preparation System to achieve control over the exam.

Part B: What's on the Test

If you haven't already done so, stop here and read Chapter 1 of this book, which gives you an overview of EMT-Paramedic written exams in general and the National Registry of Emergency Medical Technicians (NR-EMT) exam in particular.

Many states use the NR-EMT exam as their exam, but others do not. Turn to Chapter 8 for a state-by-state overview of certification requirements. If you haven't already gotten the full rundown on certification procedures as part of your training program, you can contact the state EMS agency listed in Chapter 8 for details.

STEP 2: CONQUER TEST ANXIETY

Time to complete: 20 minutes
Activity: Take the Test Stress Test

Having complete information about the exam is the first step in getting control of the exam. Next, you have to overcome one of the biggest obstacles to test success: test anxiety. Test anxiety can not only impair your performance on the exam itself; it can even keep you from preparing! In Step 2, you'll learn stress management techniques that will help you succeed on your exam. Learn these strategies now, and practice them as you work through the exams in this book, so they'll be second nature to you by exam day.

COMBATING TEST ANXIETY

The first thing you need to know is that a little test anxiety is a good thing. Everyone gets nervous before a big exam—and if that nervousness motivates you to prepare thoroughly, so much the better. It's said that Sir Laurence Olivier, one of the foremost British actors of this century, threw up before every performance. His stage fright didn't impair his performance; in fact, it probably gave him a little extra edge—just the kind of edge you need to do well, whether on a stage or in an examination room.

On the next page is the Test Stress Test. Stop here and answer the questions on that page, to find out whether your level of test anxiety is something you should worry about.

Stress Management Before the Test

If you feel your level of anxiety getting the best of you in the weeks before the test, here is what you need to do to bring the level down again:

- **Get prepared.** There's nothing like knowing what to expect and being prepared for it to put you in control of test anxiety. That's why you're reading this book. Use it faithfully, and remind yourself that you're better prepared than most of the people taking the test.
- **Practice self-confidence.** A positive attitude is a great way to combat test anxiety. This is no time to be humble or shy. Stand in front of the mirror and say to your reflection, "I'm prepared. I'm full of self-confidence. I'm going to ace this test. I know I can do it." Say it into a tape recorder and play it back once a day. If you hear it often enough, you'll believe it.
- **Fight negative messages.** Every time someone starts telling you how hard the exam is or how it's almost impossible to get a high score, start telling them your self-confidence messages above. If the someone with the negative messages is *you*, telling yourself *you don't do well on exams, you just can't do this*, don't listen. Turn on your tape recorder and listen to your self-confidence messages.

(continued on page 6)

Test Stress Test

You only need to worry about test anxiety if it is extreme enough to impair your performance. The following questionnaire will provide a diagnosis of your level of test anxiety. In the blank before each statement, write the number that most accurately describes your experience.

0 = Never   1 = Once or twice   2 = Sometimes   3 = Often

_____ I have gotten so nervous before an exam that I simply put down the books and didn't study for it.

_____ I have experienced disabling physical symptoms such as vomiting and severe headaches because I was nervous about an exam.

_____ I have simply not showed up for an exam because I was scared to take it.

_____ I have experienced dizziness and disorientation while taking an exam.

_____ I have had trouble filling in the little circles because my hands were shaking too hard.

_____ I have failed an exam because I was too nervous to complete it.

_____ **Total: Add up the numbers in the blanks above.**

Your Test Stress Score

Here are the steps you should take, depending on your score. If you scored:

- **Below 3,** your level of test anxiety is nothing to worry about; it's probably just enough to give you that little extra edge.
- **Between 3 and 6,** your test anxiety may be enough to impair your performance, and you should practice the stress management techniques listed in this section to try to bring your test anxiety down to manageable levels.
- **Above 6,** your level of test anxiety is a serious concern. In addition to practicing the stress management techniques listed in this section, you may want to seek additional, personal help. Call your local high school or community college and ask for the academic counselor. Tell the counselor that you have a level of test anxiety that sometimes keeps you from being able to take the exam. The counselor may be willing to help you or may suggest someone else you should talk to.

- **Visualize.** Imagine yourself reporting for duty on your first day as a paramedic. Think of yourself responding to calls, interacting with patients, preserving health and saving lives. Visualizing success can help make it happen—and it reminds you of why you're going to all this work in preparing for the exam.
- **Exercise.** Physical activity helps calm your body down and focus your mind. Besides, being in good physical shape can actually help you do well on the exam. Go for a run, lift weights, go swimming—and do it regularly.

Stress Management on Test Day

There are several ways you can bring down your level of test anxiety on test day. They'll work best if you practice them in the weeks before the test, so you know which ones work best for you.

- **Deep breathing.** Take a deep breath while you count to five. Hold it for a count of one, then let it out on a count of five. Repeat several times.
- **Move your body.** Try rolling your head in a circle. Rotate your shoulders. Shake your hands from the wrist. Many people find these movements very relaxing.
- **Visualize again.** Think of the place where you are most relaxed: lying on the beach in the sun, walking through the park, or whatever. Now close your eyes and imagine you're actually there. If you practice in advance, you'll find that you only need a few seconds of this exercise to experience a significant increase in your sense of well-being.

When anxiety threatens to overwhelm you right there during the exam, there are still things you can do to manage the stress level:

- **Repeat your self-confidence messages.** You should have them memorized by now. Say them quietly to yourself, and believe them!
- **Visualize one more time.** This time, visualize yourself moving smoothly and quickly through the test answering every question right and finishing just before time is up. Like most visualization techniques, this one works best if you've practiced it ahead of time.
- **Find an easy question.** Skim over the test until you find an easy question, and answer it. Getting even one circle filled in gets you into the test-taking groove.
- **Take a mental break.** Everyone loses concentration once in a while during a long test. It's normal, so you shouldn't worry about it. Instead, accept what has happened. Say to yourself, "Hey, I lost it there for a minute. My brain is taking a break." Put down your pencil, close your eyes, and do some deep breathing for a few seconds. Then you're ready to go back to work.

Try these techniques ahead of time, and see if they don't work for you!

STEP 3: MAKE A PLAN

Time to complete: 30 minutes
Activity: Construct a study plan

Maybe the most important thing you can do to get control of yourself and your exam is to make a study plan. Too many people fail to prepare simply because they fail to plan. Spending hours on the day before the exam poring over sample test questions not only raises your level of test anxiety, it also is simply no substitute for careful preparation and practice over time.

Don't fall into the cram trap. Take control of your preparation time by mapping out a study schedule. On the following pages are two sample schedules, based on the amount of time you have before you take the EMT-Paramedic written exam. If you're the kind of person who needs deadlines and assignments to motivate you for a project, here they are. If you're the kind of person who doesn't like to follow other people's plans, you can use the suggested schedules here to construct your own.

Even more important than making a plan is making a commitment. You can't review everything you learned in your paramedic course in one night. You have to set aside some time every day for study and practice. Try for at least 20 minutes a day. Twenty minutes daily will do you much more good than two hours on Saturday.

Don't put off your study until the day before the exam. Start now. A few minutes a day, with half an hour or more on weekends, can make a big difference in your score.

SCHEDULE A: THE 30-DAY PLAN

If you have at least a month before you take the EMT-Paramedic exam, you have plenty of time to prepare—as long as you don't waste it! If you have less than a month, turn to Schedule B.

Time	Preparation
Days 1–4	Skim over the written materials from your training program, particularly noting 1) areas you expect to be emphasized on the exam and 2) areas you don't remember well. On Day 4, concentrate on those areas.
Day 5	Take the first practice exam in Chapter 3.
Day 6	Score the first practice exam. Use the outline of skills on the test given in Chapter 1 to show you which are your strongest and weakest areas. Identify *two* areas that you will concentrate on before you take the second practice exam.
Days 7–10	Study the two areas you identified as your weak points. Don't worry about the other areas.
Day 11	Take the second practice exam in Chapter 4.
Day 12	Score the second practice exam. Identify *one* area to concentrate on before you take the third practice exam.
Days 13–18	Study the one area you identified for review. In addition, review both practice exams you've taken so far, with special attention to the answer explanations.
Day 19	Take the third practice exam in Chapter 5.
Day 20	Once again, identify *one* area to review, based on your score on the third practice exam.
Days 20–21	Study the one area you identified for review.
Days 22–25	Take an overview of *all* your training materials, consolidating your strengths and improving on your weaknesses.
Days 26–27	Review all the areas that have given you the most trouble in the three practice exams you've taken so far.
Day 28	Take the fourth practice exam in Chapter 6. Note how much you've improved!
Day 29	Review one or two weak areas.
Day before the exam	Relax. Do something unrelated to the exam and go to bed at a reasonable hour.

SCHEDULE B: THE 10-DAY PLAN

If you have two weeks or less before you take the exam, you may have your work cut out for you. Use this 10-day schedule to help you make the most of your time.

Time	Preparation
Day 1	Take the first practice exam in Chapter 3 and score it using the answer key at the end. Turn to the list of subject areas on the exam in Chapter 1, and find out which areas need the most work, based on your exam score.
Day 2	Review one area that gave you trouble on the first practice exam.
Day 3	Review another area that gave you trouble on the first practice exam.
Day 4	Take the second practice exam in Chapter 4 and score it.
Day 5	If your score on the second practice exam doesn't show improvement on the two areas you studied, review them. If you did improve in those areas, choose a new weak area to study today.
Day 6	Take the third practice exam in Chapter 5 and score it.
Day 7	Choose your weakest area from the third practice exam to review.
Day 8	Review any areas that you have not yet reviewed in this schedule.
Day 9	Take the fourth practice exam in Chapter 6 and score it.
Day 10	Use your last study day to brush up on any areas that are still giving you trouble.
Day before the exam	Relax. Do something unrelated to the exam and go to bed at a reasonable hour.

STEP 4: LEARN TO MANAGE YOUR TIME

Time to complete: 10 minutes to read, many hours of practice!
Activities: Practice these strategies as you take the sample tests in this book

Steps 4, 5, and 6 of the EasySmart Test Preparation System put you in charge of your exam by showing you test-taking strategies that work. Practice these strategies as you take the sample tests in this book, and then you'll be ready to use them on test day.

First, you'll take control of your time on the exam. Most EMT-Paramedic exams have a time limit, which may give you more than enough time to complete all the questions—or may not. It's a terrible feeling to hear the examiner say, "Five minutes left," when you're only three-quarters of the way through the test. Here are some tips to keep that from happening to *you*.

- **Follow directions.** If the directions are given orally, listen to them. If they're written on the exam booklet, read them carefully. Ask questions *before* the exam begins if there's anything you don't understand. If you're allowed to write in your exam booklet, write down the beginning time and the ending time of the exam.
- **Pace yourself.** Glance at your watch every few minutes, and compare the time to how far you've gotten in the test. When one-quarter of the time has elapsed, you should be a quarter of the way through the test, and so on. If you're falling behind, pick up the pace a bit.
- **Keep moving.** Don't dither around on one question. If you don't know the answer, skip the question and move on. Circle the number of the question in your test booklet in case you have time to come back to it later.
- **Keep track of your place on the answer sheet.** If you skip a question, make sure you skip on the answer sheet too. Check yourself every 5–10 questions to make sure the question number and the answer sheet number are still the same.
- **Don't rush.** Though you should keep moving, rushing won't help. Try to keep calm and work methodically and quickly.

STEP 5: LEARN TO USE THE PROCESS OF ELIMINATION

Time to complete: 20 minutes
Activity: Complete worksheet on Using the Process of Elimination

After time management, your next most important tool for taking control of your exam is using the process of elimination wisely. It's standard test-taking wisdom that you should always read all the answer choices before choosing your answer. This helps you find the right answer by eliminating wrong answer choices. And, sure enough, that standard wisdom applies to your exam, too.

Let's say you're facing a question that goes like this:

13. Which of the following lists of signs and symptoms indicates cardiac compromise?
   a. headache, dizziness, nausea, confusion
   b. dull chest pain, sudden sweating, difficulty breathing
   c. wheezing, labored breathing, chest pain
   d. difficulty breathing, high fever, rapid pulse

You should always use the process of elimination on a question like this, even if the right answer jumps out at you. Sometimes the answer that jumps out isn't right after all. Let's assume, for the purpose of this exercise, that you're a little rusty on your signs and symptoms of cardiac compromise, so you need to use a little intuition to make up for what you don't remember. Proceed through the answer choices in order.

So you start with answer **a**. This one is pretty easy to eliminate; none of these signs and symptoms is consistent with cardiac compromise. Mark an X next to choice **a** so you never have to look at it again.

On to the next. "Dull chest pain" looks good, though if you're not up on your cardiac signs and symptoms you might wonder if it should be "acute chest pain" instead. "Sudden sweating" and "difficulty breathing"? Check. And that's what you write next to answer **b**—a check mark, meaning "good answer, I might use this one."

Choice **c** is a possibility. Maybe you don't really expect wheezing in cardiac compromise, but you know "chest pain" is right, and let's say you're not sure whether "labored breathing" is a sign of cardiac difficulty. Put a question mark next to **c**, meaning "well, maybe."

Choice **d** strikes you about the same, with "difficulty breathing" being a good sign of cardiac compromise. But wait a minute. "High fever"? Not really. "Rapid pulse"? Well, maybe. This doesn't really sound like cardiac compromise, and you've already got a better answer picked out in choice **b**. If you're feeling sure of yourself, put an X next to this one. If you want to be careful, put a question mark.

Now your question looks like this:

13. Which of the following lists of signs and symptoms indicates cardiac compromise?
   ✕ **a.** headache, dizziness, nausea, confusion
   ✔ **b.** dull chest pain, sudden sweating, difficulty breathing
   ? **c.** wheezing, labored breathing, chest pain
   ? **d.** difficulty breathing, high fever, rapid pulse

You've got just one check mark, for a good answer. If you're pressed for time, you should simply mark answer **b** on your answer sheet. If you've got the time to be extra careful, you could compare your check-mark answer to your question-mark answers to make sure that it's better.

It's good to have a system for marking good, bad, and maybe answers. We're recommending this one:

× = bad
✔ = good
? = maybe

If you don't like these marks, devise your own system. Just make sure you do it long before test day—while you're working through the practice exams in this book—so you won't have to worry about it during the test.

Even when you think you're absolutely clueless about a question, you can often use process of elimination to get rid of one answer choice. If so, you're better prepared to make an educated guess, as you'll see in Step 6. More often, the process of elimination allows you to get down to only *two* possibly right answers. Then you're in a strong position to guess. And sometimes, even though you don't know the right answer, you find it simply by getting rid of the wrong ones, as you did in the example above.

Try using your powers of elimination on the questions in the worksheet Using the Process of Elimination beginning on the next page. The questions aren't about paramedic work; they're just designed to show you how the process of elimination works. The answer explanations for this worksheet show one possible way you might use the process to arrive at the right answer.

The process of elimination is your tool for the next step, which is knowing when to guess.

Using the Process of Elimination

Use the process of elimination to answer the following questions.

1. Ilsa is as old as Meghan will be in five years. The difference between Ed's age and Meghan's age is twice the difference between Ilsa's age and Meghan's age. Ed is 29. How old is Ilsa?
   a. 4
   b. 10
   c. 19
   d. 24

2. "All drivers of commercial vehicles must carry a valid commercial driver's license whenever operating a commercial vehicle." According to this sentence, which of the following people need NOT carry a commercial driver's license?
   a. a truck driver idling his engine while waiting to be directed to a loading dock
   b. a bus operator backing her bus out of the way of another bus in the bus lot
   c. a taxi driver driving his personal car to the grocery store
   d. a limousine driver taking the limousine to her home after dropping off her last passenger of the evening

3. Smoking tobacco has been linked to
   a. increased risk of stroke and heart attack
   b. all forms of respiratory disease
   c. increasing mortality rates over the past ten years
   d. juvenile delinquency

4. Which of the following words is spelled correctly?
   a. incorrigible
   b. outragous
   c. domestickated
   d. understandible

Answers

Here are the answers, as well as some suggestions as to how you might have used the process of elimination to find them.

1. **d.** You should have eliminated answer **a** off the bat. Ilsa can't be four years old if Meghan is going to be Ilsa's age in five years. The best way to eliminate other answer choices is to try plugging them in to the information given in the problem. For instance, for answer **b,** if Ilsa is 10, then Meghan must be 5. The difference in their ages is 5. The difference between Ed's age, 29, and Meghan's age, 5, is 24. Is 24 two times 5? No. Then answer **b** is wrong. You could eliminate answer **c** in the same way and be left with answer **d.**

2. **c.** Note the word *not* in the question, and go through the answers one by one. Is the truck driver in choice **a** "operating a commericial vehicle"? Yes, idling counts as "operating," so he needs to have a commercial driver's license. Likewise, the bus operator in answer **b** is operating a commercial vehicle; the question doesn't say the operator has to be on the street. The limo driver in **d** is operating a commercial vehicle, even if it doesn't have passenger in it. However, the cabbie in answer **c** is *not* operating a commercial vehicle, but his own private car.

3. **a.** You could eliminate answer **b** simply because of the presence of the word *all.* Such absolutes hardly ever appear in correct answer choices. Choice **c** looks attractive until you think a little about what you know—aren't *fewer* people smoking these days, rather than more? So how could smoking be responsible for a higher mortality rate? (If you didn't know that *mortality rate* means the rate at which people die, you might keep this choice as a possibility, but you'd still be able to eliminate two answers and have only two to choose from.) And choice **d** is plain silly, so you could eliminate that one, too. And you're left with the correct choice, **a.**

4. **a.** How you used the process of elimination here depends on which words you recognized as being spelled incorrectly. If you knew that the correct spellings were *outrageous, domesticated,* and *understandable,* then you were home free. Surely you knew that at least one of those words was wrong!

STEP 6: KNOW WHEN TO GUESS

Time to complete: 20 minutes
Activity: Complete worksheet on Your Guessing Ability
Armed with the process of elimination, you're ready to take control of one of the big questions in test-taking: Should I guess? The first and main answer is Yes. Some exams have what's called a "guessing penalty," in which a fraction of your wrong answers is subtracted from your right answers—but EMT-Paramedic exams don't tend to work like that. The number of questions you answer correctly yields your raw score. So you have nothing to lose and everything to gain by guessing.

The more complicated answer to the question "Should I guess?" depends on you—your personality and your "guessing intuition." There are two things you need to know about yourself before you go into the exam:

- Are you a risk-taker?
- Are you a good guesser?

You'll have to decide about your risk-taking quotient on your own. To find out if you're a good guesser, complete the worksheet Your Guessing Ability that begins on page 16. Frankly, even if you're a play-it-safe person with lousy intuition, you're still safe in guessing every time. The best thing would be if you could overcome your anxieties and go ahead and mark an answer. But you may want to have a sense of how good your intuition is before you go into the exam.

STEP 7: REACH YOUR PEAK PERFORMANCE ZONE

Time to complete: 10 minutes to read; weeks to complete!
Activity: Complete the Physical Preparation Checklist
To get ready for a challenge like a big exam, you have to take control of your physical, as well as your mental, state. Exercise, proper diet, and rest will ensure that your body works with, rather than against, your mind on test day, as well as during your preparation.

EXERCISE

If you don't already have a regular exercise program going, the time during which you're preparing for an exam is actually an excellent time to start one. And if you're already keeping fit—or trying to get that way—don't let the pressure of preparing for an exam fool you into quitting now. Exercise helps reduce stress by pumping wonderful good-feeling hormones called endorphins into your system. It also increases the oxygen supply throughout your body, including your brain, so you'll be at peak performance on test day.

(continued on page 19)

Your Guessing Ability

The following are ten really hard questions. You're not supposed to know the answers. Rather, this is an assessment of your ability to guess when you don't have a clue. Read each question carefully, just as if you did expect to answer it. If you have any knowledge at all of the subject of the question, use that knowledge to help you eliminate wrong answer choices. Use this answer grid to fill in your answers to the questions.

ANSWER GRID

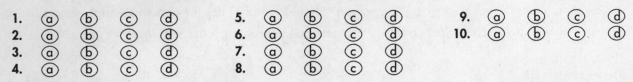

1. September 7 is Independence Day in
    a. India
    b. Costa Rica
    c. Brazil
    d. Australia

2. Which of the following is the formula for determining the momentum of an object?
    a. $p = mv$
    b. $F = ma$
    c. $P = IV$
    d. $E = mc^2$

3. Because of the expansion of the universe, the stars and other celestial bodies are all moving away from each other. This phenomenon is known as
    a. Newton's first law
    b. the big bang
    c. gravitational collapse
    d. Hubble flow

4. American author Gertrude Stein was born in
    a. 1713
    b. 1830
    c. 1874
    d. 1901

5. Which of the following is NOT one of the Five Classics attributed to Confucius?
   a. the I Ching
   b. the Book of Holiness
   c. the Spring and Autumn Annals
   d. the Book of History

6. The religious and philosophical doctrine that holds that the universe is constantly in a struggle between good and evil is known as
   a. Pelagianism
   b. Manichaeanism
   c. neo-Hegelianism
   d. Epicureanism

7. The third Chief Justice of the U.S. Supreme Court was
   a. John Blair
   b. William Cushing
   c. James Wilson
   d. John Jay

8. Which of the following is the poisonous portion of a daffodil?
   a. the bulb
   b. the leaves
   c. the stem
   d. the flowers

9. The winner of the Masters golf tournament in 1953 was
   a. Sam Snead
   b. Cary Middlecoff
   c. Arnold Palmer
   d. Ben Hogan

10. The state with the highest per capita personal income in 1980 was
    a. Alaska
    b. Connecticut
    c. New York
    d. Texas

Answers

Check your answers against the correct answers below.

1. c.	**5.** b.	**9.** d.
2. a.	**6.** b.	**10.** a.
3. d.	**7.** b.	
4. c.	**8.** a.	

How Did You Do?

You may have simply gotten lucky and actually known the answer to one or two questions. In addition, your guessing was more successful if you were able to use the process of elimination on any of the questions. Maybe you didn't know who the third Chief Justice was (question 7), but you knew that John Jay was the first. In that case, you would have eliminated answer **d** and therefore improved your odds of guessing right from one in four to one in three.

According to probability, you should get 2 1/2 answers correct, so getting either two or three right would be average. If you got four or more right, you may be a really terrific guesser. If you got one or none right, you may be a really bad guesser.

Keep in mind, though, that this is only a small sample. You should continue to keep track of your guessing ability as you work through the sample questions in this book. Circle the numbers of questions you guess on as you make your guess; or, if you don't have time while you take the practice tests, go back afterward and try to remember which questions you guessed at. Remember, on a test with four answer choices, your chances of getting a right answer is one in four. So keep a separate "guessing" score for each exam. How many questions did you guess on? How many did you get right? If the number you got right is at least one-fourth of the number of questions you guessed on, you are at least an average guesser, maybe better—and you should always go ahead and guess on the real exam. If the number you got right is significantly lower than one-fourth of the number you guessed on, you would, frankly, be safe in guessing anyway, but maybe you'd feel more comfortable if you guessed only selectively, when you can eliminate a wrong answer or at least have a good feeling about one of the answer choices.

A half hour of vigorous activity—enough to raise a sweat—every day should be your aim. If you're really pressed for time, every other day is OK. Choose an activity you like and get out there and do it. Jogging with a friend always makes the time go faster, or take a radio.

But don't overdo. You don't want to exhaust yourself. Moderation is the key.

DIET

First of all, cut out the junk. Go easy on caffeine and nicotine, and eliminate alcohol and any other drugs from your system at least two weeks before the exam. Promise yourself a binge the night after the exam, if need be.

What your body needs for peak performance is simply a balanced diet. Eat plenty of fruits and vegetables, along with protein and carbohydrates. Foods that are high in lecithin (an amino acid), such as fish and beans, are especially good "brain foods."

The night before the exam, you might "carbo-load" the way athletes do before a contest. Eat a big plate of spaghetti, rice and beans, or whatever your favorite carbohydrate is.

REST

You probably know how much sleep you need every night to be at your best, even if you don't always get it. Make sure you do get that much sleep, though, for at least a week before the exam. Moderation is important here, too. Extra sleep will just make you groggy.

If you're not a morning person and your exam will be given in the morning, you should reset your internal clock so that your body doesn't think you're taking an exam at 3 a.m. You have to start this process well before the exam. The way it works is to get up half an hour earlier each morning, and then go to bed half an hour earlier that night. Don't try it the other way around; you'll just toss and turn if you go to bed early without having gotten up early. The next morning, get up another half an hour earlier, and so on. How long you will have to do this depends on how late you're used to getting up. Use the Physical Preparation Checklist on the next page to make sure you're in tip-top form.

STEP 8: GET YOUR ACT TOGETHER

Time to complete: 10 minutes to read; time to complete will vary
Activity: Complete Final Preparations worksheet
You're in control of your mind and body; you're in charge of test anxiety, your preparation, and your test-taking strategies. Now it's time to take charge of external factors, like the testing site and the materials you need to take the exam.

FIND OUT WHERE THE TEST IS AND MAKE A TRIAL RUN

The testing agency or your EMS instructor will notify you when and where your exam is being held. Do you know how to get to the testing site? Do you know how long it will take to get there? If not, make a trial run, preferably on the same day of the week at the same time of day. Make note, on the worksheet Final Preparations on page 23,

(continued on page 22)

Physical Preparation Checklist

For the week before the test, write down 1) what physical exercise you engaged in and for how long and 2) what you ate for each meal. Remember, you're trying for at least half an hour of exercise every other day (preferably every day) and a balanced diet that's light on junk food.

Exam minus 7 days
Exercise: _____ for _____ minutes
Breakfast: _____
Lunch: _____
Dinner: _____
Snacks: _____

Exam minus 6 days
Exercise: _____ for _____ minutes
Breakfast: _____
Lunch: _____
Dinner: _____
Snacks: _____

Exam minus 5 days
Exercise: _____ for _____ minutes
Breakfast: _____
Lunch: _____
Dinner: _____
Snacks: _____

Exam minus 4 days
Exercise: _____ for _____ minutes
Breakfast: _____
Lunch: _____
Dinner: _____
Snacks: _____

Exam minus 3 days

Exercise: _____ for _____ minutes

Breakfast: _____

Lunch: _____

Dinner: _____

Snacks: _____

Exam minus 2 days

Exercise: _____ for _____ minutes

Breakfast: _____

Lunch: _____

Dinner: _____

Snacks: _____

Exam minus 1 day

Exercise: _____ for _____ minutes

Breakfast: _____

Lunch: _____

Dinner: _____

Snacks: _____

of the amount of time it will take you to get to the exam site. Plan on arriving 10–15 minutes early so you can get the lay of the land, use the bathroom, and calm down. Then figure out how early you will have to get up that morning, and make sure you get up that early every day for a week before the exam.

GATHER YOUR MATERIALS

The night before the exam, lay out the clothes you will wear and the materials you have to bring with you to the exam. Plan on dressing in layers; you won't have any control over the temperature of the examination room. Have a sweater or jacket you can take off if it's warm. Use the checklist on the worksheet Final Preparations on page 23 to help you pull together what you'll need.

Don't Skip Breakfast

Even if you don't usually eat breakfast, do so on exam morning. A cup of coffee doesn't count. Don't do dough-nuts or other sweet foods, either. A sugar high will leave you with a sugar low in the middle of the exam. A mix of protein and carbohydrates is best: cereal with milk and just a little sugar, or eggs with toast, will do your body a world of good.

STEP 9: DO IT!

Time to complete: 10 minutes, plus test-taking time
Activity: Ace the EMT-Paramedic exam!
Fast forward to exam day. You're ready. You made a study plan and followed through. You practiced your test-taking strategies while working through this book. You're in control of your physical, mental, and emotional state. You know when and where to show up and what to bring with you. In other words, you're better prepared than most of the other people taking the EMT-Paramedic exam with you. You're psyched.

Just one more thing. When you're done with the exam, you will have earned a reward. Plan a celebration. Call up your friends and plan a party, or have a nice dinner for two—whatever your heart desires. Give yourself something to look forward to.

And then do it. Go into the exam, full of confidence, armed with test-taking strategies you've practiced till they're second nature. You're in control of yourself, your environment, and your performance on the exam. You're ready to succeed. So do it. Go in there and ace the exam. And look forward to your future career as a paramedic!

Final Preparations

Getting to the Exam Site

Location of exam site: _____

Date: _____

Departure time: _____

Do I know how to get to the exam site? Yes _____ No _____
If no, make a trial run.

Time it will take to get to exam site: _____

Things to lay out the night before

Clothes I will wear   _____

Sweater/jacket   _____

Watch   _____

Photo ID   _____

4 No. 2. pencils   _____

_____   _____

_____   _____

PARAMEDIC PRACTICE EXAM 1

3

CHAPTER SUMMARY

This is the first of four practice exams in this book based on the National Registry EMT-Paramedic written exam. Use this test to find out how much you remember from your training program and where your strengths and weaknesses lie.

Like the other tests in this book, this test is based on the National Registry's written exam for Paramedics. See Chapter 1 for a complete description of this exam.

Take this first exam in as relaxed a manner as you can, without worrying about timing. You can time yourself on the other three exams. You should, however, make sure that you have enough time to take the entire exam at one sitting, at least two hours. Find a quiet place where you can work without being interrupted.

The answer sheet you should use is on the following page, and then comes the exam. The correct answers, each fully explained, come after the exam. When you have read and understood the answer explanations, turn to Chapter 1 for an explanation of how to score your exam.

1.	ⓐ	ⓑ	ⓒ	ⓓ		46.	ⓐ	ⓑ	ⓒ	ⓓ		91.	ⓐ	ⓑ	ⓒ	ⓓ
2.	ⓐ	ⓑ	ⓒ	ⓓ		47.	ⓐ	ⓑ	ⓒ	ⓓ		92.	ⓐ	ⓑ	ⓒ	ⓓ
3.	ⓐ	ⓑ	ⓒ	ⓓ		48.	ⓐ	ⓑ	ⓒ	ⓓ		93.	ⓐ	ⓑ	ⓒ	ⓓ
4.	ⓐ	ⓑ	ⓒ	ⓓ		49.	ⓐ	ⓑ	ⓒ	ⓓ		94.	ⓐ	ⓑ	ⓒ	ⓓ
5.	ⓐ	ⓑ	ⓒ	ⓓ		50.	ⓐ	ⓑ	ⓒ	ⓓ		95.	ⓐ	ⓑ	ⓒ	ⓓ
6.	ⓐ	ⓑ	ⓒ	ⓓ		51.	ⓐ	ⓑ	ⓒ	ⓓ		96.	ⓐ	ⓑ	ⓒ	ⓓ
7.	ⓐ	ⓑ	ⓒ	ⓓ		52.	ⓐ	ⓑ	ⓒ	ⓓ		97.	ⓐ	ⓑ	ⓒ	ⓓ
8.	ⓐ	ⓑ	ⓒ	ⓓ		53.	ⓐ	ⓑ	ⓒ	ⓓ		98.	ⓐ	ⓑ	ⓒ	ⓓ
9.	ⓐ	ⓑ	ⓒ	ⓓ		54.	ⓐ	ⓑ	ⓒ	ⓓ		99.	ⓐ	ⓑ	ⓒ	ⓓ
10.	ⓐ	ⓑ	ⓒ	ⓓ		55.	ⓐ	ⓑ	ⓒ	ⓓ		100.	ⓐ	ⓑ	ⓒ	ⓓ
11.	ⓐ	ⓑ	ⓒ	ⓓ		56.	ⓐ	ⓑ	ⓒ	ⓓ		101.	ⓐ	ⓑ	ⓒ	ⓓ
12.	ⓐ	ⓑ	ⓒ	ⓓ		57.	ⓐ	ⓑ	ⓒ	ⓓ		102.	ⓐ	ⓑ	ⓒ	ⓓ
13.	ⓐ	ⓑ	ⓒ	ⓓ		58.	ⓐ	ⓑ	ⓒ	ⓓ		103.	ⓐ	ⓑ	ⓒ	ⓓ
14.	ⓐ	ⓑ	ⓒ	ⓓ		59.	ⓐ	ⓑ	ⓒ	ⓓ		104.	ⓐ	ⓑ	ⓒ	ⓓ
15.	ⓐ	ⓑ	ⓒ	ⓓ		60.	ⓐ	ⓑ	ⓒ	ⓓ		105.	ⓐ	ⓑ	ⓒ	ⓓ
16.	ⓐ	ⓑ	ⓒ	ⓓ		61.	ⓐ	ⓑ	ⓒ	ⓓ		106.	ⓐ	ⓑ	ⓒ	ⓓ
17.	ⓐ	ⓑ	ⓒ	ⓓ		62.	ⓐ	ⓑ	ⓒ	ⓓ		107.	ⓐ	ⓑ	ⓒ	ⓓ
18.	ⓐ	ⓑ	ⓒ	ⓓ		63.	ⓐ	ⓑ	ⓒ	ⓓ		108.	ⓐ	ⓑ	ⓒ	ⓓ
19.	ⓐ	ⓑ	ⓒ	ⓓ		64.	ⓐ	ⓑ	ⓒ	ⓓ		109.	ⓐ	ⓑ	ⓒ	ⓓ
20.	ⓐ	ⓑ	ⓒ	ⓓ		65.	ⓐ	ⓑ	ⓒ	ⓓ		110.	ⓐ	ⓑ	ⓒ	ⓓ
21.	ⓐ	ⓑ	ⓒ	ⓓ		66.	ⓐ	ⓑ	ⓒ	ⓓ		111.	ⓐ	ⓑ	ⓒ	ⓓ
22.	ⓐ	ⓑ	ⓒ	ⓓ		67.	ⓐ	ⓑ	ⓒ	ⓓ		112.	ⓐ	ⓑ	ⓒ	ⓓ
23.	ⓐ	ⓑ	ⓒ	ⓓ		68.	ⓐ	ⓑ	ⓒ	ⓓ		113.	ⓐ	ⓑ	ⓒ	ⓓ
24.	ⓐ	ⓑ	ⓒ	ⓓ		69.	ⓐ	ⓑ	ⓒ	ⓓ		114.	ⓐ	ⓑ	ⓒ	ⓓ
25.	ⓐ	ⓑ	ⓒ	ⓓ		70.	ⓐ	ⓑ	ⓒ	ⓓ		115.	ⓐ	ⓑ	ⓒ	ⓓ
26.	ⓐ	ⓑ	ⓒ	ⓓ		71.	ⓐ	ⓑ	ⓒ	ⓓ		116.	ⓐ	ⓑ	ⓒ	ⓓ
27.	ⓐ	ⓑ	ⓒ	ⓓ		72.	ⓐ	ⓑ	ⓒ	ⓓ		117.	ⓐ	ⓑ	ⓒ	ⓓ
28.	ⓐ	ⓑ	ⓒ	ⓓ		73.	ⓐ	ⓑ	ⓒ	ⓓ		118.	ⓐ	ⓑ	ⓒ	ⓓ
29.	ⓐ	ⓑ	ⓒ	ⓓ		74.	ⓐ	ⓑ	ⓒ	ⓓ		119.	ⓐ	ⓑ	ⓒ	ⓓ
30.	ⓐ	ⓑ	ⓒ	ⓓ		75.	ⓐ	ⓑ	ⓒ	ⓓ		120.	ⓐ	ⓑ	ⓒ	ⓓ
31.	ⓐ	ⓑ	ⓒ	ⓓ		76.	ⓐ	ⓑ	ⓒ	ⓓ		121.	ⓐ	ⓑ	ⓒ	ⓓ
32.	ⓐ	ⓑ	ⓒ	ⓓ		77.	ⓐ	ⓑ	ⓒ	ⓓ		122.	ⓐ	ⓑ	ⓒ	ⓓ
33.	ⓐ	ⓑ	ⓒ	ⓓ		78.	ⓐ	ⓑ	ⓒ	ⓓ		123.	ⓐ	ⓑ	ⓒ	ⓓ
34.	ⓐ	ⓑ	ⓒ	ⓓ		79.	ⓐ	ⓑ	ⓒ	ⓓ		124.	ⓐ	ⓑ	ⓒ	ⓓ
35.	ⓐ	ⓑ	ⓒ	ⓓ		80.	ⓐ	ⓑ	ⓒ	ⓓ		125.	ⓐ	ⓑ	ⓒ	ⓓ
36.	ⓐ	ⓑ	ⓒ	ⓓ		81.	ⓐ	ⓑ	ⓒ	ⓓ		126.	ⓐ	ⓑ	ⓒ	ⓓ
37.	ⓐ	ⓑ	ⓒ	ⓓ		82.	ⓐ	ⓑ	ⓒ	ⓓ		127.	ⓐ	ⓑ	ⓒ	ⓓ
38.	ⓐ	ⓑ	ⓒ	ⓓ		83.	ⓐ	ⓑ	ⓒ	ⓓ		128.	ⓐ	ⓑ	ⓒ	ⓓ
39.	ⓐ	ⓑ	ⓒ	ⓓ		84.	ⓐ	ⓑ	ⓒ	ⓓ		129.	ⓐ	ⓑ	ⓒ	ⓓ
40.	ⓐ	ⓑ	ⓒ	ⓓ		85.	ⓐ	ⓑ	ⓒ	ⓓ		130.	ⓐ	ⓑ	ⓒ	ⓓ
41.	ⓐ	ⓑ	ⓒ	ⓓ		86.	ⓐ	ⓑ	ⓒ	ⓓ		131.	ⓐ	ⓑ	ⓒ	ⓓ
42.	ⓐ	ⓑ	ⓒ	ⓓ		87.	ⓐ	ⓑ	ⓒ	ⓓ		132.	ⓐ	ⓑ	ⓒ	ⓓ
43.	ⓐ	ⓑ	ⓒ	ⓓ		88.	ⓐ	ⓑ	ⓒ	ⓓ		133.	ⓐ	ⓑ	ⓒ	ⓓ
44.	ⓐ	ⓑ	ⓒ	ⓓ		89.	ⓐ	ⓑ	ⓒ	ⓓ		134.	ⓐ	ⓑ	ⓒ	ⓓ
45.	ⓐ	ⓑ	ⓒ	ⓓ		90.	ⓐ	ⓑ	ⓒ	ⓓ		135.	ⓐ	ⓑ	ⓒ	ⓓ

136.	(a)	(b)	(c)	(d)		151.	(a)	(b)	(c)	(d)		166.	(a)	(b)	(c)	(d)
137.	(a)	(b)	(c)	(d)		152.	(a)	(b)	(c)	(d)		167.	(a)	(b)	(c)	(d)
138.	(a)	(b)	(c)	(d)		153.	(a)	(b)	(c)	(d)		168.	(a)	(b)	(c)	(d)
139.	(a)	(b)	(c)	(d)		154.	(a)	(b)	(c)	(d)		169.	(a)	(b)	(c)	(d)
140.	(a)	(b)	(c)	(d)		155.	(a)	(b)	(c)	(d)		170.	(a)	(b)	(c)	(d)
141.	(a)	(b)	(c)	(d)		156.	(a)	(b)	(c)	(d)		171.	(a)	(b)	(c)	(d)
142.	(a)	(b)	(c)	(d)		157.	(a)	(b)	(c)	(d)		172.	(a)	(b)	(c)	(d)
143.	(a)	(b)	(c)	(d)		158.	(a)	(b)	(c)	(d)		173.	(a)	(b)	(c)	(d)
144.	(a)	(b)	(c)	(d)		159.	(a)	(b)	(c)	(d)		174.	(a)	(b)	(c)	(d)
145.	(a)	(b)	(c)	(d)		160.	(a)	(b)	(c)	(d)		175.	(a)	(b)	(c)	(d)
146.	(a)	(b)	(c)	(d)		161.	(a)	(b)	(c)	(d)		176.	(a)	(b)	(c)	(d)
147.	(a)	(b)	(c)	(d)		162.	(a)	(b)	(c)	(d)		177.	(a)	(b)	(c)	(d)
148.	(a)	(b)	(c)	(d)		163.	(a)	(b)	(c)	(d)		178.	(a)	(b)	(c)	(d)
149.	(a)	(b)	(c)	(d)		164.	(a)	(b)	(c)	(d)		179.	(a)	(b)	(c)	(d)
150.	(a)	(b)	(c)	(d)		165.	(a)	(b)	(c)	(d)		180.	(a)	(b)	(c)	(d)

PARAMEDIC EXAM 1

1. During a stress reaction, the signs of a Stage I alarm include
   a. normal vital signs
   b. increased vital signs that quickly return to normal
   c. increased pulse rate and pupillary dilatation
   d. lowered pulse rate and blood pressure

2. Which root word means *blue*?
   a. cyan-
   b. melan-
   c. buce-
   d. hyster-

3. The E of the ABCDE's of primary assessment stands for
   a. edema
   b. expiration
   c. erythema
   d. expose

4. The secondary assessment of a patient begins after you have
   a. controlled immediate threats to the patient's life
   b. transported the patient to the hospital
   c. secured the scene and gained access to the patient
   d. contacted medical control

Answer questions 5–6 on the basis of the information below.

You are called to the scene of an elderly patient complaining of severe abdominal and back pain. Upon further questioning, the patient states that the pain is "all over the left side." On palpation you feel a pulsating mass in the abdomen.

5. This patient is most likely suffering from
   a. pulsating diaphragm lesions
   b. acute arterial occlusion
   c. acute pulmonary embolism
   d. abdominal aortic aneurysm

6. This patient's vital signs have been worsening steadily over the length of the call. Treatment for this patient should consist of
   a. shock position, high-flow oxygen, PASG, and IV volume replacement
   b. low-flow oxygen, nitroglycerin, and atropine
   c. PASG with legs inflated only, IV, and dopamine
   d. IV, low-flow oxygen, and isoproterenol

7. *Rales* are best described as
   a. coarse, wet sounds
   b. high-pitched whistles
   c. fine crackling sounds
   d. gasping sounds

8. The posterior tibial pulse is assessed near the
   a. arch of the foot
   b. ankle bone
   c. base of the thumb
   d. base of the ear

9. Which question would you ask to assess the P part of the AMPLE acronym?
   a. "Are you taking any prescription medicines?"
   b. "What have you had to eat and drink in the past 24 hours?"
   c. "Have you recently been sick or had any surgery?"
   d. "What were you doing when you felt sick?"

10. Which patient should be transported immediately, with minimal on-scene care and attempts at stabilization en route?
    a. female, age 45, pulse 132, systolic BP 78
    b. male, age 60, respiratory rate 12, pulse 115
    c. female, age 28, systolic BP 96, one suspected long bone fracture
    d. male, age 54, Glasgow Coma Scale score 14, respiratory rate 15

11. The collective change in vital signs associated with increasing intracranial pressure consists of
    a. quickening pulse rate, shallow respirations, increasing blood pressure
    b. slowing pulse rate, deep or erratic respirations, increasing blood pressure
    c. rapid and shallow pulse, deep respirations, decreasing blood pressure
    d. quickening pulse rate, shallow respirations, decreasing blood pressure

12. If your patient has an open abdominal wound with a loop of bowel obtruding, you should apply
    a. a gauze pad and tell the patient to hold it in place
    b. an occlusive dressing secured on three sides
    c. a wet sterile dressing and then an occlusive dressing
    d. a clean gauze dressing taped on all four sides

13. Which patient is NOT likely to be a candidate for rapid transport?
    a. a 33-year-old female, hit by a car travelling 40 mph
    b. a 28-year-old male, pulse 134, BP 80/50
    c. a 48-year-old male, fell 30 feet down an elevator shaft
    d. a 56-year-old female, burns to 9 percent of BSA

14. An unconscious patient who has one dilated pupil that is reactive to light is showing early signs of
    a. transient ischemic attacks
    b. cerebral aneurysm
    c. status epilepticus
    d. increased intracranial pressure

15. Your patient converses with you and answers most questions appropriately but is unsure of where she is or who you are. Her mental status is best described as
    a. unresponsive
    b. responsive to painful stimuli
    c. responsive to verbal stimuli
    d. alert

Answer questions 16–20 on the basis of the information below.

You respond on a 28-year-old male who fell approximately 25 feet from a scaffolding and landed feet first.

16. You might expect all of the following injuries EXCEPT
    a. sternal fracture
    b. lumbar spinal pain
    c. femur fracture
    d. ankle fracture

17. Because the victim landed on his feet at first, the force of the fall might result in compression fractures of the
    a. lumbar vertebrae
    b. cervical vertebrae
    c. thoracic vertebrae
    d. coccyx vertebrae

18. After landing on his feet, the patient then fell forward. This forward fall might result in all of the following EXCEPT
    a. wrist injuries
    b. shoulder injuries
    c. clavicle fractures
    d. pelvic fractures

19. Because this was a 25-foot fall, another possible injury with grave results might be
    a. lounge avulsions
    b. calcaneus fractures
    c. aortic tears
    d. pneumothorax

20. Treatment for this patient should consist of
    a. IV via micro-drip, oxygen, splinting
    b. large bore IV, oxygen, spinal immobilization, splinting
    c. spinal immobilization, sodium bicarbonate, splinting
    d. spinal immobilization, cardiac monitoring, epinephrine

21. A positive tilt test suggests that a patient
    a. has appendicitis
    b. is hypovolemic
    c. has peritonitis
    d. is a diabetic

22. A patient with an acute abdomen who shows no signs of hemorrhage and has stable vital signs should be positioned
    a. in whatever position is most comfortable for the patient
    b. in a prone position
    c. in shock position
    d. sitting upright

23. Secondary assessment of the abdomen of a patient who is complaining of abdominal pain should consist of
    a. percussion
    b. auscultation
    c. gentle palpation
    d. repeated tests for rebound tenderness

24. Your patient is a 28-year-old diver who has been using SCUBA equipment and shows signs of reduced level of consciousness just after a dive. You should suspect
    a. Type I decompression sickness
    b. Type II decompression sickness
    c. air embolism
    d. pneumomediastinum

25. Drug dosages are lower in elderly patients than in young adults primarily because elderly patients
    a. weigh more on average
    b. have a slower rate of elimination
    c. forget to take their medication
    d. sell drugs to obtain needed food supplies

26. Which statement about the pain that accompanies an MI is INCORRECT?
    a. Patients often describe the pain as "crushing."
    b. The pain is present when the patient is at rest.
    c. The pain is relieved by sublingual nitroglycerin.
    d. The pain is not usually brought on by exertion.

27. Which set of vital signs is consistent with left heart failure?
    a. BP 100/60, P 48 and regular, R 8 and shallow
    b. BP 130/80, P 68 and irregular, R 14 and normal
    c. BP 160/100, P 108 and irregular, R 26 and labored
    d. BP 170/110, P 76 and irregular, R 22 and shallow

28. Which of the following is an example of an open-ended question?
    a. What kinds of things make you feel sad?
    b. Do you feel sad right now?
    c. Do you want to go to the hospital?
    d. Will you feel better if your wife comes along with us?

29. Which of the following distress signals requires immediate corrective action from the paramedic?
    a. decreased alertness to surroundings
    b. increased or decreased food intake
    c. complaints of feeling overwhelmed
    d. nausea

Answer questions 30–33 on the basis of the information below.

You are called to the home of an elderly female who is having difficulty breathing. She has a history of chronic congestive heart failure.

30. Which vital-sign pattern is possible for this patient?
    a. increased respiratory rate, decreased pulse rate, flushed dry skins
    b. deep labored respirations, decreased pulse rate, hot dry skins
    c. shallow rapid respirations, increased pulse rate, cool clammy skins
    d. shallow rapid respirations, decreased pulse rate, cool clammy skins

31. Which of the following are common medications associated with patients with chronic CHF?
a. thiamine, nitroglycerine, and albuterol
b. penicillin, digoxin, and theophylline
c. diuretics, calcium, and Coumadin
d. diuretics, potassium, and digoxin

32. The lung sounds you would expect to hear from this patient are
a. basilar wheezes
b. rales and/or rhonchi
c. clear but diminished sounds in the upper lobes
d. rhonchi in the upper lobes only

33. Which of the following best describes the pathophysiology of CHF?
a. heart failure resulting in pulmonary edema
b. aortic failure resulting in pulmonary edema
c. pneumonia resulting in pulmonary edema
d. superior vena cave failure resulting in pulmonary edema

34. The purpose of performing Sellick's maneuver is to
a. visualize the upper airway structures
b. prevent the tongue from blocking the airway
c. protect a patient with possible spinal injury
d. prevent vomiting during attempts at intubation

35. In order to maintain adequate oxygenation, an attempt to intubate a patient should last no longer than
a. 10 seconds
b. 15 seconds
c. 30 seconds
d. 45 seconds

36. To ensure proper placement of the endotracheal tube, you should
a. confirm tube placement by two different methods
b. place the tube only under medical direction
c. check breath sounds in the chest before and after placement
d. visualize the open glottis, then withdraw the laryngoscope before tube placement

37. The digital intubation method is used for patients who
a. have short, fat necks
b. are very old or very young
c. have arthritis
d. have suspected spinal injury

38. Nasotracheal intubation should NOT be attempted in patients who
a. are very obese
b. have suspected basilar skull fracture
c. have recently undergone oral surgery
d. are suspected of having spinal injury

39. When suctioning a patient, you should always
   a. begin suctioning after the catheter is placed in the patient's airway
   b. limit attempts at suctioning to no more than 45 seconds at a time
   c. ventilate the patient after every three suction attempts
   d. insert the catheter while the suctioning apparatus is turned on

40. Your patient exhibits signs and symptoms of shock, including cold, clammy skin; air hunger; distended neck veins; tracheal displacement; and absent breath sounds on one side. You should suspect
   a. tension pneumothorax
   b. flail chest
   c. massive hemothorax
   d. pericardial tamponade

41. Signs of circulatory overload in a patient who is receiving IV fluids include
   a. dyspnea, rales, and rhonchi
   b. agitation and cold, clammy skin
   c. falling blood pressure
   d. Trauma Score lower than 10

42. For an adult patient who is conscious but who has a complete airway obstruction, your FIRST action should be to
   a. deliver five rapid abdominal thrusts
   b. use the jaw-thrust/chin-lift technique
   c. pinch the patient's nostrils and attempt to give two ventilations
   d. attempt finger sweeps

43. If the patient is not too hypoxic, treatment for someone who is suffering an exacerbation of either emphysema or chronic bronchitis is to
   a. transport to the hospital rapidly
   b. administer high-flow oxygen, establish an IV line, place the patient on an EKG monitor, and administer bronchodilators as ordered
   c. establish an airway, position the patient seated or semi-seated, administer low-flow oxygen, establish an IV line
   d. establish an airway, administer oxygen at the highest possible concentration, establish an IV line, transport rapidly

44. The most commonly used drug and method of delivery for patients with asthma is
   a. corticosteroids given intravenously
   b. epinephrine given via inhaler
   c. albuterol given via inhaler
   d. methylprednisolone given intramuscularly

45. A recommended way to measure respiratory rate is to
   a. use a Wright Meter to determine peak expiratory flow rate
   b. tell the patient to remain quiet while you count his or her respirations
   c. carry on a conversation with the patient to distract him or her while you count
   d. place your hand on the patient's wrist as if you were measuring his or her pulse

Answer questions 46–49 on the basis of the information below.

You respond to a college fraternity where you encounter a 19-year-old male with a partially obstructed airway. According to witnesses, he was eating pizza and drinking beer when he began to cough and grab his throat. The patient is able to speak in a hoarse whisper only, and he has been coughing repeatedly for about 20 minutes.

46. The best treatment for this patient would be
   a. chest thrusts
   b. back blows
   c. continued repeated coughing
   d. a laryngoscopy and McGill forceps

47. Should this patient suddenly become unable to cough or speak, treatment would then include
   a. chest thrusts
   b. back blows
   c. abdominal thrusts
   d. a laryngoscopy and McGill forceps

48. Should this patient become unconscious, the treatment may then include all of the following EXCEPT
   a. chest thrusts
   b. back blows
   c. repositioning the airway
   d. a laryngoscopy and McGill forceps

49. Should the obstruction be relieved, which of the following treatments should be performed?
   a. encourage the patient to seek private medical attention the next morning
   b. have the patient's friends monitor him through the night and, if necessary, drive him to the emergency room
   c. utilize direct laryngoscopy to ensure that the airway is clear
   d. insist upon transport by medics to the emergency room

50. The breathing pattern characterized by periods of apnea followed by periods in which respirations first increase, then decrease, in depth and frequency is
   a. central neurogenic hyperventilation
   b. apneustic respirations
   c. Cheyne-Stokes breathing
   d. diaphragmatic respirations

51. The pathophysiological result of near drowning in sea water is
   a. ventricular fibrillation
   b. pulmonary edema
   c. pulmonary embolism
   d. metabolic alkalosis

Answer questions 52–57 on the basis of the information below.

You respond along with fire unit to the scene of a structure fire. Fire fighters have rescued a 25-year-old female who is unconscious and unresponsive to verbal or painful stimuli. The victim was located in a smoke-filled bedroom on the floor above the actual fire. A physical exam reveals cherry-red mucous membranes. Vital signs are a blood pressure of 146/80; a pulse of 128, strong and regular with a sinus tachycardia on the EKG; and a respiratory rate of 40, rapid but apparently effective with generally clear lung sounds and a mild expiratory wheeze. You note no burn injuries.

52. What would account for the patient's level of consciousness?
   a. Toxic byproducts of combustion have depressed her central nervous system.
   b. The environment that she was found in was sufficiently hot to cause a form of heat stroke.
   c. She is suffering from carbon monoxide poisoning.
   d. She is suffering from carbon dioxide poisoning.

53. Pulse oximetry readings should be scrutinized because high
   a. carbon monoxide levels can cause an inaccurately high reading of the percentage of oxygen saturation
   b. carbon monoxide levels can cause an inaccurately low reading of the percentage of oxygen saturation
   c. carbon dioxide levels can cause an inaccurately high reading of the percentage of oxygen saturation
   d. carbon dioxide levels can cause an inaccurately low reading of the percentage of oxygen saturation

54. Treatment for this type of toxic exposure should include all of the following EXCEPT
   a. high-flow oxygen
   b. sodium bicarbonate
   c. transport to a hyperbaric facility
   d. close monitoring for onset of seizures

55. Other signs of this type of exposure include all of the following EXCEPT
   a. cyanotic skins
   b. cherry-red skins
   c. chest pain
   d. hyperactivity

56. Common sources of the colorless, odorless gas that is responsible for this patient's condition include all of the following EXCEPT
   a. engine exhaust
   b. cellular respiration/cellular metabolism
   c. burning of combustible materials
   d. improperly ventilated space heaters

57. Which of the following best describes the difficulty the rescuer faces in reversing this patient's condition?
   a. As compared to oxygen, carbon monoxide has a 200x affinity for hemoglobin.
   b. As compared to oxygen, carbon dioxide has a 200x affinity for hemoglobin.
   c. Carbon monoxide is weakly associated with hemoglobin and is therefore difficult to remove from the blood.
   d. Carbon dioxide is weakly associated with hemoglobin and is therefore difficult to remove from the blood.

58. Which of the following is a disease that is associated with cigarette smoking and is related to but distinct from emphysema?
   a. chronic bronchitis
   b. pleurisy
   c. pneumothorax
   d. hemothorax

59. The primary drug for the management of anaphylaxis is
   a. diphenhydramine HCL
   b. methylprednisolone
   c. atropine
   d. epinephrine

60. You have started an IV line, but the fluid is not flowing properly. The first thing you should do is
   a. remove the cannula and try another site
   b. make sure the constricting band has been removed
   c. request help from medical control
   d. lower the IV bag below the level of the patient's arm

61. Which patient would benefit from application of the PASG?
   a. 10-year-old male, suspected spinal fracture, no blood loss
   b. 72-year-old female, suspected cardiogenic shock
   c. 40-year-old male, suspected lower extremity fracture, low blood pressure
   d. 67-year-old female, suspected ankle sprain, high blood pressure

62. Care for the patient with cardiac contusion is similar to care for the patient with
   a. closed abdominal trauma
   b. pericardial tamponade
   c. tension pneumothorax
   d. myocardial infarction

63. Which statement about use of Nitronox in the field is INCORRECT?
   a. Nitronox is a long-acting agent that is administered intravenously.
   b. Nitronox is used to manage pain in patients with chest trauma.
   c. Nitronox may cause nausea and vomiting.
   d. Nitronox should not be used for patients with head injury.

64. The Seldinger technique allows you to
   a. calculate the amount of fluid replacement a patient needs
   b. pass a large-gauge catheter into a peripheral vein
   c. infuse fluids quickly under pressure
   d. estimate the patient's Trauma Score accurately and quickly

65. Which statement about care of the patient who is suffering from complications of dialysis is correct?
    a. You should obtain blood pressure readings on the arm on which the shunt is located.
    b. You should use the shunt for easy IV access.
    c. Monitoring for dysrhythmias is unnecessary in dialysis patients.
    d. Start an IV only if ordered by medical control.

66. The leading cause of death in the elderly is
    a. respiratory emergency
    b. trauma
    c. cancer
    d. cardiovascular disease

67. Which information CANNOT be determined from a single-lead ECG?
    a. heart rate
    b. heartbeat regularity
    c. time period of electrical impulse
    d. presence of an infarct

68. The QRS complex on an ECG tracing reflects
    a. atrial depolarization
    b. ventricular depolarization
    c. ventricular repolarization
    d. atrial resting phase

69. A QRS complex is considered ABNORMAL if it lasts longer than
    a. 0.04 seconds
    b. 0.08 seconds
    c. 0.10 seconds
    d. 0.12 seconds

70. Treatment for a patient whose ECG shows premature atrial contractions includes
    a. observation only, if the patient is asymptomatic
    b. vagal maneuvers and adenosine, 6 mg, rapid IV push over 1–3 seconds
    c. lidocaine, 1–1.5 mg/kg IV push
    d. digoxin, beta blockers, or diltiazem

71. The term *bradycardia* refers to
    a. a heart rate lower than 60
    b. a heart rate greater than 150
    c. congestive heart failure
    d. sinus tachycardia

72. The clinical significance of a first-degree AV block is that it
    a. signals the onset of rapid cardiovascular decompensation
    b. indicates that the heart rate may drop
    c. can lead to syncope and angina
    d. may foreshadow a more advanced dysrhythmia

73. Wolf-Parkinson-White syndrome is characterized by
    a. QRS complex shorter than 0.12 seconds
    b. short P-R interval and long QRS complex
    c. lengthened and bizarre QRS complex
    d. inverted P waves and normal QRS complex

74. In which situation would you consider having the patient perform a Valsalva maneuver to slow the heart rate?
a. male, age 34, paroxysmal junctional tachycardia
b. male, age 68, idioventricular rhythm
c. female, age 74, premature ventricular contractions
d. female, age 39, ventricular tachycardia

75. Which rhythm is likely to foreshadow the development of other, more serious dysrhythmias?
a. paroxysmal junctional tachycardia
b. isolated premature atrial contractions
c. accelerated junctional rhythm
d. sinus dysrhythmia

76. Prolonged sinus tachycardia accompanying an acute myocardial infarction suggests that
a. cardiogenic shock may develop
b. damage to the heart is minimal
c. hypervolemia is the underlying cause
d. the diagnosis of MI is incorrect

77. To check for jugular vein distention, you should position the patient
a. lying flat on his or her back
b. sitting upright
c. standing up
d. seated at a 45-degree angle

78. A carotid artery bruit indicates the presence of
a. good peripheral perfusion
b. blockage of the vessel
c. jugular vein distention
d. congestive heart failure

79. Intermittent *claudication* refers to
a. difficulty breathing due to congestive heart failure
b. nausea and vomiting
c. dizziness
d. pain in the leg brought on by walking

80. The pain of stable angina is brought on by
a. exercise or stress
b. imminent MI
c. difficulty breathing
d. overuse of nitroglycerin

81. In the care of patients with suspected MI, epinephrine is used to
a. alleviate pain
b. avoid ventricular fibrillation
c. alleviate tachycardias
d. relieve anxiety

82. A patient's signs and symptoms include orthopnea, spasmodic coughing, agitation, cyanosis, rales, jugular vein distention, elevated blood pressure, pulse, and respirations. You should suspect
a. left heart failure
b. right heart failure
c. stable angina
d. cardiogenic shock

83. The management of right heart failure by itself consists of
  a. high-flow oxygen, IV of D5W with minidrip set, baseline ECG, medications including dopamine and norepinephrine, rapid transport
  b. high-flow oxygen, IV of D5W with minidrip set, baseline ECG, medications including morphine sulfate and furosemide, rapid transport
  c. high-flow oxygen, IV of D5W with minidrip set, baseline ECG
  d. shock treatment, including oxygen, IV fluids, and PASG

84. Sodium nitroprusside (Nipride) is used in the treatment of
  a. deep venous thrombosis
  b. myocardial infarction
  c. hypertensive emergency
  d. cardiogenic shock

85. Which of the following drugs is an antidysrhythmic agent?
  a. furosemide
  b. lidocaine
  c. nitroglycerin
  d. isoproterenol

86. In performing emergency synchronized cardioversion, you would synchronize the electrical shock with the
  a. P wave
  b. R wave
  c. P-R interval
  d. QRS complex

87. The P wave on an ECG strip reflects what event inside the heart?
  a. atrial depolarization
  b. ventricular polarization
  c. ventricular repolarization
  d. atrial repolarization

88. Treatment for a patient who is experiencing an attack of stable angina consists of
  a. oxygen and defibrillation
  b. rest, oxygen, nitroglycerin or Procardia
  c. reassurance, oxygen, start IV, ECG monitoring, pain relief
  d. seat patient upright, start IV, ECG, furosemide

89. The wheezing associated with left heart failure results from
  a. fluid in the alveoli
  b. chronic asthma
  c. associated right heart failure
  d. chest pain

90. The function of epinephrine in patients in cardiac arrest is to
  a. decrease anxiety
  b. treat bradycardia
  c. manage tachycardia
  d. manage dysrhythmia

91. A primary reason for administering high-flow oxygen to a patient with MI is to
  a. help limit the infarct size
  b. prevent pulmonary edema
  c. ease pain and reduce anxiety
  d. treat ventricular dysrhythmias

92. The primary use of procainimide in MI patients is to
   a. manage bradycardia
   b. relieve anxiety
   c. reduce pain
   d. treat dysrhythmia

Answer questions 93–96 on the basis of the information below.

You respond on a 22-year-old male who is complaining of rapid onset of chest pain and hemiplegia. The patient states that the pain is tearing and sharp and that it started shortly after he completed a SCUBA dive to 85 feet. The patient's diving partner stated that the patient surfaced too rapidly.

93. This patient is most likely suffering from
   a. acute pulmonary edema
   b. nitrogen narcosis
   c. decompression sickness
   d. pulmonary embolism

94. Treatment for this patient consists of
   a. IV, low-flow oxygen, and transport to the nearest emergency department
   b. IV, high-flow oxygen, and transport to a recompression chamber
   c. IV, demand valve positive pressure ventilation and monitoring, and transport to the nearest emergency department
   d. IV, monitoring, low-flow oxygen, and transport to a recompression chamber

95. Due to his rapid ascent, this patient may also be suffering from which other diving-related emergency?
   a. nitrogen narcosis
   b. acute pulmonary edema
   c. decompression sickness
   d. pneumonia

96. This second possible problem is associated with
   a. an increase in carbon dioxide in the interstitial spaces
   b. nitrogen bubbles entering tissue spaces and smaller blood vessels
   c. an increase in oxygen levels in the interstitial spaces
   d. nitrogen gases collecting in the alveolar space

97. Skeletal muscle is also referred to as
   a. voluntary muscle
   b. cardiac muscle
   c. involuntary muscle
   d. smooth muscle

98. The term *abduction* refers to
   a. movement toward the body
   b. the act of bending
   c. movement away from the body
   d. the act of rotating the arm

99. You would be likely to receive an order to administer intravenous thiamine to a patient who appeared to be
   a. in status epilepticus
   b. in shock
   c. hyperventilating
   d. profoundly intoxicated

100. In a patient with a head injury, you would use the halo sign to check for
   a. pupil reactivity
   b. increased intracranial pressure
   c. brain stem injury
   d. cerebrospinal fluid leakage

101. The rule for splinting fractures that are within three inches of a joint or dislocation is to
   a. manipulate the joint to ensure the presence of distal pulses before splinting
   b. splint the injury in the position the patient is found
   c. use the ladder splint after manipulating the joint
   d. not splint the injury

102. A greenstick fracture is one that is
   a. open
   b. impacted
   c. partial
   d. comminuted

103. To care for a patient with a suspected pelvic fracture, you should
   a. apply the PASG, start two IVs, and monitor for signs of shock
   b. immobilize the patient to a spine board and transport immediately
   c. align the lower limbs, apply splints, and administer analgesics
   d. do not immobilize; monitor distal pulse and sensation and transport immediately

104. Your patient has a chemical burn to her face and eyes. You should
   a. cover the area with a dry, sterile dressing
   b. apply rubbing alcohol
   c. apply a neutralizing agent
   d. flush the area with clean, cool water

105. Local cooling should be used to treat minor burns that cover no more than
   a. 5 percent of BSA
   b. 10 percent of BSA
   c. 20 percent of BSA
   d. 30 percent of BSA

106. A burn wound that blisters is an example of a
   a. first-degree burn
   b. second-degree burn
   c. third-degree burn
   d. chemical burn

107. An adult who has burns over both sides of one arm and both sides of one leg would be estimated to have total burns over
   a. 9 percent of BSA
   b. 18 percent of BSA
   c. 27 percent of BSA
   d. 36 percent of BSA

108. Your patient is a comatose 56-year-old male. His breath smells fruity and sweet, and his respirations are very deep and rapid. After undertaking the primary assessment, you should
a. draw blood, start an IV of 0.9 percent sodium chloride, and administer insulin
b. draw blood, start an IV of normal saline, and administer 50 percent dextrose
c. administer oxygen, start an IV of Ringer's lactate, and transport immediately
d. administer oxygen, monitor vital signs, and administer beta-blockers as directed

109. Signs of hypoglycemia include
a. nausea and vomiting; tachycardia; abdominal pain; deep, rapid respirations
b. weak, rapid pulse; cold, clammy skin; headache; irritability; coma
c. shallow, rapid breathing; low blood pressure; warm, dry skin; irritability
d. decreased blood pressure, pulse, and respirations; loss of consciousness

110. Naloxone is given to patients who are suspected of having
a. narcotics overdose
b. Wernicke's syndrome
c. Korsakoff's psychosis
d. increased intracranial pressure

111. Another word for *syncope* is
a. seizure
b. aura
c. fainting
d. stroke

112. A patient presents with symptoms of flushing, itching, hives, difficulty breathing, decreased blood pressure, and dizziness. You should suspect
a. diabetic coma
b. anaphylaxis
c. acute appendicitis
d. stroke

113. The first drug given to patients with severe allergic reactions is
a. epinephrine
b. diphenhydramine (Benadryl)
c. albuterol
d. insulin

114. The purpose of giving inhaled beta agonists to patients with severe allergic reactions is to
a. increase heart rate and strengthen the heart's contractile force
b. block histamine receptors
c. suppress the inflammatory response
d. reverse bronchospasm and laryngeal edema

115. The correct dosage of syrup of ipecac for an adult patient is
a. 15 mL, followed by 15 mL/kg of fluids
b. 30 mL, followed by 15 mL/kg of fluids
c. 25 g, mixed with water
d. 50 g, mixed with water

116. Classic symptoms of overdose narcotics are
a. euphoria, dilated pupils
b. hyperactivity, hypertension
c. respiratory depression, constricted pupils
d. cardiac dysrhythmias, altered mental status

117. Your patient is a farmer who has employed a crop duster to spray his fields. The farmer is exhibiting nausea and vomiting, diarrhea, and excessive salivation. You should suspect
   a. organophosphate poisoning
   b. bee or wasp sting
   c. snake bite
   d. overdose of amphetamines

118. Your patient is a 26-year-old man who is alert to verbal stimuli and has a body temperature of 104° F. The patient also complains of muscle cramps and headache. A friend with whom he has been playing tennis reports that the patient has drunk only 1 liter of water in the past 3 hours. You should suspect
   a. heat stroke
   b. water intoxication
   c. heat exhaustion
   d. myocardial infarction

119. Which patient presents the signs and symptoms of moderate hypothermia?
   a. male, age 34, core temperature 85.8° F
   b. female, age 28, core temperature 88.8° F
   c. female, age 47, core temperature 95.8° F
   d. male, age 39, core temperature 96.4° F

120. The correct treatment for a frostbitten body part is to
   a. warm the affected part in water maintained at 100–106° F
   b. rub the affected part in ice or snow
   c. keep the affected part frozen; thawing should be attempted only in the hospital
   d. cover the frozen part tightly in occlusive dressings

121. Which of the following statements regarding the complications in assessing elderly patients is NOT accurate?
   a. Elderly patients are sometimes unable to describe their symptoms accurately.
   b. Elderly patients are likely to fake illnesses.
   c. Elderly patients may suffer from more than one disease at a time.
   d. Elderly patients may be unable to communicate clearly.

122. Degeneration of the vertebrates is referred to as
   a. spondylosis
   b. osteoporosis
   c. kyphosis
   d. fibrosis

123. Your patient is a 46-year-old man with a long history of mental illness. He appears depressed and withdrawn. Suddenly, he begins to sob uncontrollably. You should
   a. administer a sedative
   b. attempt to calm him by putting your arms around him
   c. maintain a quiet, listening attitude
   d. ask him what is making him feel sad

124. Depression is an example of a
   a. psychiatric illness
   b. psychosis
   c. mood disorder
   d. organic disease

125. In the field, Benadryl (diphenhydramine) may be administered to schizophrenic patients to
   a. treat manic symptoms
   b. counteract catatonic symptoms
   c. raise blood pressure and respiratory rate
   d. counteract medication reactions

126. Which of the following represents a significant mechanism of injury?
   a. a child is in a medium-speed car accident
   b. an adult falls from a 6-foot-high ledge
   c. an adult pedestrian is hit by a bicycle
   d. a child falls from a 6-foot-high ledge

127. Your patient is a 10-year-old boy who has fallen off his bicycle. When obtaining the history of the accident, you should
   a. insist on speaking only to the responsible adult
   b. suspect child abuse until the possibility is eliminated
   c. suspect abnormal musculoskeletal development
   d. obtain as much information as possible from the child

Answer questions 128–132 on the basis of the information below.

You arrive to find a 6-year-old boy on the floor of his classroom, unconscious, incontinent, and responsive to pain only. The substitute teacher states that the child began to shake violently for approximately 2 minutes and has been unconscious ever since. She knows that he takes phenobarbital because she gave him one at lunch, but she is unable to provide further medical history.

128. This child most likely suffers from
   a. diabetes mellitus
   b. diabetes insipidus
   c. seizure disorder
   d. diabetes juvenalis

129. Phenobarbital is an example of a
   a. synthetic form of insulin
   b. sedative/anticonvulsant
   c. hypoglycemic
   d. diuretic

130. If this child is on medication, why did he have this episode at school?
   a. Medications only limit the number of seizures a person has; they do not always obliterate the seizures.
   b. Medication for this disorder does not completely control the amount of glucose available for cellular metabolism.
   c. This child may have had too much to eat at school, thus overriding the medication's ability to regular blood sugar.
   d. This child obviously only takes his medication while he is at school.

131. Treatment for this patient should include
   a. a 50% dextrose solution
   b. a 25% dextrose solution
   c. valium
   d. oxygen and monitoring

132. This patient should be transported to a hospital because
   a. he needs a lumbar puncture to determine if he has meningitis
   b. medication levels need to be determined by laboratory analysis
   c. glucose levels need to be determined by laboratory analysis
   d. this will absolve the school of any responsibility for this child

133. Normal systolic blood pressure in a 3-year-old is
   a. 50–70
   b. 70–95
   c. 80–100
   d. 90–120

134. The average 6-year-old weighs approximately
   a. 45 pounds, or 20 kg
   b. 56 pounds, or 25 kg
   c. 70 pounds, or 32 kg
   d. 75 pounds, or 34 kg

135. In cases of suspected child abuse, the paramedic's primary goal is to make sure that the
   a. abuser is punished severely
   b. abuser is arrested
   c. child is removed from the family
   d. child receives necessary treatment

136. All pediatric patients who have had seizures should be
   a. given diazepam
   b. transported to a hospital
   c. evaluated for signs of child abuse
   d. given acetaminophen

137. Your patient is Carlos, age 10 months. Carlos is wheezing and has a fever of 100.6° F. You should suspect
   a. asthma
   b. epiglottitis
   c. bronchiolitis
   d. croup

138. Cardiac arrest in children is most commonly associated with all of the following EXCEPT
   a. drowning
   b. choking
   c. smoke inhalation
   d. underlying cardiac disease processes

139. Assessment of a patient who is a victim of sexual assault should include
   a. complete vaginal exam
   b. detailed questions about the assault
   c. reassurance and respect
   d. a bath and douche

140. A *primipara* is a woman who has
   a. never had a child
   b. delivered her first child
   c. had more than one child
   d. been pregnant only once

141. Which statement characterizes normal changes in vital signs during pregnancy?
   a. Blood pressure falls; pulse rate rises.
   b. Blood pressure falls; pulse rate falls.
   c. Blood pressure rises; pulse rate rises.
   d. Blood pressure rises; pulse rate falls.

142. You are recording vital signs in a 34-year-old woman who is 8 months pregnant. Blood pressure is 100/70, pulse rate is 80, and respirations are 17 per minute and normal. You also hear a mild systolic flow murmur. You should
a. transport the patient immediately
b. establish an IV, administer high-flow oxygen, and monitor vital signs every 2 minutes
c. document your findings; this is normal
d. assess the patient for signs and symptoms of left heart failure

143. Your patient is a 29-year-old woman who is 9 months pregnant with her third child. She reports bright red vaginal bleeding, but no pain. You should
a. perform a vaginal exam
b. check for crowning
c. wait for delivery and then transport both mother and child to the hospital
d. treat for signs and symptoms of shock and transport immediately

144. Your patient is a 35-year-old woman who is 8 months pregnant. You note that her blood pressure is 140/90 and edema is present. The patient is anxious and complains of headache. You should suspect
a. pregnancy-induced hypertension
b. preeclampsia
c. eclampsia
d. abruptio placentae

145. You are assisting in a delivery in the field. As the baby's head is born, you realize that the umbilical cord is wrapped around the baby's neck. You should
a. attempt to slip it over the head
b. cut the cord immediately
c. transport immediately
d. position the patient as for a prolapsed cord

146. A neonate that had a pink body and blue extremities, a pulse rate of 90, a positive grimace response, active motion, and irregular respiratory effort would have an Apgar score of
a. 4
b. 6
c. 8
d. 10

147. Care for a newborn born with evidence of meconium staining includes
a. suctioning, followed by removal of meconium under direct visualization
b. suctioning, followed by resuscitation with the bag-valve-mask unit
c. reporting the presence of meconium to the medical control physician after administering oxygen
d. chest compressions, followed by administration of high-flow oxygen

148. You would NOT administer positive-pressure ventilations to a newborn if which of the following conditions were present?
a. apnea
b. heart rate less than 100
c. central cyanosis after oxygen is administered
d. meconium staining

Answer questions 149–151 on the basis of the information below.

You respond to the home of a 2-year-old female who is experiencing labored and difficult breathing. The child's mother states that she has had a cold for the past several days and a seal-like bark for the past 20 minutes. A physical exam reveals a fever of 102° F and hot, dry skin. Inspiratory stridor is heard upon auscultation of lung sounds. Vital signs are a blood pressure of 100/70, a pulse rate of 100, and a respiratory rate of 40, labored and with sternal in-drawing noted.

149. This patient is most likely suffering from
   a. upper respiratory obstruction
   b. asthma
   c. pneumonia
   d. croup

150. Treatment of this child would consist of
   a. examination of the oropharynx with a tongue blade
   b. direct visualization of the vocal chords
   c. albuterol
   d. nebulized saline mist

151. A related disease or condition that can result in rapid and total airway obstruction is
   a. bronchitis
   b. epiglottitis
   c. bronchiolitis
   d. laryngitis

152. The term *ethics* refers to
   a. professional standards of care
   b. rules, standards, and morals
   c. upgrading standards of care
   d. continuing education programs

153. A *tiered* response system is one that
   a. dispatches responders at various levels, depending on the incident
   b. dispatches ALS responders first to all emergencies
   c. does not have ALS responders
   d. uses laypersons as first responders

154. Congress passed the Emergency Medical Services System Act in
   a. 1966
   b. 1971
   c. 1972
   d. 1973

155. Ultimate responsibility for patient care in the field always rests with the
   a. paramedic
   b. EMT
   c. medical control physician
   d. mobile intensive care nurse

156. A state law that defines the scope of practice and role of paramedics and other prehospital workers is called
   a. delegation of authority
   b. a good Samaritan law
   c. a medical practice act
   d. durable power of attorney

157. Which of the following situations represents *expressed consent*?
   a. The patient says, "Help me. My chest hurts."
   b. The patient is a small child with no parent present.
   c. The patient is unconscious.
   d. The patient says, "I don't need any help. Just let me die."

158. An intoxicated person refuses treatment or transport. You should first
   a. do as the patient wishes and leave
   b. find a family member to give consent for treatment
   c. try to persuade the person to accept help
   d. carefully document the refusal

159. The paramedic's report about the patient's medical condition should include all of the following EXCEPT the patient's
   a. complete medical history
   b. age, sex, and weight
   c. chief complaint
   d. estimated time of arrival at the hospital

160. The function of a safety officer is to
   a. teach the unit members to work safely
   b. decide if a scene is safe to enter
   c. ensure that all unit members are wearing safety gear
   d. ensure patient safety before the BLS unit arrives

161. *Packaging* refers to
   a. bandaging wounds to protect them from dirt and foreign bodies.
   b. using force to remove a patient from a dangerous environment
   c. freeing a patient from wreckage
   d. preparing the patient for transfer to an ambulance

162. At a mass casualty incident, which sector should the incident commander establish first?
   a. extrication sector
   b. triage sector
   c. transportation sector
   d. supply sector

163. Which officer will coordinate with police to block streets and provide access at an MCI?
   a. triage officer
   b. transportation officer
   c. supply officer
   d. staging officer

164. The purpose of the START method is to
   a. coordinate the efforts of multiple response units
   b. ensure access of response units to an MCI
   c. rapidly triage large numbers of patients
   d. communicate with medical personnel as efficiently as possible

165. The first step in triage at a mass casualty incident is to
   a. clear the walking wounded from the scene
   b. assess the victims' respiratory status
   c. assess the victims' hemodynamic status
   d. evaluate the victims' mental status

166. In the METTAG system, a yellow tag means that the victim
  a. does not need care or transportation
  b. is not seriously injured
  c. is in critical condition
  d. is dead

167. Continual reexperiencing of a traumatic event is a characteristic of
  a. anxiety
  b. burnout
  c. cumulative stress reaction
  d. delayed stress reaction

168. Your patient has died. What should you say to her family members?
  a. "Your mother has gone on a long journey."
  b. "I'm sorry to tell you that your mother is dead."
  c. "Mrs. Smith expired at 1300 hours."
  d. "The doctor will speak to you when we arrive at the hospital."

169. One of the best ways for EMS personnel to deal with job-related stress is to
  a. take sleeping pills at night
  b. take time away from family
  c. discuss the situation with co-workers
  d. eliminate all physical exercises

170. The prefix *blast-* means
  a. shoot
  b. to or toward
  c. germ or cell
  d. not

171. Which suffix refers to pain?
  a. -cyte
  b. -ptosis
  c. -algia
  d. -scope

172. The symbol NaCl stands for
  a. nitrous oxide
  b. sodium bicarbonate
  c. calcium
  d. sodium chloride

173. Which patient is most likely to require immediate transport?
  a. 25-year-old male, fractured wrist
  b. 45-year-old male, fractured pelvis
  c. 38-year-old female, fractured tibia
  d. 52-year-old female, fractured humerus

Answer questions 174–176 on the basis of the information below.

You respond to a 25-patient mass-casualty incident at a store. The 911 caller stated that she smelled something "funny" and then started to feel weak and nauseous. You are the second unit on the scene. The initial unit is nowhere to be seen, and they do not answer their radios.

174. What should be your first concern in this situation?
  a. The other crew is treating patients inside and needs your help.
  b. This is a potential hazardous materials incident.
  c. The other crew has been overcome and needs your immediate assistance.
  d. You need more oxygen than your rig carries.

175. You decide to call for the hazardous materials team. After you make the call your next step should be to
a. begin decontaminating each victim in the back of your ambulance
b. begin assisting in clothing removal of all patients
c. stand back and wait for the Haz-Mat team
d. call for an oxygen vendor to respond

176. After you are instructed by the Haz-Mat team to begin treating decontaminated patients, you should
a. take universal precautions and wear protective equipment
b. begin with the least symptomatic patient
c. thoroughly treat the first patient you encounter
d. thoroughly question the first patient for purposes of documentation

177. For which procedure is it NOT necessary to wear a gown?
a. emergency childbirth
b. drawing blood
c. suctioning
d. cleaning instruments

178. Intermediate-level disinfection with a solution of bleach and water is used for
a. routine housecleaning
b. items that have come into contact with mucous membranes
c. invasive instruments
d. items that have come into contact with intact skin

179. Which infection is transmitted through contact with blood or body secretions?
a. hepatitis A
b. hepatitis B
c. varicella
d. tuberculosis

180. A major concern in treating a patient with organophospate poisoning is
a. exposure of rescuers to the poison
b. repeated dysthymias
c. crush syndrome-like symptoms
d. CVA

ANSWERS

1. **c.** At the beginning of a stress reaction (Stage I), vital signs such as pulse rate increase and pupils are dilated.

2. **a.** The root word *cyan-* means *blue*, as in *cyanosis*.

3. **d.** After assessing airway, breathing, circulation, and disability, you expose vital body parts to assess for injury.

4. **a.** The purpose of the secondary assessment is to detect additional problems after you have controlled immediate threats to the patient's life.

5. **d.** This patient is exhibiting the classic signs and symptoms of an abdominal aortic aneurysm. Further palpation may cause the aneurysm to rupture.

6. **a.** This choice gives the appropriate treatment for an abdominal aortic aneurysm.

7. **c.** Rales, which indicate fluid in the lungs and minor obstruction, are often described as fine, crackling sounds.

8. **b.** The posterior tibial pulse is assessed just below and posterior to where the ankle bone protrudes.

9. **c.** The P in the AMPLE acronym stands for past medical problems.

10. **a.** Indications for immediate transport include pulse rate greater than 120 or less than 50, systolic BP less than 90, and respiratory rate less than 10 or greater than 29.

11. **b.** This change in vital signs comprises Cushing's Reflex, a sign of increasing intracranial pressure.

12. **c.** The wet sterile dressing keeps the organs moist, and the occlusive dressing provides a barrier against contamination.

13. **d.** This patient's injuries do not suggest the need for rapid transport.

14. **d.** One dilated pupil may be an early sign of increased intracranial pressure.

15. **c.** The patient is responsive to verbal stimuli but not alert, because she is not oriented to her surroundings.

16. **a.** Falls in which the victim lands on his or her feet often result in fractures along the skeletal pathway.

17. **a.** The lumbar spine is especially prone to compression fractures because it supports the entire weight of the upper body.

18. **d.** Pelvic fractures are more likely if the patient falls backwards.

19. **c.** In falls over 20 feet, rapid deceleration can cause the heart to pull downward with such force that the aorta may be completely bisected leading to a rapid death.

20. **d.** For a patient who has had this type of fall, spinal mobilization, cardiac monitoring, and epinephrine is the appropriate treatment.

21. **b.** A positive tilt test in a patient with acute abdominal pain suggests that the patient is hypovolemic and may have impending shock.

22. **a.** Patients who are stable should be in a position of comfort.

23. c. Use gentle palpation only in the field.

24. c. Air embolism presents as neurological deficits during or after ascent from a dive, as well as sharp pain in the chest.

25. b. The dosage of many common medications is up to 50 percent lower in elderly adults, primarily because of a decreased rate of elimination.

26. c. The pain of MI is not relieved by sublingual nitroglycerin; intravenous morphine or nitroglycerin is usually necessary.

27. c. A patient with left heart failure will present with elevated blood pressure, elevated and sometimes irregular pulse, and labored respirations.

28. a. Open-ended questions cannot be answered by a simple "yes" or "no"; such questions help keep lines of communication open.

29. a. Decreased alertness to surroundings is an early sign of shock and should always alert the paramedic to take corrective action.

30. c. The vital signs given in this choice are most likely for a patient with CHF who is complaining of difficulty breathing.

31. d. Diuretics, potassium, and digoxin are the common medications used to treat CHF.

32. b. The pulmonary edema associated with CHF commonly results in rales and/or rhonchi, especially in the lower lobes.

33. a. CHF results from the heart's inability to pump efficiently.

34. d. Sellick's maneuver is used to prevent patients from vomiting during intubation.

35. c. Tube placement should take no longer than 30 seconds; if it does, hyperventilate the patient again before the next attempt.

36. a. To ensure proper placement, always confirm by two different methods: after watching the tube pass through the vocal cords, assess the chest *and* check the proximal end of the tube for breath condensation.

37. d. Because the digital method does not require hyper-extending the patient's neck, it is used for patients with suspected spinal or cervical injury.

38. b. Nasal intubation is not recommended in patients who have suspected nasal fracture, nasal obstruction, or basilar skull fracture.

39. a. Attempts at suctioning should be limited to no more than 10 seconds. You should ventilate the patient after each attempt, and you should not turn on the apparatus until the catheter is placed properly.

40. a. The signs and symptoms of tension pneumothorax, the presence of air in the pleural space, are listed.

41. a. Dyspnea, rales, and rhonchi are classic signs of fluid overload.

42. a. For the conscious patient, your first action would be abdominal thrusts.

43. c. Low-flow oxygen is appropriate for this patient if he or she is not too hypoxic. If a patient with emphysema or chronic bronchitis is hypoxic, he or she needs more oxygen.

44. c. Albuterol, a bronchodilator sold under the trade names Proventil and Ventolin, is frequently given via inhaler in the field.

45. d. Place your hand on the patient's wrist as if you were measuring his or her pulse and count for 30 seconds. This will prevent the patient from consciously changing the respiratory rate.

46. c. AHA standards dictate that a conscious partial obstructed airway should be dealt with by encouraging coughing and continuous monitoring of patient status.

47. c. AHA standards dictate that a conscious adult with airway obstruction should be given abdominal thrusts.

48. b. AHA standards do not include back blows for an adult choking victim.

49. d. Because portions of the obstruction may be retained, transport to an ER for chest X rays and observation is essential.

50. c. Cheyne-Stokes respirations are characterized by periods of apnea lasting 10–60 seconds, followed by periods in which respirations gradually decrease, then increase, in depth and rate.

51. b. Because sea water is hypertonic, fluid is drawn from the blood stream into the alveoli, causing pulmonary edema.

52. c. This victim of smoke inhalation is exhibiting the classic signs and symptoms of carbon monoxide poisoning.

53. a. This is a common finding with the use of pulse oximetry.

54. b. Of the four choices, only sodium bicarbonate is not indicated for carbon monoxide poisoning.

55. d. Hyperactivity is not a sign of carbon monoxide exposure. Generally, patients are lethargic due to being hypoxic.

56. b. Choices **a, c,** and **d** are all common sources of colorless, odorless gases associated with this patient's condition.

57. a. Choice **a** indicates the difficulty the rescuer faces in reversing carbon monoxide poisoning.

58. a. In addition to emphysema, chronic bronchitis is associated with cigarette smoking.

59. d. To manage anaphylaxis, epinephrine is the first medication used, followed by diphenhydramine. Epinephrine reverses the physiological effects of the reaction while diphenhydramine slows and stops the reaction itself.

60. b. Proper flow cannot be achieved if the constricting band is not removed.

61. c. Indications for use of the PASG are to control bleeding, stabilize fractures, and raise blood pressure.

62. d. Patients with cardiac contusion can present the symptoms of myocardial infarction, including life-threatening dysrhythmias. Care is similar to care of cardiac patients.

63. a. Nitronox is a short-acting agent that the patient self-administers by mask. The other statements are correct.

64. b. The Seldinger technique uses a wire dilator to allow you to place a large catheter into a vein you have punctured with a small catheter.

65. d. Fluid administration in dialysis patients should be under the direct authority of medical control.

66. d. Cardiovascular disease is the leading cause of death in the elderly.

67. **d.** A single-lead ECG, used for routine monitoring, can be used to determine the heart rate, regularity, and the length of time it takes for the impulse to travel through the heart.

68. **b.** The QRS complex reflects the underlying ventricular depolarization.

69. **d.** The QRS complex normally lasts 0.04 to 0.12 seconds; anything longer than 0.12 seconds is considered to be abnormal.

70. **a.** If the patient is asymptomatic, this arrhythmia requires observation only.

71. **a.** Bradycardia refers to a heart rate lower than 60 beats per minute.

72. **d.** First-degree AV block in itself calls for observation only; however, it may indicate the development of a more advanced heart block.

73. **b.** Wolf-Parkinson-White syndrome is characterized by a short P-R interval and lengthened QRS complex.

74. **a.** When PJT is caused by stress or excessive caffeine intake in a patient with no history of heart disease, the Valsalva maneuver can be successful at slowing the heart rate.

75. **c.** Because the underlying cause is usually ischemia, accelerated junctional rhythm can deteriorate into more serious dysrhythmias.

76. **a.** In a patient with acute MI, sinus tachycardia suggests that cardiogenic shock may develop.

77. **d.** Check for jugular vein distention with the patient elevated at a 45-degree angle.

78. **b.** A bruit, noisy blood flow in a vessel, indicates partial blockage.

79. **d.** Intermittent claudication, a symptom of atherosclerosis, refers to severe pain in the calf muscle brought on by exercise.

80. **a.** Attacks of stable angina are brought on by exercise or by stress and are usually easily managed.

81. **b.** Epinephrine is used to avoid life-threatening dysrhythmias such as ventricular fibrillation.

82. **a.** Listed are classic signs and symptoms of left heart failure with pulmonary edema.

83. **c.** Right heart failure, unless it is accompanied by left heart failure with pulmonary edema, is not a true medical emergency and does not require *rapid* transport.

84. **c.** Sodium nitroprusside is used in the treatment of hypertensive emergency.

85. **b.** Lidocaine is a first-line drug in the treatment of dysrhythmias.

86. **b.** Emergency synchronized cardioversion is synchronized with the R wave in order to avoid the refractory period.

87. **a.** The P wave reflects atrial depolarization at the beginning of the cardiac cycle.

88. **b.** The correct protocol for stable angina is rest, oxygen, and nitroglycerin.

89. **a.** The wheezing is the lung's reflex response to the fluid that builds up in the alveoli in left-sides pump failure.

90. **d.** Epinephrine can help manage life-threatening dysrhythmias by increasing the cardiac contractile force and automaticity.

91. **a.** Oxygen can help limit the size of the infarct by increasing oxygen delivery to the heart muscle.

92. d. Procainimide is used to treat dysrhythmias, especially in patients who are allergic to lidocaine.

93. d. A too-rapid ascent from a SCUBA dive may result in a pulmonary embolism due to lung overinflation.

94. b. An IV, 100% oxygen via a non-rebreather mask, and transport to the emergency department is essential for this patient.

95. c. Due to the depth of the dive and the rapid ascent, this patient may also be suffering from decompression sickness.

96. b. In this patient, nitrogen bubbles may have entered tissue spaces and blood vessels.

97. a. Skeletal muscle is also referred to as voluntary muscle because it is under voluntary control and thus allows for movement.

98. c. Abduction refers to movement away from the body.

99. d. Intravenous thiamine is used to reverse the effects of acute thiamine deficiency in alcoholics.

100. d. The halo test, the presence of a ring of lighter fluid around a blood stain, indicates whether cerebrospinal fluid is leaking from the patient's nose or ears.

101. b. Do not manipulate joint injuries before splinting.

102. c. A greenstick fracture is a partial fracture that is on one side of the long bone only.

103. a. The protocol for pelvic fracture is given here.

104. d. The correct treatment for most chemical burns is to flush the area with cool water immediately and to continue this treatment even during transport.

105. b. Cooling of larger areas may lead to hypothermia.

106. b. Blisters are characteristic of second-degree burns.

107. c. Using the rule of nines, this patient has burns over 27 percent of her body surface area (both sides of one arm = 9 percent; both sides of one leg = 18 percent).

108. a. This patient is showing signs and symptoms of diabetic ketoacidosis.

109. b. This option lists the classic signs of hypoglycemia.

110. a. Naloxone (Narcan) is a narcotic antagonist that is given to patients suspected of taking an overdose of narcotics.

111. c. Syncope is transient loss of consciousness resulting from inadequate blood flow to the brain.

112. b. Hives, accompanied by difficulty breathing, strongly suggest anaphylaxis.

113. a. Epinephrine is the first-line drug for patients with severe allergic reactions. Other drugs, such as Benadryl or albuterol, are given after epinephrine.

114. d. Beta agonists such as albuterol help in the treatment of severe allergic reactions by relaxing the airway and thus relieving bronchospasm.

115. b. The usual dose for an adult is 30 mL, followed by approximately 2 to 3 glasses (15 mL/kg body weight) of water or other fluids.

116. c. Respiratory depression and constricted pupils ("pinpoint pupils") are classic symptoms.

117. a. The symptoms of organophosphate absorption are described by the acronym SLUDGE: excessive salivation, lacrimation, urination, diarrhea, gastrointestinal distress, emesis.

118. c. The temperature of 104° F and the low fluid intake suggest heat exhaustion.

119. b. Moderate hypothermia is characterized by a core temperature between 86 and 94° F.

120. a. The correct treatment is gradual warming in a water bath maintained between 100 and 106° F.

121. b. Assessment of an elderly patient's condition may be complicated by several factors, but the elderly are not likely to fake illness.

122. a. Spondylosis, or degeneration of the body of the vertebrae, makes the spine more vulnerable to injury.

123. c. Allow the patient to express emotion; do not interrupt his expression with questions or comments.

124. c. Depression is a mood disorder; depressed patients feel hopeless and helpless and manifest many physical symptoms as well.

125. d. Benadryl is used to counter extrapyramidal reactions in patients who are taking antipsychotic drugs.

126. a. A medium-speed car accident is a significant mechanism of injury for a child but not for an adult unless other significant findings (lack of seatbelts, another person killed in the same car) are present.

127. d. With a child of this age, obtain as much information as possible from the patient himself; this will allow the child to feel responsibility. The adult caretaker can fill in relevant details.

128. c. Phenobarbital is commonly associated with seizure disorder.

129. b. Phenobarbital is a sedative/anticonvulsant.

130. a. Anticonvulsants serve to limit the number of seizures a patient has.

131. d. The other medications listed in choices **a, b,** and **c** are not indicated for post-ictal patients.

132. b. This patient needs to be transported to a hospital because medication levels should be assessed by laboratory methods.

133. c. Average systolic blood pressure in a 3-year-old is 80 to 100.

134. a. The average 6-year-old weighs about 45 pounds.

135. d. In many states, medical personnel are legally required to report all cases of suspected abuse and neglect, but a paramedic's first responsibility is to ensure that the child is transported to the hospital to receive necessary treatment.

136. b. The cause of seizure activity can be determined only in the hospital.

137. c. Wheezing in a child younger than age 1 is most often due to bronchiolitis.

138. d. Most childhood cardiac arrests are the result of preventable accidents such as those in choices **a, b,** and **c.**

139. c. Do not perform a vaginal exam or ask detailed questions about the assault in the field; treat the patient with respect.

140. b. The term *primipara* refers to a woman who has just delivered her first child.

141. a. During pregnancy, a woman's blood pressure usually falls, while her pulse rate rises.

142. c. A mild systolic murmur in a pregnant patient whose vital signs are normal is not a cause for concern.

143. d. Bright red bleeding in late pregnancy is assumed to be placenta previa, a medical emergency. Treat the mother for shock and transport immediately.

144. b. The patient shows signs and symptoms of preeclampsia and should be transported to the hospital.

145. a. First attempt to slip the cord over the baby's head. If this is impossible, clamp the cord in two places and cut it between the clamps.

146. b. The score would consist of one point each for appearance, pulse rate, grimace, and respiratory effort, and two points for activity.

147. a. Do not resuscitate until the meconium is cleared from the respiratory tree.

148. d. All the other choices are criteria for ventilating a newborn; meconium staining in itself is not.

149. d. This patient is exhibiting the classic signs and symptoms of croup.

150. d. A nebulized saline mist is the appropriate treatment for croup.

151. b. Epiglottitis, a condition whereby the patient's airway can become totally obstructed, is related to croup.

152. b. Ethics refers to rules, standards, and morals that govern the actions of a profession.

153. a. In a tiered system, responders are dispatched to calls depending upon the nature of the incident as stated by the 911 caller.

154. d. The Emergency Medical services Systems Act, passed in 1973, provided funding to develop regional systems.

155. c. No matter who is actually providing care or giving directions to the responder, ultimate responsibility always rests with the medical control physician.

156. c. A medical practice act defines the scope of practice and role of medical personnel.

157. a. Expressed consent means that the patient gives you permission to treat him or her, either verbally or in writing.

158. c. If a person who needs help refuses to accept it, you should try to persuade the person to accept aid and explain the consequences of refusing it. Only after doing so should you accept and document the refusal of care.

159. a. Although some details of the medical history, such as allergies, surgeries, and medications, are relevant, a detailed history is not.

160. b. The function of the safety officer is to evaluate the scene and make the "go/no go" decision for the operation.

161. d. Packaging refers to the emergency care procedures that must be performed before a patient can be moved from the scene to an ambulance.

162. a. The extrication sector should be the first to be established, followed by the triage and transportation sectors.

163. d. The staging officer's responsibilities include coordinating with police, ensuring access for vehicles, maintaining a log of available units, and coordinating requests for resources.

164. c. The purpose of the START method is to triage large numbers of patients as quickly as possible.

165. a. The first step in triage at an MCI is to direct the walking wounded to a safe place where they can be cared for and reassessed later.

166. b. A yellow tag indicates that the victim's injuries are not serious and that transportation can be delayed.

167. d. Delayed stress reaction, or post-traumatic stress disorder, is characterized by reexperiencing of the traumatic event, diminished responsiveness to everyday life, and physical and cognitive symptoms.

168. b. When your patient dies, speak to the family members kindly but straightforwardly.

169. c. Sharing your feelings about a stressful event can help relieve them.

170. c. The prefix *blast-* refers to a germ or a cell, as in the term *blastoma*.

171. c. The suffix *-algia* refers to pain, as in the word *neuralgia*.

172. d. The chemical symbol NaCl stands for sodium chloride, or salt.

173. b. Because of the possibility of severe blood loss, patients with fractures of the pelvis or femur are most likely to need immediate transport.

174. b. This is a hazardous materials incident until proven otherwise. Do not rush in after fallen rescuers because you too may become a victim.

175. c. Stay clear of the incident. Use a public address system to calm victims and explain what is going on. It is important that they not leave the scene for fear of future contamination.

176. a. Always wear personal protective equipment to help avoid becoming personally contaminated.

177. b. Wearing a gown is recommended for all the other procedures listed.

178. d. Intermediate-level disinfection is used for all instruments and supplies that have come into contact with intact skin.

179. b. Hepatitis B is a blood-borne disease that is transmitted through contact with blood or body secretions.

180. a. Exposure to organophosphate is a major concern. Proper isolation procedures are paramount to rescuer safety. Dispose of all patient clothing according to Environmental Protection Agency guidelines.

PARAMEDIC PRACTICE EXAM 2

CHAPTER SUMMARY

This is the second of four practice exams in this book based on the National Registry EMT-Paramedic written exam. Having taken one exam already, you should feel more confident in your ability to pick the correct answers. Use this test to see how knowing what to expect makes you feel more prepared.

L
ike the first exam in this book, this test is based on that of the National Registry of EMTs. It should not, however, look to you just like the first test you took, because you know more now about how the test is put together. You have seen how different types of questions are presented and are perhaps beginning to notice patterns in the order of questions. You see that questions on each area are grouped together. This pattern will help you develop your own test-taking strategy.

If you're following the advice of this book, you've done some studying between the first exam and this one. This second exam will give you a chance to see how much you've improved.

For this second exam, pay attention to the different types of questions there are and the relationship between quetions on the same topic. Also, you might want to try timing yourself, to get an idea of which sections take you longer. The answer sheet follows this page, and the test is followed by the answer key. Pay attention to the answer explanations in the key, especially for the questions you missed.

1.	(a)	(b)	(c)	(d)	46.	(a)	(b)	(c)	(d)	91.	(a)	(b)	(c)	(d)
2.	(a)	(b)	(c)	(d)	47.	(a)	(b)	(c)	(d)	92.	(a)	(b)	(c)	(d)
3.	(a)	(b)	(c)	(d)	48.	(a)	(b)	(c)	(d)	93.	(a)	(b)	(c)	(d)
4.	(a)	(b)	(c)	(d)	49.	(a)	(b)	(c)	(d)	94.	(a)	(b)	(c)	(d)
5.	(a)	(b)	(c)	(d)	50.	(a)	(b)	(c)	(d)	95.	(a)	(b)	(c)	(d)
6.	(a)	(b)	(c)	(d)	51.	(a)	(b)	(c)	(d)	96.	(a)	(b)	(c)	(d)
7.	(a)	(b)	(c)	(d)	52.	(a)	(b)	(c)	(d)	97.	(a)	(b)	(c)	(d)
8.	(a)	(b)	(c)	(d)	53.	(a)	(b)	(c)	(d)	98.	(a)	(b)	(c)	(d)
9.	(a)	(b)	(c)	(d)	54.	(a)	(b)	(c)	(d)	99.	(a)	(b)	(c)	(d)
10.	(a)	(b)	(c)	(d)	55.	(a)	(b)	(c)	(d)	100.	(a)	(b)	(c)	(d)
11.	(a)	(b)	(c)	(d)	56.	(a)	(b)	(c)	(d)	101.	(a)	(b)	(c)	(d)
12.	(a)	(b)	(c)	(d)	57.	(a)	(b)	(c)	(d)	102.	(a)	(b)	(c)	(d)
13.	(a)	(b)	(c)	(d)	58.	(a)	(b)	(c)	(d)	103.	(a)	(b)	(c)	(d)
14.	(a)	(b)	(c)	(d)	59.	(a)	(b)	(c)	(d)	104.	(a)	(b)	(c)	(d)
15.	(a)	(b)	(c)	(d)	60.	(a)	(b)	(c)	(d)	105.	(a)	(b)	(c)	(d)
16.	(a)	(b)	(c)	(d)	61.	(a)	(b)	(c)	(d)	106.	(a)	(b)	(c)	(d)
17.	(a)	(b)	(c)	(d)	62.	(a)	(b)	(c)	(d)	107.	(a)	(b)	(c)	(d)
18.	(a)	(b)	(c)	(d)	63.	(a)	(b)	(c)	(d)	108.	(a)	(b)	(c)	(d)
19.	(a)	(b)	(c)	(d)	64.	(a)	(b)	(c)	(d)	109.	(a)	(b)	(c)	(d)
20.	(a)	(b)	(c)	(d)	65.	(a)	(b)	(c)	(d)	110.	(a)	(b)	(c)	(d)
21.	(a)	(b)	(c)	(d)	66.	(a)	(b)	(c)	(d)	111.	(a)	(b)	(c)	(d)
22.	(a)	(b)	(c)	(d)	67.	(a)	(b)	(c)	(d)	112.	(a)	(b)	(c)	(d)
23.	(a)	(b)	(c)	(d)	68.	(a)	(b)	(c)	(d)	113.	(a)	(b)	(c)	(d)
24.	(a)	(b)	(c)	(d)	69.	(a)	(b)	(c)	(d)	114.	(a)	(b)	(c)	(d)
25.	(a)	(b)	(c)	(d)	70.	(a)	(b)	(c)	(d)	115.	(a)	(b)	(c)	(d)
26.	(a)	(b)	(c)	(d)	71.	(a)	(b)	(c)	(d)	116.	(a)	(b)	(c)	(d)
27.	(a)	(b)	(c)	(d)	72.	(a)	(b)	(c)	(d)	117.	(a)	(b)	(c)	(d)
28.	(a)	(b)	(c)	(d)	73.	(a)	(b)	(c)	(d)	118.	(a)	(b)	(c)	(d)
29.	(a)	(b)	(c)	(d)	74.	(a)	(b)	(c)	(d)	119.	(a)	(b)	(c)	(d)
30.	(a)	(b)	(c)	(d)	75.	(a)	(b)	(c)	(d)	120.	(a)	(b)	(c)	(d)
31.	(a)	(b)	(c)	(d)	76.	(a)	(b)	(c)	(d)	121.	(a)	(b)	(c)	(d)
32.	(a)	(b)	(c)	(d)	77.	(a)	(b)	(c)	(d)	122.	(a)	(b)	(c)	(d)
33.	(a)	(b)	(c)	(d)	78.	(a)	(b)	(c)	(d)	123.	(a)	(b)	(c)	(d)
34.	(a)	(b)	(c)	(d)	79.	(a)	(b)	(c)	(d)	124.	(a)	(b)	(c)	(d)
35.	(a)	(b)	(c)	(d)	80.	(a)	(b)	(c)	(d)	125.	(a)	(b)	(c)	(d)
36.	(a)	(b)	(c)	(d)	81.	(a)	(b)	(c)	(d)	126.	(a)	(b)	(c)	(d)
37.	(a)	(b)	(c)	(d)	82.	(a)	(b)	(c)	(d)	127.	(a)	(b)	(c)	(d)
38.	(a)	(b)	(c)	(d)	83.	(a)	(b)	(c)	(d)	128.	(a)	(b)	(c)	(d)
39.	(a)	(b)	(c)	(d)	84.	(a)	(b)	(c)	(d)	129.	(a)	(b)	(c)	(d)
40.	(a)	(b)	(c)	(d)	85.	(a)	(b)	(c)	(d)	130.	(a)	(b)	(c)	(d)
41.	(a)	(b)	(c)	(d)	86.	(a)	(b)	(c)	(d)	131.	(a)	(b)	(c)	(d)
42.	(a)	(b)	(c)	(d)	87.	(a)	(b)	(c)	(d)	132.	(a)	(b)	(c)	(d)
43.	(a)	(b)	(c)	(d)	88.	(a)	(b)	(c)	(d)	133.	(a)	(b)	(c)	(d)
44.	(a)	(b)	(c)	(d)	89.	(a)	(b)	(c)	(d)	134.	(a)	(b)	(c)	(d)
45.	(a)	(b)	(c)	(d)	90.	(a)	(b)	(c)	(d)	135.	(a)	(b)	(c)	(d)

136.	(a) (b) (c) (d)	151.	(a) (b) (c) (d)	166.	(a) (b) (c) (d)
137.	(a) (b) (c) (d)	152.	(a) (b) (c) (d)	167.	(a) (b) (c) (d)
138.	(a) (b) (c) (d)	153.	(a) (b) (c) (d)	168.	(a) (b) (c) (d)
139.	(a) (b) (c) (d)	154.	(a) (b) (c) (d)	169.	(a) (b) (c) (d)
140.	(a) (b) (c) (d)	155.	(a) (b) (c) (d)	170.	(a) (b) (c) (d)
141.	(a) (b) (c) (d)	156.	(a) (b) (c) (d)	171.	(a) (b) (c) (d)
142.	(a) (b) (c) (d)	157.	(a) (b) (c) (d)	172.	(a) (b) (c) (d)
143.	(a) (b) (c) (d)	158.	(a) (b) (c) (d)	173.	(a) (b) (c) (d)
144.	(a) (b) (c) (d)	159.	(a) (b) (c) (d)	174.	(a) (b) (c) (d)
145.	(a) (b) (c) (d)	160.	(a) (b) (c) (d)	175.	(a) (b) (c) (d)
146.	(a) (b) (c) (d)	161.	(a) (b) (c) (d)	176.	(a) (b) (c) (d)
147.	(a) (b) (c) (d)	162.	(a) (b) (c) (d)	177.	(a) (b) (c) (d)
148.	(a) (b) (c) (d)	163.	(a) (b) (c) (d)	178.	(a) (b) (c) (d)
149.	(a) (b) (c) (d)	164.	(a) (b) (c) (d)	179.	(a) (b) (c) (d)
150.	(a) (b) (c) (d)	165.	(a) (b) (c) (d)	180.	(a) (b) (c) (d)

PARAMEDIC EXAM 2

1. Your patient is a 27-year-old male who has fallen from a 24-foot ladder. After noting that the patient is conscious and talking, you would FIRST
   a. look at his chest to begin assessing the airway
   b. manually stabilize his neck
   c. feel for a radial pulse
   d. palpate for a carotid pulse

2. You note snoring in your initial assessment of a trauma patient. You should
   a. manually stabilize the cervical spine
   b. perform the chin-lift/jaw-thrust maneuver
   c. perform the head-tilt/chin-lift maneuver
   d. institute advance cardiac life support measures

3. Capillary refill time is most accurate as an indicator of circulatory status in
   a. patients who smoke
   b. elderly patients
   c. infants and children
   d. healthy adult patients

4. The E in the assessment ABCDEs refers to
   a. expiration
   b. edema
   c. erythema
   d. expose

5. Under the START triage method, which patient would receive immediate treatment to support hemodynamic status without further assessment?
   a. male, radial pulse present, skin warm and dry
   b. female, radial pulse present, capillary refill time 1 sec
   c. male, radial pulse present, skin pale and cyanotic
   d. female, radial pulse present capillary refill time 0.5 sec

6. The root word *myo-* refers to
   a. muscle
   b. heart
   c. self
   d. opening

7. Which prefix means *white?*
   a. cyan-
   b. erythro-
   c. chole-
   d. leuk-

8. Which of the following is an example of epithelial tissue?
   a. the heart
   b. the skin
   c. the carpal ligament
   d. the liver

9. A wound that is described as distal to the knee might be located on the
a. hip
b. stomach
c. thigh
d. calf

Answer questions 10–13 on the basis of the information below.

You respond on a 63-year-old male who is complaining of sudden onset of extreme substernal chest pain that, he says, "feels like my insides are tearing." The patient also states that the pain radiates to the middle of his back between his shoulder blades.

10. This patient is most likely suffering from
a. dissecting aortic aneurysm
b. abdominal aortic aneurysm
c. acute arterial occlusion
d. acute pulmonary embolism

11. Which of the following are predisposing factors for this patient's condition?
a. hypotension and chronic angina pectoris
b. hypertension and possibly family history
c. chronic angina pectoris and possibly family history
d. hypotension and possibly family history

12. Which of the following medications may be ordered by medical control if the diagnosis is fairly accurate?
a. dopamine
b. atropine sulfate
c. morphine sulfate
d. isoproterenol

13. Progression of this condition may cause
a. stroke, pericardial tamponade, acute myocardial infarction
b. acute arterial occlusion, acute pulmonary embolism, encephalitis
c. deep venous thrombosis, varicose veins, arterial atherosclerotic disease
d. arterial atherosclerotic disease, pulmonary embolism, acute arterial occlusion

14. Your patient has survived a vehicle rollover in which another passenger died. He is alert, is not complaining of pain, and his vital signs are as follows: pulse, 100; systolic BP, 90; respirations, 28. In deciding when to transport this patient, you should
a. carry out a lengthy secondary assessment and take time to stabilize his injuries at the scene
b. suspect that the patient has serious underlying injuries and transport immediately
c. allow the patient to rest quietly for 15 minutes before reassessing his condition
d. consult with medical direction about the suspicious vital signs

15. Which statement about motorcycle wrecks is INCORRECT?
a. They can result in severe trauma, even at low speeds.
b. Use of a helmet can reduce the incidence and severity of head injury.
c. Use of a helmet can reduce the incidence and severity of spinal injury.
d. Use of leather clothing can protect the rider against some soft-tissue injury.

16. Battle's sign is an indication of
   a. basilar skull fracture
   b. orbital skull fracture
   c. subarachnoid hemorrhage
   d. cervical spinal trauma

17. A contrecoup injury is a brain injury that
   a. results from cerebral edema
   b. causes subdural or epidural hematoma
   c. is on the opposite side of the head from the impact site
   d. results from open skull fracture

18. Your patient is a car-crash victim who vomited suddenly and now is becoming disoriented. You should suspect
   a. subdural hematoma
   b. brainstem injury
   c. basilar skull fracture
   d. inner-ear injury

19. A patient who opens her eyes when pinched, pulls her hand away when pinched, and who speaks only in garbled sounds would have a Glasgow Coma Scale score of
   a. 5
   b. 7
   c. 9
   d. 11

20. Your patient, a trauma victim, is agitated and apprehensive. She is increasingly cyanotic, and breath sounds are rapidly diminishing over her left lung. She is exhibiting signs and symptoms of shock, and her trachea is displaced toward the right. You should suspect
   a. hemothorax
   b. tension pneumothorax

   c. cardiac tamponade
   d. flail chest

21. A child has third-degree burns over the front of her trunk and the front of her right leg. According to the rule of nines, what percentage of her body surface is affected?
   a. 18 1/2 percent
   b. 22 1/2 percent
   c. 25 percent
   d. 33 percent

22. Your patient is a 34-year-old woman who has been in an automobile crash. Her respiratory rate is 34 with normal chest expansion, her systolic blood pressure is 78, and her capillary return is delayed. This patient's Glasgow Trauma Scale score is
   a. 4
   b. 6
   c. 8
   d. 10

23. Which group of vital sign changes is associated with Cushing's reflex?
   a. decreased blood pressure, decreased pulse rate, decreased respiratory rate, decreased temperature
   b. increased blood pressure, decreased pulse rate, decreased respiratory rate, increased temperature
   c. decreased blood pressure, increased pulse rate, increased respiratory rate, decreased temperature
   d. increased blood pressure, increased pulse rate, increased respiratory rate, increased temperature

24. The correct procedure for examining the abdomen of a patient who is complaining of abdominal pain is to ask the patient to point to where it hurts and then
   a. begin palpating there
   b. palpate all four quadrants, ending at the painful area
   c. begin auscultation and percussion away from the site of the pain
   d. begin auscultation and percussion at the site of the pain

25. Which question would evaluate the O portion of the OPQRST algorithm?
   a. "What makes the pain feel better?"
   b. "Describe the pain for me."
   c. "What were you doing when the pain began?"
   d. "How long ago did the pain begin?"

26. Your patient is a 58-year-old woman who complains of severe abdominal pain. The tilt test is positive. You should place this patient in
   a. Trendelenburg's position
   b. supine position
   c. prone position
   d. shock position

27. *Ascites* refers to
   a. chronic alcoholism
   b. fluid in the abdomen
   c. severe abdominal pain
   d. a ruptured aortic aneurysm

28. Which type of hepatitis is spread via the fecal-oral route?
   a. hepatitis A
   b. hepatitis B
   c. hepatitis C
   d. hepatitis D

29. Your patient is an 83-year-old woman who has fallen down her front steps and has possibly fractured her ankle. Which assessment finding may be considered abnormal in this patient?
   a. altered mental status
   b. respirations regular
   c. pulse 68
   d. blood pressure 128/86

30. All of the following drugs commonly cause toxicity in elderly patients EXCEPT
   a. lidocaine
   b. nitroglycerin
   c. digitalis
   d. theophylline

31. Which dysrhythmia is considered normal in an otherwise healthy person?
   a. sinus bradycardia
   b. sinus arrest
   c. atrial fibrillation
   d. paroxysmal supraventricular tachycardia

32. Which statement about the vital signs of a patient with MI is correct?
   a. Respiratory and pulse rates will be elevated while blood pressure will be depressed.
   b. Vital signs are insignificant because management depends on the underlying heart rhythm.
   c. Vital signs vary greatly since they are related to the extent of heart damage.
   d. Elevated respiratory and pulse rates are associated with a favorable outcome.

33. Your patient's ECG strip shows 7 electrical complexes within a 6-second interval. This means that the patient's heart rate is
   a. 21 beats/min
   b. 42 beats/min
   c. 60 beats/min
   d. 70 beats/min

34. Your patient is a 24-year-old female who shows signs and symptoms of pelvic inflammatory disease. The goal of prehospital care for this patient is to
   a. begin definitive therapy
   b. perform a complete physical exam to identify associated medical problems
   c. make the patient as comfortable as possible
   d. identify all the patient's sexual contacts

35. All of the following factors increase a patient's respiratory rate EXCEPT
   a. anxiety
   b. sleep
   c. fever
   d. hypoxia

36. While ventilating a patient with a bag-valve mask, you note decreasing compliance. You should
   a. remove the device and intubate the patient
   b. request permission to sedate the patient
   c. assess the cause of this finding
   d. treat the patient for signs and symptoms of shock

37. A pulse oximetry reading of 88 percent indicates
   a. normal oxygenation
   b. mild hypoxia
   c. moderate hypoxia
   d. severe hypoxia

38. Sellick's maneuver is used to
   a. prevent regurgitation during attempts at intubation
   b. open the airway of a patient with suspected neck trauma
   c. move the tongue aside during attempts at intubation
   d. aid in removal of an esophageal obturator airway in the field

39. In order to visualize the patient's vocal cords during oral intubation, you should align the patient's
   a. nostrils, back of the head, and shoulders
   b. mouth, pharynx, and trachea
   c. pharynx, trachea, and bronchi
   d. nostrils, mouth, and vocal cords

40. All of the following are signs of esophageal intubation EXCEPT
   a. air leak
   b. gurgling sounds in the epigastrium
   c. cyanosis and general worsening of the patient's condition
   d. cardiac arrhythmias

Answer questions 41–43 on the basis of the information below.

You are called to the home of a 68-year-old female who is complaining of severe dyspnea. She states that it started about 45 minutes ago and has been getting progressively worse. She has a heart history but denies chest pain at this time. Her breathing is very congested. During your assessment, you notice accessory muscle use and wet rales on both sides.

41. Of the following, which is this patient most likely suffering from?
   a. pulmonary embolism
   b. acute pulmonary edema
   c. pneumonia
   d. lung cancer

42. This patient should be treated with which of the following medications?
   a. diphenydramine
   b. isoproterenol
   c. verpamil
   d. morphine sulfate

43. Which of the following drugs should be used with extreme caution with this patient?
   a. atrophine sulfate
   b. theophylline
   c. epinephrine
   d. aminophylline

44. In most cases, treatment of metabolic acidosis consists of
   a. having the patient rebreathe carbon dioxide
   b. ventilating the patient adequately
   c. administering sodium bicarbonate
   d. determining and treating the underlying cause

45. Which drug is an example of a beta agonist?
   a. aminophylline
   b. ipratropium (Atrovent)
   c. furosemide
   d. albuterol

46. If a patient's pleural space expands because air enters from an interior wound, it is
   a. a closed pneumothorax
   b. an open pneumothorax
   c. a tension pneumothorax
   d. traumatic asphyxia

47. Nitronox is useful in managing care of patients with chest trauma because it
   a. reduces intracranial pressure
   b. reduces inflammation and prevents spine damage
   c. depresses respiration and therefore preserves respiratory effort
   d. eases pain and thus helps the patient breathe more deeply

48. *Stridor* refers to a
   a. rattling sound associated with fluid in the upper airway
   b. whistling sound heard on expiration
   c. gurgling sound resulting from fluid in the lower airways
   d. high-pitched sound heard on inspiration

49. The correct treatment for a choking victim who can speak is to
   a. administer five abdominal thrusts
   b. administer five chest thrusts
   c. ask the victim to cough forcefully
   d. open the airway, give two ventilations, and then administer five abdominal thrusts

50. The primary treatment for a patient with chronic emphysema who is NOT severely hypoxic consists of
   a. ventilating with high-flow oxygen
   b. administering low-flow oxygen
   c. establishing two large-bore IVs
   d. administering intubation and high-flow oxygen

51. A Wright meter is used to determine
   a. peak expiratory flow rate in an asthma patient
   b. oxygen saturation level in any respiratory patient
   c. carbon dioxide level in a patient who is hyperventilating
   d. hemoglobin saturation in an emphysema patient

52. The classes of drugs most commonly used by asthma patients are
   a. beta blockers and narcotics
   b. antiarrhythmics
   c. bronchodilators and steroids
   d. anticholinergics and diuretics

Answer questions 53–56 on the basis of the information below.

You are called to the home of a 17-year-old female who was found by her parents hanging from a rope in the garage. The patient was cut down by her father approximately 6 minutes prior to your arrival, but she is unconscious and unresponsive to pain or voice. She is breathing spontaneously but has coarse inspiratory stridor.

53. This patient's inspiratory stridor is most probably due to
   a. a crushed or torn trachea
   b. bronchoconstriction due to trauma
   c. a foreign-body obstruction
   d. a cervical spine injury

54. Upon examination of the patient's upper chest and neck, you note the presence of a large swollen area that extends from her throat to her shoulder. When you press on this area, you feel crackles under the skin. This is called
   a. traumatic asphyxia
   b. hangman's fracture
   c. subcutaneous emphysema
   d. subcutaneous embolism

55. This patient has left a note indicating her desire to die. Considering this, which of the following statements is true?
   a. Begin treatment, once consent is given by her parents.
   b. The note constitutes an advanced directive for health care, so resuscitative measures should be stopped.
   c. The note constitutes a Do Not Resuscitate order, so resuscitative measures should be stopped.
   d. The note constitutes a durable power of attorney, so resuscitative measures should be stopped.

56. Treatment of this patient should include all of the following EXCEPT
   a. spinal precautions
   b. high-flow oxygen via a non-rebreather mask
   c. larygoscopy to determine the extent of damage
   d. monitoring for further airway compromise

57. Possible side effects of albuterol include
   a. GI bleeding
   b. palpitations, anxiety
   c. drowsiness, confusion
   d. skin rash, dry mouth

58. In a patient suffering from anaphylaxis, the FIRST sign of laryngeal edema is often
   a. wheezing
   b. coughing
   c. hoarseness
   d. difficulty breathing

59. The disease process of emphysema involves
   a. a build-up of fluid in the lungs due to increased capillary permeability
   b. deflation of a portion of the lung due to the rupture of a bleb
   c. bronchoconstriction due to increased airway resistance
   d. a loss of elasticity in the alveoli due to prolonged insult

Answer questions 60–65 on the basis of the information below.

You are called to the home of a 78-year-old male who is having difficulty breathing. The patient is sitting upright in a tripod position, and you note profound accessory muscle use. His skins are pale, cool, and clammy. His vital signs are: blood pressure of 180/72; heart rate of 90 with a strong and regular pulse; a respiratory rate of 40, shallow and labored with a coarse rattling sound upon expiration. Auscultation of lung sounds reveals coarse rales to about the nipple line and no air movement to the bases of the lungs. The patient can speak in only one- or two-word sentences. Family bystanders inform you that the patient was sleeping when this episode began and this has happened several times since his MI one year ago. He has mild pedal edema and no distended neck veins. His family first noticed the patient having dyspnea about 25–30 minutes ago.

60. This patient is most likely exhibiting the signs and symptoms of
   a. pneumonia
   b. chronic obstructive pulmonary disease
   c. congestive heart failure
   d. asthma

61. Medications used to intervene would include all of the following EXCEPT
   a. morphine sulfate
   b. nitroglycerin
   c. furosemide
   d. dobutamine

62. Patients with a history of this disease, or signs and symptoms of this disease, may exhibit all of the following symptoms prior to an acute event EXCEPT
   a. high fever
   b. paroxysmal nocturnal dyspnea
   c. dyspnea upon exertion
   d. generally increasing dyspnea over several hours

63. Priorities for the management of this patient include all of the following EXCEPT
   a. decreasing venous return to the heart
   b. increasing venous return to the heart
   c. decreasing myocardial oxygen demand
   d. improving oxygenation and ventilation

64. This patient would most likely benefit from which of the following?
   a. moving him to a supine position
   b. assisting him in walking to the ambulance
   c. having him breathe deeply into a paper sack
   d. giving him intermittent positive pressure ventilation

65. If this patient were to be experiencing right-side heart failure, you would expect to find all of the following symptoms EXCEPT
   a. tachycardia
   b. profound peripheral edema
   c. jugular venous distention
   d. fever

66. Which transfusion is certain to cause a severe transfusion reaction?
   a. Type A blood given to a Type AB individual
   b. Type AB blood given to a Type O individual
   c. Type O blood given to a Type AB individual
   d. Type B blood given to a Type AB individual

67. An isotonic solution is one that
   a. has an electrolyte composition like that of blood plasma
   b. is used only in patients who are severely dehydrated
   c. has a higher solute composition than the body cells
   d. has a lower solute composition than the body cells

68. Cardiogenic shock most often results from severe
   a. spinal cord injury
   b. allergic reaction
   c. ventricular failure
   d. internal or external hemorrhage

69. The PASG can be used to
   a. control bleeding in a patient with abruptio placentae
   b. prevent shock in a patient with an impaled object in the abdomen
   c. support the respiratory efforts of a patient with severe dyspnea
   d. stabilize lower-extremity fractures in a hypotensive patient

PARAMEDIC PRACTICE EXAM 2

70. Which of the following is a diuretic?
a. nitroglycerin
b. morphine sulfate
c. nitrous oxide
d. furosemide

71. Which statement about use of the PASGs for a shock patient with an impaled object in the abdomen is correct?
a. Do not use the PASG for patients with impaled-object wounds.
b. Inflate the lower compartments of the PASG only.
c. Request medical direction before inflating the PASG.
d. Remove the object before inflating the PASG.

72. While giving IV fluids to a shock trauma patient, it is MOST important for you to continuously monitor the patient's
a. breath sounds
b. capillary refill
c. blood pressure
d. pupillary response

73. Morphine sulfate is used in the management of MI patients to
a. help distinguish between angina and MI
b. relieve pain and reduce myocardial oxygen demand
c. relieve ventricular dysrhythmias
d. substitute for Lidocaine in allergic patients

74. Paroxysmal nocturnal dyspnea is commonly a sign of
a. myocardial infarction
b. ruptured aortic aneurysm
c. left-sided heart failure
d. right-sided heart failure

75. Management of left-sided heart failure includes
a. high-flow oxygen, minidrip IV of D5W, placement of ECG leads, careful monitoring
b. high-flow oxygen, minidrip IV of D5W, placement of electrodes, administration of morphine sulfate and nitroglycerin, rapid transport
c. oxygen, administration of sublingual nifedipine, administration of sodium nitro-prusside via IV infusion, administration of labetolol via IV bolus
d. high-flow oxygen, placement of ECG leads, defibrillation

76. Which of the following is an antidysrhythmic drug?
a. epinephrine
b. isoproterenol
c. nitroglycerin
d. procainamide

77. The preferred field treatment for patients with third-degree AV block who are symptomatic consists of
a. pacemaker insertion
b. lidocaine
c. transcutaneous cardiac pacing
d. bretylium followed by synchronized cardioversion

78. Treatment for a patient suspected of having an abdominal aortic aneurysm consists of
   a. provide oxygen, apply PASG, give intravenous fluids, transport rapidly
   b. provide oxygen, carefully palpate the abdomen, give intravenous fluids, transport rapidly
   c. establish and maintain airway, provide oxygen, transport rapidly
   d. provide oxygen, administer Procardia, transport rapidly

79. Furosemide is used in the prehospital management of
   a. asystole
   b. dysrhythmias
   c. cardiogenic shock
   d. congestive heart failure

80. Vagal maneuvers are used to treat which type of dysrhythmias?
   a. PACs
   b. atrial fibrillation
   c. atrial flutter
   d. PSVTs

81. Which part of the ECG tracing reflects repolarization of the ventricles?
   a. P wave
   b. QRS complex
   c. R wave
   d. T wave

82. The length of the normal P–R interval is
   a. 0.04–0.12 seconds
   b. 0.12–0.20 seconds
   c. 0.20–0.28 seconds
   d. 0.28–0.36 seconds

83. The term *tachycardia* refers to a heart rate that is
   a. less than 60 beats per minute
   b. irregular
   c. ineffective
   d. greater than 100 beats per minute

84. Which dysrhythmia often results from use of mild stimulants such as caffeine or nicotine?
   a. sinus bradycardia
   b. atrial flutter
   c. premature atrial contractions
   d. accelerated junctional rhythm

85. In a patient with ventricular tachycardia, the QRS complex is
   a. absent
   b. 0.04–0.12 seconds
   c. greater than 0.12 seconds and bizarre in shape
   d. shorter than 0.04 seconds and flattened

86. A patient with nonperfusing ventricular tachycardia would receive the same treatment as a patient with
   a. ventricular fibrillation
   b. perfusing ventricular tachycardia
   c. atrial fibrillation
   d. PSVTs

87. Which of the following is an indication that an MI patient is developing cardiogenic shock?
   a. increasing pain
   b. rising temperature
   c. falling blood pressure
   d. sinus bradycardia

88. Which of the following are signs and symptoms of right heart failure?
   a. tachycardia, peripheral edema, jugular vein distention
   b. bradycardia, carotid bruits, falling blood pressure
   c. respiratory distress, hypoxia, cyanosis
   d. chest pain, diaphoresis, anxiety, dyspnea, nausea and vomiting

89. The first sign of a potentially lethal dysrhythmia in an MI patient is often
   a. changing pulse rate
   b. increasing pain
   c. loss of consciousness
   d. nausea and vomiting

90. Easing the patient's anxiety and relieving pain are major goals for prehospital care of MI patients because anxiety and pain can
   a. signal development of a lethal dysrhythmia
   b. mask underlying symptoms
   c. prevent the patient from cooperating with treatment
   d. increase heart rate and oxygen demand

91. Dopamine is used to
   a. relieve pain
   b. increase cardiac output
   c. reduce blood pressure
   d. treat dysrhythmias

92. In prehospital care, bretylium is used to
   a. relieve pain
   b. decrease anxiety
   c. dilate peripheral blood vessels
   d. treat dangerous dysrhythmias

93. Causes of pulseless electrical activity include all of the following EXCEPT
   a. right-sided heart failure
   b. massive myocardial infarction
   c. hypovolemia
   d. cardiac tamponade

94. To avoid masking the elevated enzyme levels that are used to diagnose MI in the hospital, when treating suspected MI patients, you should NOT administer
   a. high-flow oxygen
   b. intramuscular drugs
   c. beta blockers
   d. diazepam or lidocaine

95. Your patient is a 67-year-old male who is complaining of chest pain, which continues after two doses of nitroglycerin. He reports a history of angina and says that all his previous attacks have been relieved by nitroglycerin. You should
   a. take a detailed history to determine the cause of this attack
   b. assume that the patient is having an MI and treat accordingly
   c. check for signs and symptoms of shock
   d. assume that the patient's medication has expired and give two more doses

96. The most common complication of MI is
   a. cardiogenic shock
   b. unstable angina
   c. dysrhythmia
   d. chest pain

97. The first-line treatment for malignant PVCs is
   a. lidocaine
   b. bretylium
   c. procainamide
   d. observation only

98. Your patient's ECG indicates atrial fibrillation. Which additional finding would indicate the need for immediate cardioversion?
   a. PSVTs
   b. wide-complex tachycardia
   c. atrial flutter
   d. ventricular tachycardia

99. The inferior border of the thoracic cavity is the
   a. neck
   b. pelvic floor
   c. diaphragm
   d. second intercostal space

Answer questions 100–102 on the basis of the information below.

You are called by the police department to a neighborhood where you encounter a male patient approximately 20–30 years old. The police officer states that neighbors called because the patient was "freaking out." Witnesses say they saw him smoking something just before he started acting in a bizarre manner. During your assessment you notice that the patient is hyperactive and anxious. His pupils are dilated, and he is hypertensive and tachycardic.

100. This patient is most likely experiencing
   a. insulin shock
   b. cocaine overdose
   c. narcotic overdose
   d. delirium tremens

101. The appropriate treatment for this patient consists of
   a. oxygen, IV, and ECG monitoring
   b. oxygen, IV, and naloxone
   c. activated charcoal, IV, and ECG monitoring
   d. activated charcoal, IV, and shock management

102. When treating this patient you should be prepared for which of the following complications?
   a. febrile seizures and septic shock
   b. CNS depression and hypoglycemia
   c. life-threatening dysrhythmias and seizures
   d. diuresis and bradychardia

103. The primary use of thiamine in emergency care is to treat patients with
   a. signs and symptoms of shock
   b. delirium tremens from chronic alcoholism
   c. diabetic emergency
   d. cardiogenic shock

104. Methylprednisolone is used to
   a. decrease intracranial pressure in patients with head injury
   b. control seizures and reduce anxiety
   c. reduce bleeding in patients with head trauma
   d. reduce swelling in patients with suspected spinal cord injury

105. Your patient has a suspected hand injury. You can immobilize the hand in the neutral position by
  a. taping it flat against the chest
  b. putting the arm in a sling and allowing the hand to dangle
  c. placing a covered roll of bandaging in the palm
  d. securing the hand tightly to a board with the palm and fingers slightly flexed

106. When splinting a limb with a suspected fracture, one paramedic applies the splint while the other paramedic
  a. holds the limb in place and monitors the distal pulse
  b. reassures the patient and provides support
  c. checks limb alignment and administers high-flow oxygen
  d. applies PASGs and monitors vital signs

107. It is standard practice to apply the PASG for fractures of
  a. one lower limb
  b. one upper limb
  c. the ribs
  d. the pelvis

108. How should you care for your patient's amputated finger while en route to the hospital?
  a. Place the finger in a plastic bag and immerse the bag in cold water or ice.
  b. Immerse the finger in a pail full of ice water.
  c. Bandage the severed end and place it in a plastic bag.
  d. Bandage the hand with the severed finger in contact with the wound.

109. A patient's hand and arm have been burned by dry lime. You should
  a. use a neutralizing acid to offset the effect of the chemical burn
  b. brush the lime away and then flood the skin with cool water
  c. immediately immerse the injured limb in a pail of cold water
  d. use alcohol to dissolve the lime, then flood with water

110. A patient in a very early stage of hypoglycemia may complain of
  a. dimness of sight
  b. dry mouth
  c. nausea
  d. hunger

111. Patients may develop hypoglycemia if they take too much insulin or if they
  a. exercise too much
  b. overeat
  c. develop a mild infection
  d. develop a heart arrhythmia

112. Central neurogenic hyperventilation is associated with
  a. diabetes mellitus
  b. central nervous system trauma
  c. asthma
  d. chronic bronchitis and emphysema

113. Flaccid paralysis is usually a sign of injury to the
  a. cerebrum
  b. upper brainstem
  c. spinal cord
  d. parietal lobe

114. For a patient with an altered mental status, after you secure the airway and immobilize the cervical spine, your next priority of care is to
    a. draw blood for glucose determination and establish an IV
    b. monitor cardiac rhythm and prepare to defibrillate if necessary
    c. administer naloxone and thiamine
    d. hyperventilate with oxygen and administer dexamethasone

115. You are called to the home of a 36-year-old man who is having a seizure. His wife reports that he has not taken his "seizure pills" lately and that he has now had three seizures in a row without regaining consciousness. After securing the airway and ventilating with the bag-valve mask, you should
    a. draw blood, administer dextrose, and transport immediately
    b. monitor blood glucose level and administer naloxone and thiamine
    c. secure the patient to a long spine board until the seizures are over
    d. begin an IV, monitor cardiac rhythm, and administer diazepam

116. The primary treatment for severe anaphylaxis is
    a. 0.3–0.5 mg of epinephrine 1:10,000 given intravenously
    b. 0.1–0.3 mg of epinephrine 1:10,000 given subcutaneously
    c. 0.3–0.5 mg of epinephrine 1:1,000 given intravenously
    d. 0.1–0.3 mg of epinephrine 1:1,000 given subcutaneously

117. Atropine sulfate is administered to patients who have
    a. taken an overdose of narcotics
    b. taken an overdose of cocaine
    c. been exposed to organophosphates
    d. been exposed to carbon monoxide

118. Your patient is a 64-year-old man who is experiencing seizures and hallucinations. His wife reports that he is a chronic alcoholic who stopped drinking two days ago. After providing supportive treatment, you should request permission to administer
    a. thiamine
    b. sodium bicarbonate
    c. naloxone
    d. diazepam

119. You can distinguish between water intoxication and heat exhaustion by determining your patient's
    a. temperature
    b. fluid intake
    c. level of consciousness
    d. glucose level

120. The most important consideration for a patient who is suffering from decompression sickness is to
    a. decontaminate the patient using copious amounts of cold, running water
    b. monitor the ECG and defibrillate if necessary
    c. provide oxygen at 100 percent concentration with a nonrebreathing mask
    d. administer painkillers, such as Nitronox, as needed

121. When interviewing patients who are dis-
     traught or potentially violent, you should do
     all of the following EXCEPT
     a. remove the patient from the crisis situation
     b. encourage the patient to explain the situa-
        tion freely and in his or her own words
     c. tell the patient when he or she is distorting
        reality
     d. avoid arguing with or shouting at the
        patient

122. A patient who talks non-stop and is restless
     and overactive can best be described as
     a. manic
     b. depressed
     c. anxious
     d. drunk

123. The abbreviation CVP stands for
     a. cerebral vascular pressure
     b. central venous pressure
     c. cyanotic ventral pulses
     d. central peripheral pulses

124. The metatarsal are bones of the
     a. toes
     b. feet
     c. fingers
     d. hands

125. Unusual respiratory patterns in a patient with
     a head injury indicate the need for
     a. ventilation with 100 percent oxygen
     b. administration of epinephrine 1:1000
     c. rapid transport because of brain stem injury
     d. percutaneous transtracheal catheter venti-
        lation

Answer questions 126–128 on the basis of the
information below.

You respond on a 56-year-old male who appears to
be intoxicated. He is belligerent, disoriented, and has
a laceration on his forehead. You have made several
attempts to convince him of the need for treatment,
but he refuses treatment or transport.

126. Given this situation, you should
     a. leave the patient and return to service
     b. call for medical direction
     c. transport the patient against his will in
        restraints
     d. bandage the laceration and leave the scene

127. In the above situation, which of the following
     is most important?
     a. returning to service as soon as possible
     b. obtaining billing information
     c. properly documenting your advice to the
        patient and his refusal
     d. restraining the patient in the supine position

128. Two hours later, you are called back for this
     same patient, who is now unconscious and
     responsive to painful stimuli only. Which of
     the following treatment modalities is appropri-
     ate for this patient?
     a. dextrose IV and transport to a detoxifica-
        tion center
     b. blood glucose test, thiamine IV, monitor,
        oxygen, and transport to an emergency
        department
     c. oxygen, albuterol, and transport to an emer-
        gency department
     d. 1000 cc Ringer's lactate IV and transport to
        an emergency department

129. Normal pulse rate in a newborn is
   a. 100–160
   b. 80–100
   c. 60–80
   d. 40–60

130. The normal respiratory rate in a 3-year-old child is
   a. 50–60/min
   b. 40–50/min
   c. 30–40/min
   d. 20–30/min

131. Which set of vital signs is ABNORMAL?
   a. male, age 2 weeks: respirations 40, pulse 120, systolic BP 66
   b. female, age 1 year: respirations 36, pulse 125, systolic BP 70
   c. male, age 4 years: respirations 24, pulse 100, systolic BP 90
   d. female, age 11 years: respirations 18, pulse, 78, systolic BP 96

132. Children are particularly prone to head injuries because they have
   a. small airways in relation to their head size
   b. large tongues in relation to the size of the airway
   c. an inability to balance and use their small muscle groups
   d. large heads in relation to their body size

133. Your patient is a 4-year-old girl who awoke in the middle of the night with a cough that her mother describes as sounding "like a dog barking." The patient feels more comfortable sitting up. Vital signs are: respirations, 26/min; pulse, 100; temperature, 101° F. On physical exam, you hear stridor on inspiration. You should suspect
   a. airway obstruction
   b. croup
   c. epiglottitis
   d. asthma

134. The initial amount of fluid given to a severely dehydrated child is
   a. 20 mL/kg
   b. 30 mL/kg
   c. 40 mL/kg
   d. 50 mL/kg

Answer questions 135–138 on the basis of the information below.

You are called to the home of a 21-year-old female in labor. She is two weeks from her expected due date and is having contractions that last 1.5 minutes and are 3 minutes apart. This is her second pregnancy; her first child was delivered vaginally at full term.

135. Your first course of action for this patient is to
   a. examine her for crowning
   b. place her on the gurney and transport immediately
   c. call her physician and advice that the birth will take place at the scene
   d. examine her for effacement

136. Your patient suddenly tells you she feels something slippery between her legs. Upon examination you notice a 2-inch segment of the umbilical cord protruding from the vagina. This is known as
a. prolapsed cord
b. abruptio umbilicus
c. placenta previa
d. abruptio previa

137. Your immediate treatment for this patient is to
a. provide high-flow oxygen and transport Code 3
b. take pressure off the cord
c. wrap the cord in a moist sterile dressing
d. leave the cord as it is and transport

138. You are ready to transport this patient. In what position should she be placed for the duration of the transport?
a. supine with hips elevated and knees up
b. left lateral recumbent
c. prone with hips elevated
d. sitting position

139. You arrive at the scene of an imminent delivery in the field. The First Responder, who called for assistance, reports that the patient is a 32-year-old female who is "G4, P3." This means that the
a. the patient is pregnant for the seventh time and has 3 living children
b. the patient's cervix has dilated 4 centimeters in 3 hours
c. the patient has been pregnant 4 times and delivered 3 children
d. patient has had 4 contractions in the past 3 hours

140. Your patient is a 28-year-old female who reports that she is 9 weeks pregnant. She is complaining of severe abdominal pain, shoulder pain, and vaginal bleeding. Vital signs are unremarkable, but a physical exam reveals tenderness in the lower-left quadrant. You should suspect
a. pelvic inflammatory disease
b. ectopic pregnancy
c. spontaneous abortion
d. abruptio placentae

141. *Effacement* refers to the
a. direction the fetus is facing during birth
b. position of the fetus in the uterus
c. thinning of the cervix during the first stage of labor
d. opening of the cervix during the last stage of labor

142. Your patient is a 33-year-old woman who is 9 months pregnant. She complains of severe abdominal pain and abdominal tenderness, but no vaginal bleeding. You should suspect
a. abruptio placentae
b. placenta previa
c. threatened abortion
d. eclampsia

143. Signs and symptoms of preeclampsia in a pregnant patient include
a. high blood pressure only
b. high blood pressure, headaches, edema, visual disturbances
c. high blood pressure, headaches, edema, visual disturbances, seizures
d. abdominal pain and bright-red bleeding

144. The third stage of labor begins when the
   a. contractions are 5 minutes apart
   b. cervix is fully dilated
   c. fetus is born
   d. placenta is delivered

145. The correct procedure for cutting the umbilical cord after the birth of the fetus is to
   a. milk the cord of all blood and cut it no more than 5 centimeters from the infant
   b. clamp the cord close to the infant and cut it between the infant and the clamp
   c. clamp the cord in two places, and cut it near the infant and near the placenta
   d. clamp the cord in two places 5 centimeters apart and cut it between the clamps

146. A healthy neonate's heart rate at birth is
   a. 80–100 beats per minute
   b. 100–120 beats per minute
   c. 120–150 beats per minute
   d. 150–180 beats per minute

147. The presence of meconium on the neonate or in the amniotic fluid indicates that the fetus
   a. may have been distressed
   b. is premature
   c. will require resuscitation
   d. has congenital anomalies

148. You would perform chest compressions on any newborn whose heart rate is less than
   a. 120
   b. 100
   c. 80
   d. 60

149. Medications and drugs are most often delivered to a newborn through the
   a. common iliac vein
   b. umbilical vein
   c. ductus arteriosus
   d. jugular vein

Answer questions 150–152 on the basis of the information below.

You respond on a 2-year-old female who is postictal. The patient's parents report that the child was sleeping when she began to shake and turn blue. She has had a runny nose, but she has had no medications lately. There is no history of seizures.

150. This patient is most likely suffering from
   a. Type I diabetes
   b. a hypoglycemic seizure
   c. an anaphylactic seizure
   d. a febrile seizure

151. Which of the following vital signs would you expect this patient to have?
   a. increased temperature, tachycardia, increased respirations
   b. increased temperature, decreased blood pressure, decreased heart rate
   c. increased temperature, increased blood pressure, decreased heart rate
   d. increased temperature, increased blood pressure, increased heart rate

152. If this patient continues in a prolonged postictal state, the appropriate treatment would be to
   a. sign the patient out A.M.A. and refer her to her pediatrician
   b. instruct the parents to give analgesics every four hours
   c. administer oxygen and an IV and transport
   d. administer oxygen and sodium bicarbonate and transport

153. Allied health personnel include all of the following EXCEPT
   a. paramedics
   b. EMTs
   c. physicians
   d. respiratory therapists

154. Which situation would constitute a moral dilemma for a paramedic?
   a. A rape victim insists on being cared for by a female paramedic or EMT.
   b. A drunk has sustained a potentially serious head injury but refuses care or transport.
   c. A patient has signed a Do Not Resuscitate order, and his family informs the paramedic of his wishes.
   d. A patient is found unconscious, and no family members are present to authorize care.

155. The hospital component of the EMS system includes
   a. emergency room personnel
   b. laypersons trained in CPR
   c. EMTs
   d. First Responders

156. You are called to a physician's office to care for a patient who is experiencing symptoms of MI. The physician tells you that she will stabilize the patient herself and that she is assuming responsibility for care. You should
   a. defer to the on-scene physician
   b. request direction from medical control
   c. assume responsibility immediately
   d. insist that the on-scene physician communicate with medical control

157. A Type II ambulance usually consists of a
   a. conventional cab-and-chassis truck
   b. standard van, usually with a raised roof
   c. special cab-forward van with an integral body
   d. fire engine

158. A legal document that specifies what type of treatment a patient does and does not want to receive is a
   a. Do Not Resuscitate order
   b. tort
   c. living will
   d. durable power of attorney

159. In most states, a person is considered to be capable of giving consent to treatment at age
   a. 15
   b. 16
   c. 18
   d. 21

160. You are transporting a patient with a suspected MI. The medical control physician has just given you a specific order. The first thing you should to is to
   a. carry out the order
   b. question the order
   c. record the order
   d. repeat the order

161. The process of transmitting physiological data from the field to the hospital over the phone lines is called
   a. modulation
   b. biotelemetry
   c. computer-aided dispatch
   d. trunking

162. You have accessed a 34-year-old truckdriver, Tom, who has become entrapped after a vehicle rollover accident. While waiting for rescue workers, you should do all of the following EXCEPT
   a. make sure you and that all team members who are in communication with you use the patient's name
   b. explain all delays clearly to the patient
   c. explain technical aspects of the rescue to Tom in clear, simple language
   d. tell Tom you will be right back, and leave him to get needed supplies

163. You are the first paramedic unit to arrive on the scene of a multi-injury bus accident. Your FIRST responsibility is to
   a. assume command of the incident and give a preliminary report to dispatch
   b. wait until additional backup units arrive on scene
   c. extract patients from the bus and triage them
   d. review and evaluate the efficiency of site operations up until your arrival

164. At a fully activated mass-casualty incident, which officer would establish a helicopter landing site?
   a. command officer
   b. staging officer
   c. extrication officer
   d. transportation officer

165. Under the START triage method, which patient would receive immediate respiratory treatment without further assessment?
   a. male, no respiratory effort
   b. female, respirations 12/min
   c. male, respirations 28/min
   d. female, respirations 38/min

166. In the METTAG system a red tag means that the patient
   a. is dead
   b. has critical injuries
   c. has minor injuries
   d. is not injured

167. Another term for a cumulative stress reaction is
   a. burnout
   b. fight-or-flight reaction
   c. flashback
   d. anxiety

168. To alleviate stress in the first day or two after a critical incident, one of the most helpful things you can do is to
   a. take a tranquilizer
   b. go on vacation
   c. get lots of rest as well as strenuous exercise
   d. work longer-than-average shifts to keep your mind off the incident

169. On reaching the scene of a single-motor-vehicle accident, you note that the driver is pinned behind the steering wheel. You also note the presence of two sets of spider-web patterns on the windshield. This would alert you to the possible presence of
   a. a second victim
   b. multiple injuries in the driver
   c. high-speed collision
   d. hit-and-run injuries

170. Which patient is LEAST likely to need rapid transport to a trauma center rather than secondary assessment and stabilization on the scene?
   a. male, age 56, ejected from a crashed vehicle, flail chest
   b. female, age 60, burns to 10 of body surface, including face
   c. male, age 28, fell 30 feet from platform, multiple fractures suspected
   d. female, age 46, struck by car traveling 10 mph, no penetrating injuries

171. Your patient is a 27-year-old male who has taken an overdose of Norpramin. After the primary assessment and stabilization, you should
   a. start an IV and ECG, administer medications as directed, transport rapidly
   b. reassure the patient and talk him down if he hallucinates; keep him in a dark, quiet room
   c. start an IV and ECG, administer naloxone
   d. start an IV and ECG, administer propranolol according to protocol

172. For which procedure is it NOT necessary to wear a mask or protective eyewear?
   a. drawing blood
   b. inserting an EOA
   c. suctioning
   d. cleaning contaminated instruments

173. The most common job-related source of HIV infections among health-care workers is
   a. assisting at emergency childbirth
   b. direct contact with a patient's skin
   c. the accidental needle stick
   d. breathing contaminated air

174. The leading cause of death among elderly people is
   a. cancer
   b. respiratory disease
   c. accidents and falls
   d. cardiac disease

175. When confronted with a patient whom you suspect to be a victim of elder abuse, you should
   a. ask the patient if he or she needs help
   b. confront the family with your suspicions
   c. report your suspicions to the appropriate authority
   d. search the family's medical records for prior signs of abuse

176. Your patient is Amira, age 2. Before listening to Amira's chest with your stethoscope, you should reassure her by
   a. explaining in detail exactly how the stethoscope works
   b. letting her listen to your chest
   c. telling her about all of the equipment you use
   d. letting her take the stethoscope apart

177. Your patient is Garth, age 14, who has a suspected broken arm. As you stabilize the patient and prepare him for transport, it would be most appropriate for you to
   a. allow him to record his own vital signs
   b. ask him what kinds of bandages and splints you should use
   c. offer him candy if he doesn't cry
   d. reassure him and explain what you are doing

178. Care of the patient who is a victim of sexual assault includes all of the following EXCEPT
   a. cleaning and bandaging wounds
   b. maintaining privacy and confidentiality
   c. preserving physical evidence
   d. obtaining specific permission to assess and treat

179. To be able to carry on a two-way conversation with a physician while transmitting telemetry, you would need a
   a. simplex transmission system
   b. duplex transmission system
   c. multiplex transmission system
   d. quadriplex transmission system

180. The START triage algorithm calls for rapidly assessing all of the following EXCEPT
   a. circulation
   b. respiration
   c. mentation/level of consciousness
   d. neuro-muscular function

ANSWERS

1. b. The airway is always given priority, but in this case, since the patient is talking, the first step in assessment and care would be to stabilize the cervical spine.

2. b. Snoring indicates that the airway is partially obstructed by the patient's tongue. Clear the airway with the chin-lift/jaw-thrust maneuver or by inserting a nasopharyngeal airway.

3. c. Capillary refill time is a more reliable indicator of circulatory status in infants and young children than in adults.

4. d. The E refers to expose; the paramedic exposes the patient's skin to reveal injuries.

5. c. After respiratory status is assessed, the basis for judging a patient's hemodynamic status is presence or absence or a radial pulse *or* skin color and temperature. This patient is showing signs of shock.

6. a. The root word *myo-* refers to a muscle.

7. d. The prefix *leuk-* refers to *white.*

8. b. The skin is made up of epithelial tissue, whose purpose is to protect body surfaces.

9. d. *Distal* refers to a location that is further from the trunk of the body than the reference point.

10. a. This patient is exhibiting classic signs and symptoms for a dissecting aortic aneurysm.

11. b. Hypertension is present in 75–85 percent of dissecting aortic aneurysm cases.

12. c. Morphine sulfate is the appropriate medication for this patient.

13. a. These are all consequences of further dissection. Other conditions also include syncope, heart failure, and absent or reduced pulses.

14. b. Even though the patient's condition appears to be stable, the mechanism of injury indicates that serious underlying injuries, such as internal bleeding, may be present. Transport immediately in this case.

15. c. Use of a helmet can protect the rider against head injury but not against spinal injury.

16. a. Battle's sign, discoloration of the mastoid area, is an indication of basilar skull fracture.

17. c. A contrecoup injury is an injury to the brain opposite the impact site; it results from the brain's rebounding movement against the skull wall.

18. b. A patient who vomits, especially without reporting feeling nauseated, and then becomes disoriented, should be suspected of brainstem injury.

19. c. The score is 9: 2 points for eye opening, 5 points for motor response, and 2 points for speech.

20. b. The signs and symptoms of tension pneumothorax are given.

21. c. According to the rule of nines as applied to pediatric injuries, the front or back of the trunk represents 18 percent of the body surface and the front of one leg represents 7 percent.

22. **c.** Using the Glasgow Trauma Scale, the patient would receive 3 points for respiratory rate, 1 point for normal chest expansion, 3 points for systolic blood pressure, and 1 point for delayed capillary refill.

23. **b.** This option lists the vital sign changes associated with Cushing's syndrome.

24. **b.** Palpate all quadrants of the abdomen, ending where the patient says it hurts. Do not perform abdominal auscultation and percussion in the field.

25. **c.** The O part of the OPQRST algorithm stands for onset: What made the pain start?

26. **d.** A positive tilt test (decrease in blood pressure or increase in pulse rate when the patient moves from supine to sitting position) indicates the possibility of shock.

27. **b.** *Ascites* refers to an accumulation of fluid in the abdomen.

28. **a.** Hepatitis A is spread by the fecal-oral route, most commonly acquired from eating contaminated food. Hepatitis B, C, and D are blood borne.

29. **a.** Altered mental status is an abnormal finding in healthy elderly patients; pulse rate does decrease somewhat with age.

30. **b.** All the other drugs listed are commonly associated with toxicity in elderly patients.

31. **a.** Sinus bradycardia, or a slow heartbeat, is considered normal, particularly in a healthy adult.

32. **c.** Vital signs in MI patients depend on the extent of underlying heart damage and the patient's response to the insult.

33. **d.** To determine the heart rate, determine the number of electrical complexes that occur within a 6-second internal. Multiply this number by 10 to obtain the number of beats per minute.

34. **c.** The goal of prehospital care for patients with PID is to provide comfort. Do not perform a vaginal exam.

35. **b.** A patient will breathe more slowly when asleep than when awake; all the other factors listed increase respiratory rate.

36. **c.** Compliance refers to how easily air flows into the lungs. If compliance is decreasing, look for the cause by first reassessing the airway and head position and then looking for signs that the patient is developing a tension pneumothorax.

37. **c.** A pulse oximetry reading of 86–91 percent indicates moderate hypoxia.

38. **a.** Sellick's maneuver, which involves applying pressure to the cricoid cartilage, can prevent regurgitation during attempts at intubation.

39. **b.** The patient's mouth, pharynx, and trachea must be in alignment in order for oral intubation to be successful.

40. **d.** All the other choices are signs of esophageal placement of the endotracheal tube, which can quickly lead to hypoxia and brain death.

41. **b.** The rapid onset, wet rales, accessory muscles, dyspnea, and congested respirations are classic symptoms for a patient with acute pulmonary edema.

42. **d.** Morphine sulfate would be an appropriate treatment for acute pulmonary edema.

43. b. Theophylline and the beta agonists should be used with extreme caution in patients with a history of heart problems.

44. b. Treatment of metabolic acidosis consists mainly of adequate ventilation. Administration of sodium bicarbonate is rarely needed.

45. d. Albuterol is a beta agonist that is used to cause bronchodilation in patients with asthma and other respiratory emergencies.

46. a. Closed pneumothorax occurs when air enters the pleural space from an interior wound.

47. d. Nitronox is used to manage the severe pain of chest wounds and thus allow the patient to breathe more deeply.

48. d. *Stridor,* which is a sound made during inspiration, is associated with croup.

49. c. If the patient can speak, the airway is not completely obstructed. Ask the patient to cough forcefully to expel the foreign object.

50. b. Patients with emphysema or chronic bronchitis benefit from administration of low-flow oxygen.

51. a. A Wright meter is used to determine peak expiratory flow rate in an asthma patient.

52. c. Drugs used by asthma patients include bronchodilators such as albuterol and steroids such as methylprednisolone.

53. a. The inspiratory stridor most likely indicates a crushed or torn trachea.

54. c. This patient's symptoms indicate subcutaneous emphysema.

55. a. This patient is a minor and should be treated, with the consent of her parents.

56. c. Larygoscopy is not an appropriate treatment to determine the extent of a patient's injuries.

57. b. Possible side effects of albuterol (Ventolin, Proventil) include palpitations, anxiety, and headaches.

58. c. The first sign of laryngeal edema is usually a hoarse voice.

59. d. Patients with emphysema have a loss of elasticity in the alveoli due to prolonged insult.

60. c. This patient is exhibiting the classic signs and symptoms of congestive heart failure.

61. d. Morphine, nitroglycerin, and furosemide are all used in the treatment of CHF patients; dobutamine is not.

62. a. High fever is not usually associated with CHF. High fever is used as the differential diagnosis for pneumonia.

63. a. Priorities for managing this patient are indicated by choices **b, c,** and **d.**

64. d. Increased ventilatory pressures assist in driving off some of the pulmonary edema.

65. d. Choices **a, b,** and **c** are all typically associated with CHF; fever is not.

66. b. Persons with Type O blood lack both the A and B antigens. Therefore, they will have severe transfusion reactions if they receive Type AB blood.

67. a. Isotonic solutions, such as Ringer's lactate, have electrolyte composition similar to that of blood plasma.

68. c. Cardiogenic shock results most often from left ventricular failure following acute MI.

69. d. Third-trimester pregnancy, impaled objects, and dyspnea are all contraindications for use of the PASG.

70. d. Furosemide (Lasix) is a diuretic used to treat pulmonary edema and high blood pressure.

71. b. The PASG may be used for such a patient, but only the lower compartments would be inflated.

72. a. Breath sounds are particularly important because of the danger of fluid overload, which may result in pulmonary edema.

73. b. Morphine both relieves pain and reduces the oxygen demand of the myocardium.

74. c. Left-sided heart failure with pulmonary edema is often associated with PND, or difficulty breathing after retiring for the night.

75. b. The accepted protocol for management of left-sided heart failure is given.

76. d. Procainamide is a commonly used antidysrhythmic medication.

77. c. The preferred field treatment is TCP. Definitive treatment is pacemaker insertion. Lidocaine should not be used.

78. a. Treat the patient for shock and transport rapidly. Do not palpate the abdomen.

79. d. Furosemide is a diuretic that is used in treatment of congestive heart failure.

80. d. PSVTs (paroxysmal supraventricular tachycardia) may be managed by vagal maneuvers, such as the Valsalva maneuver or ice-water immersion.

81. d. The T wave reflects repolarization of the ventricles.

82. b. The length of a normal P–R interval is 0.12–0.20 seconds, or 3–5 small boxes on the ECG strip.

83. d. The term *tachycardia* refers to an abnormally fast heart rate.

84. c. Premature atrial contractions often result from ingestion of caffeine or nicotine.

85. c. Patients with ventricular dysrhythmias often manifest lengthened and bizarre QRS complexes.

86. a. Treatment for both conditions consists of immediate defibrillation; continued treatment depends on whether a normal rhythm is initiated.

87. c. Falling blood pressure, especially a systolic pressure lower than 80 mm Hg, together with decreasing level of consciousness, is a sign of cardiogenic shock.

88. a. The classic signs and symptoms of right-sided heart failure are given.

89. a. A change in the pulse rate may be the first sign that a dysrhythmia is developing; this is why recording baseline vital signs is particularly important.

90. d. Anxiety and pain can increase the heart rate and therefore the oxygen demand of the myocardium.

91. b. In cases of cardiogenic shock, dopamine may be used to increase cardiac output.

92. d. Bretylium is used to treat life-threatening dysrhythmias. It is not a first-line agent like lidocaine.

93. a. Pulseless electrical activity may occur secondary to any of the other conditions listed and carries a grave prognosis.

94. b. Intramuscular injections can mask the elevated cardiac enzyme levels that are analyzed to confirm a diagnosis of MI.

95. b. A patient with angina whose pain does not respond to nitroglycerin is most likely suffering from MI.

96. c. The most common complication of MI is dysrhythmia, and some dysrhythmias are life-threatening.

97. a. Lidocaine is used to treat malignant PVCs or nonmalignant PVCs in patients who are symptomatic or who have a history of cardiac disease.

98. d. Ventricular tachycardia (ventricular rate greater than 150) indicates the need for immediate cardioversion.

99. c. The inferior, or lower, border of the thoracic cavity is the diaphragm.

100. b. Dilated pupils, hyperactivity, tachycardia, and hypertension are classic signs of cocaine use.

101. a. Oxygen, IV, and monitoring are appropriate for this patient. Be prepared to provide respiratory support. (Naloxone is used on narcotic overdose patients.)

102. c. Dysrhythmias and seizures are both serious possible complications of cocaine use.

103. b. Thiamine is a vitamin that is given intravenously to treat patients with delirium tremens or acute alcoholism.

104. d. Methylprednisolone is an antiinflammatory drug that is used to reduce swelling and limit the extent of spinal cord injuries.

105. d. The neutral position, or position of function, for the hand means holding the palm and fingers slightly flexed.

106. a. After positioning the limb properly, one paramedic applies the splint while the other holds the limb in position and monitors the distal pulse.

107. d. Because pelvic fractures carry a high risk of significant blood loss, it is standard practice to apply the PASG to stabilize the fracture and control bleeding.

108. a. The current protocol for care of an amputated body part is given.

109. b. Brush away as much of the lime as possible, then flood the burned area with water.

110. d. The earliest manifestations of hypoglycemia are hunger, anxiety, and restlessness.

111. a. Hypoglycemia develops in patients with diabetes when they take too much insulin or get too much exercise for the amount of food they eat.

112. b. Central neurogenic hyperventilation, which is a characterized by rapid, deep, noisy breathing, is associated with CNS damage.

113. c. Flaccid paralysis is a sign of injury to the spinal cord.

114. a. The first priority for patients with altered mental status of unknown cause is a blood glucose determination to rule out hypoglycemia.

115. d. For a patient in status epilepticus, treatment consists of establishing an IV, monitoring cardiac rhythm, and administering diazepam.

116. a. This is the standard adult dosage and route.

117. c. Atropine sulfate is administered to patients exposed to organophosphates to slow or stop overstimulation of glandular secretions.

118. d. In cases of delirium tremens after alcohol withdrawal, medical control may request you to administer diazepam before or during transport.

119. b. In a patient who has been exercising in high temperatures but who is not displaying signs of heat stroke, distinguish between water intoxication and heat exhaustion by asking questions about fluid intake and time of last urination.

120. c. Provide oxygen at 100 percent concentration; intubate if the patient is not breathing spontaneously.

121. c. The purpose of the interview is to calm the patient and to obtain as much information as possible, not to tell the patient what you think.

122. a. A patient who is displaying manic symptoms is restless and extremely active and talks constantly. The patient may or may not be violent.

123. b. The abbreviation CVP stands for central venous pressure.

124. b. The metatarsals are the bones of the feet, located between the tarsals (ankle bones) and the phalanges (toes).

125. c. Unusual respiratory patterns indicate the possibility of brain-stem injury and call for rapid transport of the patient.

126. b. Medical direction should be sought if at all possible for any suspected substance abuse patient refusing treatment or transport.

127. c. It is important in this situation to make a complete documentation of the patient's refusal to accept treatment. Documentation should include the steps you took to convince him to seek medical attention, the potential consequences of his refusal, and your assessment findings.

128. b. This choice gives the most appropriate treatment protocol for this patient. Because he is unconscious, he may be treated under implied consent.

129. a. The normal pulse rate in a neonate is 100–160 per minute.

130. d. The normal respiratory rate in a 3-year-old is 20–30 per minute.

131. b. This child's respiratory rate and pulse are too high, and her pulse is too low, for her age group.

132. d. A child's relatively large head leads to a disproportionate number of head injuries.

133. b. The signs, symptoms, and assessment findings of croup are described.

134. a. Give a severely dehydrated child an initial bolus of 20 mL/kg of normal saline or Ringer's solution.

135. a. In this situation, the first step would be to examine the patient for crowning.

136. a. The protruding umbilical cord is known as a prolapsed cord.

137. b. Taking pressure off the cord by properly placing your gloved hand in the vagina helps maintain blood flow through the umbilical cord.

138. a. Since this patient requires a caesarian section, a supine position with the hips elevated and the knees up will help to slow delivery.

139. c. G4, P3 refers to a woman who has been pregnant 4 times and delivered 3 live infants.

140. b. The signs and symptoms of an ectopic pregnancy are given.

141. c. *Effacement* refers to the thinning of the cervix, which occurs during the first stage of normal labor.

142. a. The signs and symptoms of abruptio placentae, or premature separatation of the placenta, are given.

143. b. Patients with preeclampsia manifest all the signs and symptoms of the hypertensive disorders of pregnancy except seizures.

144. c. The third stage of labor begins with the birth of the fetus and ends with the delivery of the placenta.

145. d. Clamp the cord in two places, approximately 5 centimeters apart, and cut the cord between the clamps.

146. d. Heart rate at birth is normally 150–180 beats per minute; this slows to 130–140 within a few minutes.

147. a. The presence of meconium indicates that the fetus may have been distressed before birth.

148. d. Chest compressions are required when a newborn's heart rate is less than 60, or between 60 and 80 after 30 seconds of positive-pressure ventilation.

149. b. The umbilical vein, located in the umbilical cord, is used for this purpose.

150. d. Fever-induced seizures are common in young children with only minor illnesses.

151. a. These signs and symptoms are common in a child who is recently postictal from febrile seizures.

152. c. Oxygen, an IV, and transport is an appropriate treatment for this patient.

153. c. The term allied health refers to all health care workers except physicians and nurses.

154. b. This situation constitutes a dilemma, because the paramedic would have to choose between the duty to provide care and the duty to obtain consent.

155. a. The hospital component of the EMS system includes all hospital workers, including emergency room personnel.

156. a. Paramedics should refer to a physician who is present on scene.

157. b. A Type II ambulance is an integral unit consisting of a standard van, usually with a raised roof.

158. c. A living will specifies the kind of health care a person does and does not want to receive.

159. c. In most states, consent for treatment must be obtained from all patients who are 18 years old.

160. d. Always repeat orders to ensure that you have heard them correctly before carrying them out.

161. b. Transmitting physiological data over phone lines is called biotelemetry.

162. d. Leaving a patient before turning him over to personnel of equal or higher rank constitutes abandonment; also, it is important to provide psychological support to a patient who is entrapped.

163. a. The first paramedic unit to arrive at the scene of a mass-casualty incident would immediately assume command and transmit a report to dispatch, alerting them to the need for more units.

164. d. The transportation officer would coordinate all transportation needs for the incident, including a helicopter landing site.

165. d. In the START system, a patient with respirations greater than 30 per minute would receive immediate attention.

166. b. A red tag indicates a patient with critical injuries who needs rapid transport.

167. a. A cumulative stress reaction refers to a person's reaction to the continuous, long-term effects of stress; it is also called *burnout.*

168. c. Rest, alternating with strenuous exercise, is helpful in relaxing you after a stressful incident.

169. a. The spider web pattern is made when a victim's head hits the windshield. Two spider web patterns indicate that there is a second victim.

170. d. This patient has neither a serious mechanism of injury nor a condition that on the surface that warrants rapid transport. Further assessment is the most appropriate course.

171. a. Norpramin is a tricyclic antidepressant, a class of drugs responsible for many deaths by overdose. Follow the directions of medical control and transport rapidly.

172. a. Commonly accepted infection-control guidelines call for all personnel to wear masks for any procedure that carries the risk of splashing or spurting of blood or other fluids.

173. c. Accidental needle sticks are the most common source of work-related HIV infections in health-care workers.

174. d. Because cardiac disease is so common, administer many medications commonly prescribed for other types of emergencies with extreme caution.

175. c. Report your suspicions promptly; many states require you to report such suspicions, as with suspicions of child abuse.

176. b. Toddlers can often be reassured by allowing them to handle unfamiliar objects.

177. d. Respect the teenager's feelings by explaining the purpose and result of your actions and by providing reassurance.

178. a. To avoid destroying evidence, do not clean and bandage the patient's wounds unless it is absolutely necessary.

179. c. A multiplex system allows for a two-way conversation and simultaneous transmission of telemetry readings.

180. d. Neuro-muscular function is not part of the START algorithm.

C·H·A·P·T·E·R 5
PARAMEDIC PRACTICE EXAM 3

CHAPTER SUMMARY
This is the third of four practice exams in this book based on the National Registry EMT-Paramedic written exam. Use this test to identify which types of questions are still giving you problems.

Y ou are now beginning to be very familiar with the format of the National Registry EMT-Paramedic exam. Your practice test-taking experience will help you most, however, if you have created a situation as close as possible to the real one.

For this third exam, simulate a real test. Find a quiet place where you will not be disturbed. Have with you two sharpened pencils and a good eraser. Complete the test in one sitting, setting a timer or a stopwatch. You should have plenty of time to answer all of the questions when you take the real exam, but you want to practice working quickly without rushing.

As before, the answer sheet you should use is on the next page. After the exam is an answer key, with all the answers explained. These explanations will help you see where you need to concentrate further study. When you've finished the exam and scored it, turn back to Chapter 1 to see which questions correspond to which areas of your paramedic training—then you'll know which parts of your textbook to concentrate on before you take the fourth exam.

1.	(a)	(b)	(c)	(d)		46.	(a)	(b)	(c)	(d)		91.	(a)	(b)	(c)	(d)
2.	(a)	(b)	(c)	(d)		47.	(a)	(b)	(c)	(d)		92.	(a)	(b)	(c)	(d)
3.	(a)	(b)	(c)	(d)		48.	(a)	(b)	(c)	(d)		93.	(a)	(b)	(c)	(d)
4.	(a)	(b)	(c)	(d)		49.	(a)	(b)	(c)	(d)		94.	(a)	(b)	(c)	(d)
5.	(a)	(b)	(c)	(d)		50.	(a)	(b)	(c)	(d)		95.	(a)	(b)	(c)	(d)
6.	(a)	(b)	(c)	(d)		51.	(a)	(b)	(c)	(d)		96.	(a)	(b)	(c)	(d)
7.	(a)	(b)	(c)	(d)		52.	(a)	(b)	(c)	(d)		97.	(a)	(b)	(c)	(d)
8.	(a)	(b)	(c)	(d)		53.	(a)	(b)	(c)	(d)		98.	(a)	(b)	(c)	(d)
9.	(a)	(b)	(c)	(d)		54.	(a)	(b)	(c)	(d)		99.	(a)	(b)	(c)	(d)
10.	(a)	(b)	(c)	(d)		55.	(a)	(b)	(c)	(d)		100.	(a)	(b)	(c)	(d)
11.	(a)	(b)	(c)	(d)		56.	(a)	(b)	(c)	(d)		101.	(a)	(b)	(c)	(d)
12.	(a)	(b)	(c)	(d)		57.	(a)	(b)	(c)	(d)		102.	(a)	(b)	(c)	(d)
13.	(a)	(b)	(c)	(d)		58.	(a)	(b)	(c)	(d)		103.	(a)	(b)	(c)	(d)
14.	(a)	(b)	(c)	(d)		59.	(a)	(b)	(c)	(d)		104.	(a)	(b)	(c)	(d)
15.	(a)	(b)	(c)	(d)		60.	(a)	(b)	(c)	(d)		105.	(a)	(b)	(c)	(d)
16.	(a)	(b)	(c)	(d)		61.	(a)	(b)	(c)	(d)		106.	(a)	(b)	(c)	(d)
17.	(a)	(b)	(c)	(d)		62.	(a)	(b)	(c)	(d)		107.	(a)	(b)	(c)	(d)
18.	(a)	(b)	(c)	(d)		63.	(a)	(b)	(c)	(d)		108.	(a)	(b)	(c)	(d)
19.	(a)	(b)	(c)	(d)		64.	(a)	(b)	(c)	(d)		109.	(a)	(b)	(c)	(d)
20.	(a)	(b)	(c)	(d)		65.	(a)	(b)	(c)	(d)		110.	(a)	(b)	(c)	(d)
21.	(a)	(b)	(c)	(d)		66.	(a)	(b)	(c)	(d)		111.	(a)	(b)	(c)	(d)
22.	(a)	(b)	(c)	(d)		67.	(a)	(b)	(c)	(d)		112.	(a)	(b)	(c)	(d)
23.	(a)	(b)	(c)	(d)		68.	(a)	(b)	(c)	(d)		113.	(a)	(b)	(c)	(d)
24.	(a)	(b)	(c)	(d)		69.	(a)	(b)	(c)	(d)		114.	(a)	(b)	(c)	(d)
25.	(a)	(b)	(c)	(d)		70.	(a)	(b)	(c)	(d)		115.	(a)	(b)	(c)	(d)
26.	(a)	(b)	(c)	(d)		71.	(a)	(b)	(c)	(d)		116.	(a)	(b)	(c)	(d)
27.	(a)	(b)	(c)	(d)		72.	(a)	(b)	(c)	(d)		117.	(a)	(b)	(c)	(d)
28.	(a)	(b)	(c)	(d)		73.	(a)	(b)	(c)	(d)		118.	(a)	(b)	(c)	(d)
29.	(a)	(b)	(c)	(d)		74.	(a)	(b)	(c)	(d)		119.	(a)	(b)	(c)	(d)
30.	(a)	(b)	(c)	(d)		75.	(a)	(b)	(c)	(d)		120.	(a)	(b)	(c)	(d)
31.	(a)	(b)	(c)	(d)		76.	(a)	(b)	(c)	(d)		121.	(a)	(b)	(c)	(d)
32.	(a)	(b)	(c)	(d)		77.	(a)	(b)	(c)	(d)		122.	(a)	(b)	(c)	(d)
33.	(a)	(b)	(c)	(d)		78.	(a)	(b)	(c)	(d)		123.	(a)	(b)	(c)	(d)
34.	(a)	(b)	(c)	(d)		79.	(a)	(b)	(c)	(d)		124.	(a)	(b)	(c)	(d)
35.	(a)	(b)	(c)	(d)		80.	(a)	(b)	(c)	(d)		125.	(a)	(b)	(c)	(d)
36.	(a)	(b)	(c)	(d)		81.	(a)	(b)	(c)	(d)		126.	(a)	(b)	(c)	(d)
37.	(a)	(b)	(c)	(d)		82.	(a)	(b)	(c)	(d)		127.	(a)	(b)	(c)	(d)
38.	(a)	(b)	(c)	(d)		83.	(a)	(b)	(c)	(d)		128.	(a)	(b)	(c)	(d)
39.	(a)	(b)	(c)	(d)		84.	(a)	(b)	(c)	(d)		129.	(a)	(b)	(c)	(d)
40.	(a)	(b)	(c)	(d)		85.	(a)	(b)	(c)	(d)		130.	(a)	(b)	(c)	(d)
41.	(a)	(b)	(c)	(d)		86.	(a)	(b)	(c)	(d)		131.	(a)	(b)	(c)	(d)
42.	(a)	(b)	(c)	(d)		87.	(a)	(b)	(c)	(d)		132.	(a)	(b)	(c)	(d)
43.	(a)	(b)	(c)	(d)		88.	(a)	(b)	(c)	(d)		133.	(a)	(b)	(c)	(d)
44.	(a)	(b)	(c)	(d)		89.	(a)	(b)	(c)	(d)		134.	(a)	(b)	(c)	(d)
45.	(a)	(b)	(c)	(d)		90.	(a)	(b)	(c)	(d)		135.	(a)	(b)	(c)	(d)

136.	a	b	c	d
137.	a	b	c	d
138.	a	b	c	d
139.	a	b	c	d
140.	a	b	c	d
141.	a	b	c	d
142.	a	b	c	d
143.	a	b	c	d
144.	a	b	c	d
145.	a	b	c	d
146.	a	b	c	d
147.	a	b	c	d
148.	a	b	c	d
149.	a	b	c	d
150.	a	b	c	d

151.	a	b	c	d
152.	a	b	c	d
153.	a	b	c	d
154.	a	b	c	d
155.	a	b	c	d
156.	a	b	c	d
157.	a	b	c	d
158.	a	b	c	d
159.	a	b	c	d
160.	a	b	c	d
161.	a	b	c	d
162.	a	b	c	d
163.	a	b	c	d
164.	a	b	c	d
165.	a	b	c	d

166.	a	b	c	d
167.	a	b	c	d
168.	a	b	c	d
169.	a	b	c	d
170.	a	b	c	d
171.	a	b	c	d
172.	a	b	c	d
173.	a	b	c	d
174.	a	b	c	d
175.	a	b	c	d
176.	a	b	c	d
177.	a	b	c	d
178.	a	b	c	d
179.	a	b	c	d
180.	a	b	c	d

PARAMEDIC EXAM 3

1. Which organs are contained in the right upper quadrant of the abdomen?
   a. spleen, tail of pancreas, stomach, left kidney, part of the colon
   b. liver, gall bladder, head of pancreas, part of duodenum, right kidney, part of colon
   c. appendix, ascending colon, small intestine, right ovary and fallopian tube
   d. small intestine, descending colon, left ovary and fallopian tube

2. The root word *rhin-* refers to the
   a. mouth
   b. nose
   c. skin
   d. shin

3. The prefix *hypo-* means
   a. having too much of
   b. active
   c. dead
   d. deficient in

4. When using the AVPU algorithm, the P reflects the patient's
   a. response to painful stimuli
   b. perception of the immediate surroundings
   c. level of pain
   d. radial pulse

5. Secondary assessment consists of
   a. ABCs, vital signs, and history
   b. head-to-toe evaluation, vital signs, and history
   c. AVPU, head-to-toe evaluation, and vital signs
   d. vital signs and patient history

6. Pulse pressure refers to the
   a. diastolic blood pressure reading
   b. systolic blood pressure reading
   c. difference between the systolic and diastolic readings
   d. systolic blood pressure as measured by a Doppler device

7. The organs in the left upper quadrant of the abdomen include the
   a. spleen, stomach, left kidney, colon
   b. liver, gall bladder, part of duodenum, right kidney, colon
   c. appendix, ascending colon, small intestine
   d. small intestine, descending colon

8. The Adam's apple is a common name for the
   a. epiglottis
   b. cricoid cartilage
   c. thyroid cartilage
   d. arytenoid cartilage

Answer questions 9–11 on the basis of the information below.

You arrive at a golf course to find a 45-year-old male unconscious and responsive to pain by localization only. The patient was approximately 20 feet from the tee when he was struck in the head by a golf ball. His eyes are closed, and pupil examination reveals a left pupil at about 2 mm and a right pupil at about 8 mm, not reactive to light. This patient moves upper extremities to localized pain response and moves lower extremities spontaneously. He is breathing 24 full effective and deep respirations.

9. You would expect the vital signs of this patient to generally follow which of the listed groupings?
   a. RR increased, HR decreased, BP decreased
   b. RR increased, HR decreased, BP increased
   c. RR decreased, HR decreased, BP decreased
   d. RR decreased, HR increased, BP increased

10. Treatment of this patient would include all of the following EXCEPT
   a. spinal precautions
   b. oxygen
   c. open airway using modified jaw-thrust/chin-lift
   d. placing the patient's head in a sniffing position to facilitate airflow

11. A patient with a closed head injury should be closely monitored for all of the following EXCEPT
   a. changes in blood pressure
   b. changes in respiratory rate
   c. seizures
   d. development of hemopneumothorax

12. Your patient, a car accident victim, complains of seeing "a dark curtain" in front of one eye. You should suspect
   a. spinal cord injury
   b. retinal detachment
   c. orbital fracture
   d. conjunctival hemorrhage

13. The "halo" or "target" test is used to determine whether
   a. blood flowing from the ears, nose, or mouth contains cerebrospinal fluid
   b. the pupils are fixed or reactive to light
   c. the medulla oblongata has been displaced from the foramen magnum
   d. the patient shows signs of subdural or epidural hematoma

14. Signs and symptoms of traumatic asphyxia include
   a. paradoxical chest wall motion, pain on inspiration, increased respiratory rate
   b. dyspnea, bloodshot eyes, distended neck veins, cyanotic upper body
   c. agitation, air hunger, distended neck veins, signs and symptoms of shock, tracheal displacement
   d. signs and symptoms of shock, cyanosis, absent breath sounds over one lobe, flat neck veins

15. An adult patient has burns covering her head and back. Using the rule of nines, this patient's burns cover what percentage of her body surface area?
   a. 9 percent
   b. 18 percent
   c. 27 percent
   d. 36 percent

16. A burn that is pearly white and almost painless is a
   a. first-degree burn
   b. second-degree burn
   c. third-degree burn
   d. chemical burn

17. Which condition would NOT indicate the need for rapid transport?
   a. penetrating abdominal trauma
   b. ejection from a crashed vehicle
   c. first- and second-degree burns to entire chest
   d. pulse rate of 130, blood pressure 90/60, respiratory rate 36

18. A patient who opens her eyes in response to pain, speaks incomprehensibly, and withdraws in response to pain would have a Glasgow Coma Scale score of
   a. 6
   b. 7
   c. 8
   d. 9

19. Your patient is a 23-year-old man who complains of abdominal pain. The patient states that the pain began suddenly and was originally localized to the area around the umbilicus. Now, however, it has moved to the right lower quadrant. The patient also complains of nausea and vomiting, and he has a fever of 102° F. Examination displays rebound tenderness. You should suspect
   a. diverticulitis
   b. gastritis
   c. peptic ulcer
   d. appendicitis

20. A positive tilt test may indicate that a patient is
   a. diaphoretic
   b. hypovolemic
   c. in decompensated shock
   d. hypoglycemic

21. A patient with esophageal varices will typically present with
   a. acute upper-right quadrant pain
   b. vomiting of blood
   c. blood in the stools
   d. pain that migrates from the umbilicus to the upper left quadrant

22. The initial symptoms of infection with HIV consist primarily of
   a. fatigue and fever
   b. encephalopathy
   c. Kaposi's sarcoma
   d. Pneumocystis carinii pneumonia

23. Normal age-related changes include
   a. 20–25 percent weight gain
   b. increased cardiac volume and rate
   c. increased amount of body fluid
   d. increased susceptibility to shock

24. Your patient is a 78-year-old woman who is complaining of diffuse abdominal pain, nausea, and vomiting. Examination reveals abdominal distention and absent bowel sounds. You should suspect
   a. bowel obstruction
   b. aortic aneurysm
   c. esophageal varices
   d. congestive heart failure

25. Atypical signs and symptoms of myocardial infarction that are commonly seen in elderly patients include all of the following EXCEPT
a. confusion and fatigue
b. syncope
c. tearing chest pain
d. neck pain

26. Which breathing pattern is characteristic of diabetic ketoacidosis or other types of metabolic acidosis?
a. ataxic breathing
b. Biot's breathing
c. Cheyne-Stokes breathing
d. Kussmaul breathing

27. Normal vesicular breath sounds are usually described as
a. medium in pitch, medium loud, with equal inspiration and expiration phases
b. high in pitch, heard only over the trachea, harsh and loud, with a short inspiratory phase and a long expiration phase
c. low in pitch, soft, with a long inspiratory phase and a short expiratory phase
d. medium in pitch, soft, with a short inspiratory phase and a long expiratory phase

28. The primary use of the PQRST mnemonic is to
a. obtain the medical history
b. assess the neurologic status
c. assess the respiratory status
d. define the major complaint

29. Your patient is Mr. Williams, age 70. He complains of chest pain that began while he was raking leaves. You perform a primary and secondary assessment and administer oxygen and nitroglycerin. Mr. Williams then states that he feels much better. He is most likely suffering from
a. stable angina
b. unstable angina
c. myocardial infarction
d. cardiac arrest

30. The goal of primary assessment is to
a. determine how many victims are present
b. evaluate whether it is safe to enter an accident scene
c. detect immediate threats to a patient's life
d. determine the seriousness of a patient's condition

31. Signs and symptoms of hypertensive emergency include
a. pitting edema, tachycardia, and venous congestion
b. paralysis, seizures, stupor, and coma
c. severe respiratory distress, apprehension, cyanosis, and diaphoresis
d. restlessness, confusion, blurred vision, nausea, and vomiting

32. In a young, healthy adult, vital signs may NOT be good early indicators of shock because
   a. shock patients often display false-positive readings
   b. vital signs are often too low to be measured accurately
   c. the body attempts to compensate by maintaining normal vital signs
   d. signs and symptoms of shock are based on neurological findings and are not reflected in standard vital signs

33. One grain of medication is equal to
   a. 15 mg
   b. 30 mg
   c. 60 mg
   d. 1 gm

34. The physiological cause of the anxiety and restlessness that comprise the classic early signs of shock is a
   a. release of catecholamines
   b. decrease in cardiac output
   c. rise in blood pressure
   d. constriction of arterioles

Answer questions 35–37 on the basis of the information below.

You arrive to find a 65-year-old male in acute respiratory distress. You are able to hear wheezes from across the room, and you note extreme accessory muscle use. The patient has assumed a tripod position and is breathing through pursed lips. Your physical exam reveals a barrel chest and stained fingernails. The patient's vital signs are a blood pressure of 160/90, a pulse of 100 strong and irregular with an atrial fibrillation on the cardiac monitor, and a respiratory rate of 40, shallow and labored. Lung sounds are wheezes throughout all fields anteriorly and posteriorly. The patient also has diminished lung sounds in all fields.

35. This patient is most likely suffering from
   a. chronic bronchitis
   b. anaphylaxis
   c. asthma
   d. emphysema

36. Medications used to treat this patient's condition would include all of the following EXCEPT
   a. oxygen
   b. epinephrine 1:1000
   c. albuterol
   d. metaproterenol

37. This patient is breathing through pursed lips in order to
   a. provide positive end ventilatory pressure to inflate the alveoli
   b. increase his respiratory rate
   c. retain carbon dioxide
   d. "blow off" oxygen to increase serum pH

38. The pulse oximetry reading may show a falsely elevated reading in a patient who has been exposed to
  a. radioactivity
  b. carbon monoxide
  c. pyrexins .
  d. carbon tetrachloride

39. Which statement about airway obstruction caused by the tongue is INCORRECT?
  a. The tongue is the most common cause of airway obstruction in an unconscious patient.
  b. Airway blockage depends on the position of the patient's head and jaw.
  c. The epiglottis can contribute to airway blockage, especially in the presence of diminished muscle tone.
  d. The tongue can block the airway only when the patient is recumbent.

40. To open the airway of a trauma patient, you would use
  a. the head-tilt/chin-lift
  b. the jaw thrust
  c. the modified jaw thrust
  d. Sellick's maneuver

41. Bronchiolitis is caused by
  a. either infection or allergy
  b. Mycobacterium tuberculosis
  c. the respiratory syncytial virus
  d. an exacerbation of an underlying case of asthma

Answer questions 42–44 on the basis of the information below.

Your patient is a 30-year-old female who is complaining of a generalized rash and dyspnea after eating shellfish. The patient has small, red welts all over her body and says her tongue feels like it is swollen. She complains of difficulty getting air in and difficulty catching a full breath. This patient's vital signs show a blood pressure of 110/60; a pulse of 100, strong and regular; and a respiratory rate of 36, somewhat shallow and labored.

42. This patient is exhibiting the signs and symptoms of
  a. an allergic reaction
  b. an upper airway obstruction
  c. anaphylactic shock
  d. an iodine toxicity

43. Medications used to treat this patient may include all of the following EXCEPT
  a. epinephrine 1:1000
  b. epinephrine 1:10,000
  c. diphenhydramine HCL
  d. dopamine

44. This patient needs close monitoring because she could progress into
  a. an allergic reaction
  b. an upper airway obstruction
  c. anaphylactic shock
  d. iodine toxicity

45. After placing an endotracheal tube, you note that breath sounds are much stronger on the right side of the chest than on the left. This suggests that the
   a. tube has been inserted into the right main-stem bronchus
   b. patient has a pneumothorax on the right side
   c. tube has not been inserted far enough into the trachea
   d. patient has aspirated vomitus into the airway

46. Methylprednisolone is given to patients who have
   a. epidural or subdural hematoma
   b. major motor seizures
   c. suspected spinal cord injury
   d. increased intracranial pressure

47. Nitronox should NOT be given to a patient with a suspected
   a. abdominal injury
   b. pneumothorax
   c. myocardial infarction
   d. fracture

48. An assessment finding of pulsus paradoxus is associated with a diagnosis of
   a. emphysema
   b. congestive heart disease
   c. COPD
   d. MI

49. The term *tracheal tugging* refers to
   a. use of accessory respiratory muscles
   b. retraction of intercostal muscles
   c. cyanosis and nasal flaring
   d. retraction of neck tissues

50. A dull sound heard during chest percussion may be associated with
   a. pneumothorax
   b. emphysema
   c. pneumonia
   d. bronchitis

51. Pulse oximetry allows you to continuously record the patient's
   a. pulse rate and oxygen saturation
   b. respiratory rate and oxygen saturation
   c. pulse rate and temperature
   d. respiratory rate and heart rate

52. Your patient is a 66-year-old man who is extremely thin but has a noticeably distorted barrel-shaped chest. He reports a history of dyspnea that has recently gotten worse. You note that he purses his lips when breathing but that hypoxia is not apparent. You should
   a. administer high-flow oxygen and transport immediately
   b. administer low-flow oxygen and administer a bronchodilator
   c. administer high-flow oxygen, hook up an ECG monitor, and administer a bronchodilator
   d. establish and maintain an airway, assist ventilations as required, transport immediately

53. Which of the following is an antiinflammatory drug administered to asthma patients?
   a. albuterol
   b. epinephrine
   c. metaproterenol
   d. methylprednisolone

54. Kussmaul's respirations are characterized by
   a. an increase in both rate and depth
   b. an increase in rate only
   c. a decrease in both rate and depth
   d. a decrease in rate only

55. Which of the following factors increases the amount of energy necessary for respiration?
   a. loss of pulmonary surfactant
   b. decrease in airway resistance
   c. increase in pulmonary compliance
   d. a decrease in body temperature

56. The pH of normal urine is 6.0, and the pH of distilled water is 7. This means that urine is
   a. twice as acidic as distilled water
   b. ten times as acidic as distilled water
   c. twice as alkaline as distilled water
   d. ten times as alkaline as distilled water

57. Your patient is a 6-year-old child who is conscious but not breathing because of an airway obstruction. The first thing you should do is to
   a. give 5 back blows following by 5 chest thrusts
   b. perform the tongue-jaw lift and finger sweep
   c. give 5 subdiaphragmatic abdominal thrusts
   d. open the airway with a head-tilt/chin-lift

58. You should attempt to remove foreign material from a patient's airway with forceps only if you
   a. do not have access to laryngoscopy equipment
   b. have already attempted to suction the airway
   c. are unable to insert an endotracheal tube
   d. are able to visualize the obstruction directly

Answer questions 59–63 on the basis of the information below.

Your patient is a 29-year-old female complaining of the sudden onset of severe shortness of breath and chest pain. She indicates she is recovering from surgery to her left femur after an automobile crash.

59. This patient is most likely suffering from
   a. pneumonia
   b. myocardial infarction
   c. cerebral vascular accident
   d. pulmonary embolism

60. Upon further examination of this patient, you would expect to find all of the following EXCEPT
   a. labored breathing
   b. bradycardia
   c. jugular venous distension
   d. tachypnea

61. This patient's physiological problems are most likely due to
   a. the right side of the heart pumping against increased resistance
   b. the left side of the heart pumping against decreased resistance
   c. the right side of the heart pumping against decreased resistance
   d. pneumonia resulting from pulmonary edema

62. Management of this patient centers around all of the following EXCEPT
   a. an IV at a TKO rate
   b. oxygen
   c. ventilatory assistance
   d. transport in shock position

63. The common causes of this patient's problem include all of the following EXCEPT
   a. placement of a central line
   b. blood clots
   c. myocardial infarction
   d. fractures

64. The fluid therapy of choice for a patient suffering from dehydration is
   a. whole blood or packed red blood cells
   b. lactated Ringer's or normal saline
   c. blood plasma or plasma substitute
   d. plasma only

65. A patient suspected of showing early signs of shock should be placed supine with feet elevated only if
   a. head injury can be ruled out
   b. the shock is due to hypovolemia
   c. respiratory alkalosis is the underlying cause
   d. respirations are inadequate

66. Which statement about deflation of the PASG in the field setting is correct?
   a. Deflation should be accomplished rapidly in the field.
   b. Deflate the legs first and then the abdominal compartment.
   c. The PASG should never be left on a patient for more than 20 minutes.
   d. Deflation should not be attempted in the field without medical direction.

67. The usual initial dose of epinephrine 1:10,000 used in adult patients in cardiac arrest is
   a. 0.5 to 1.0 mg IV
   b. 0.3 to 0.5 mg IV
   c. 0.1 to 0.3 mg IV
   d. 0.1 mg/kg IV

68. The principal use of dopamine in emergency care is to treat patients with
   a. hypertensive crisis
   b. cardiogenic shock
   c. hypovolemic shock
   d. respiratory failure

69. A patient with a suspected CVA but with no signs or symptoms of congestive heart failure should be positioned
   a. supine with the head raised 15 degrees
   b. in a lateral recumbent position
   c. supine with the feet raised 15 degrees
   d. semi-upright

70. The vital signs of a patient with increased intracranial pressure will be characterized by
   a. increased blood pressure, decreased pulse and respiratory rate
   b. increased blood pressure, pulse, and respiratory rate
   c. decreased blood pressure, increased pulse and respiratory rate
   d. decreased blood pressure, pulse, and respiratory rate

71. The T wave on an ECG tracing represents
   a. repolarization of the ventricles
   b. depolarization of the atria
   c. depolarization of the ventricles
   d. repolarization of the atria

72. You are analyzing a patient's heart rate on an ECG strip. You note that there are 13 complexes within one 6-second interval. Therefore, the heart rate is
a. 6
b. 13
c. 78
d. 130

73. Atrial depolarization is seen on the Lead II ECG strip in the form of
a. a negative, rounded P wave
b. a positive, rounded P wave
c. two small negative deviations, with a large positive deviation in between
d. two positive, rounded T waves

74. Which of the following is an abnormal finding on an ECG strip?
a. a P-R interval of 0.16 sec
b. a P-R interval of 0.10 sec
c. a QRS complex of 0.10 sec
d. a QRS complex of 0.08 sec

75. A heart rate of 52 beats per minute is likely to be a normal finding in a
a. 6-month old infant
b. 7-year-old child
c. 24-year-old athlete
d. 76-year-old woman

76. The valsalva maneuver can improve a too-rapid or irregular heart beat by
a. forcing the patient to slow his or her respirations
b. stimulating the vagus nerve
c. inhibiting the release of acetylcholine
d. stimulating the carotid artery

77. Which arrhythmia may be a sign of digitalis toxicity?
a. atrial fibrillation with a ventricular rate of less than 60
b. premature junctional contractions
c. paroxysmal supraventricular tachycardia
d. atrial flutter with a ventricular rate greater than 120

78. Your patient is a 67-year-old man whose ECG strip shows ventricular tachycardia and who has a pulse. After administering oxygen and placing an IV line, you should
a. administer 6 mg of adenosine via rapid IV push over 1–3 seconds
b. administer 2.5–5.0 mg of verapamil via IV
c. perform synchronized cardioversion
d. administer 1.0–1.5 mg/kg lidocaine via IV

79. Which of the following is a risk factor for atherosclerosis?
a. hypotension
b. excessive exercises
c. diabetes mellitus
d. cancer

80. The pain caused by myocardial infarction is usually relieved only by
a. nitroglycerin
b. acetaminophen
c. diazepam
d. morphine

81. During the secondary assessment of a patient with a suspected MI, you note the presence of basilar rales. This is an indication that the patient
    a. is suffering from heart failure
    b. is perfusing adequately
    c. has adequate venous return
    d. is entering cardiogenic shock

82. What statement describes the use of bretylium in management of MI in the field?
    a. It is the first-line agent used to manage ventricular dysrhythmias.
    b. It is used only in patients who are allergic to lidocaine.
    c. It is used to correct bradycardias of atrial origin.
    d. It is used to correct life-threatening ventricular dysrhythmias.

83. Patients with pulmonary edema are assumed to have had an MI because MI
    a. is the underlying cause of right heart failure
    b. is a common cause of left ventricular failure
    c. causes the oxygen-carrying capacity of the blood to increase
    d. can result in pulmonary embolism

84. The primary goal of management for a patient with left ventricular failure and pulmonary edema is to
    a. prevent or control pain
    b. initiate thrombolytic therapy
    c. decrease venous return
    d. prevent serious dysrhythmias

85. Your patient is a 68-year-old male with a history of two prior MIs. Your assessment findings include a pulse rate of 124, peripheral edema, and jugular vein distention. The patient denies any chest pain or breathing difficulty. You should suspect
    a. left ventricular failure with pulmonary edema
    b. right ventricular failure
    c. pulmonary embolism
    d. myocardial infarction

86. Your patient is an 82-year-old female with a suspected MI. While en route to the hospital, you note that her systolic blood pressure, which had been stable, has started to drop, and she is becoming confused. At the same time, her heart rhythm converts to sinus tachycardia. You should suspect
    a. cardiogenic shock
    b. cardiac arrest
    c. left ventricular failure with pulmonary edema
    d. right ventricular failure

87. Your patient is a 65-year-old male who is complaining of pain in his abdomen, back, and flanks. His blood pressure is 90/60, and, on examination, you note that the femoral pulses are markedly weaker than the radial pulses. You should
    a. examine the abdomen carefully for a pulsatile mass
    b. administer dopamine to increase cardiac output
    c. treat for shock and transport rapidly
    d. administer nitroglycerin

88. Signs and symptoms of acute pulmonary embolism include
  a. rapid, labored breathing and tachycardia
  b. slow, labored breathing and cyanosis
  c. acute substernal pain and anxiety
  d. pallor, chest pain, and tachycardia

89. Your patient is a 67-year-old female who complains of increasing leg pain and tenderness. The skin over the affected area is warm and red, and Homan's sign is positive. Vital signs are unremarkable. You should
  a. massage the affected area to relieve the pain
  b. elevate the leg and transport the patient
  c. treat for signs and symptoms of shock
  d. have the patient walk for half an hour to promote blood flow to the affected leg

90. Which of the following is a sympathomimetic agent used to resuscitate cardiac arrest victims?
  a. adenosine
  b. atropine sulfate
  c. epinephrine
  d. nitroglycerin

91. Initial attempts at defibrillation in an adult should use
  a. 100 joules
  b. 200 joules
  c. 300 joules
  d. 360 joules

92. Carotid sinus massage is used for patients with which dysrhythmia?
  a. nonperfusing ventricular tachycardia
  b. ventricular fibrillation
  c. paroxysmal supraventricular tachycardia
  d. second-degree AB block (Mobitz II)

93. External cardiac pacing is used to
  a. convert ventricular fibrillation
  b. correct symptomatic bradycardias
  c. correct asystole
  d. convert PVCs

94. The usual dosage and route of administration of diazepam given before defibrillation is
  a. 2–5 mg given intramuscularly
  b. 5–10 mg directly into the vein
  c. 5–15 mg by slow IV push
  d. 15–10 mg administered rectally

95. Which drug is used in management of left heart failure?
  a. dobutamine
  b. dopamine
  c. bretylium
  d. verapamil

96. Which heart sounds are normal findings on auscultation?
  a. S1 only
  b. S1 and S2
  c. S1, S2, and S3
  d. S1, S2, S3, and S4

97. Which set of vital signs is suggestive of left ventricular failure with pulmonary edema?
  a. BP elevated, pulse slow and irregular, respirations slow and labored
  b. BP diminished, pulse slow and irregular, respirations rapid but easy
  c. BP diminished, pulse fast and regular, respirations rapid and labored
  d. BP elevated, pulse fast and irregular, respirations rapid and labored

Answer questions 98–103 on the basis of the information below.

You respond on a 44-year-old diabetic who is complaining of a general feeling of weakness. During your questioning you learn that he has been "constantly thirsty and hungry." His breath has a fruity odor, and his level of consciousness appears to be diminishing.

98. This patient is most likely suffering from
   a. diabetic ketoacidosis
   b. diabetes mellitus
   c. hypoglycemia
   d. glucose intolerance

99. Which vital signs would you expect from this patient?
   a. cool, clammy skins; bradycardia; increased respirations
   b. warm, dry skins; tachycardia; increased respirations
   c. warm, dry skins; bradycardia; decreased respirations
   d. cool, clammy skins; tachycardia; decreased respirations

100. This patient's symptoms are most likely due to
   a. high levels of insulin
   b. low levels of insulin
   c. low levels of glucose
   d. dehydration

101. Which of the following statements is most likely accurate with regard to this patient?
   a. He has not eaten in a while.
   b. He has taken too much insulin.
   c. He has not taken his insulin.
   d. He has taken his insulin but did not limit his fluid intake.

102. During transport, this patient slips into unconsciousness, and his breathing becomes very deep and rapid. This is known as
   a. Kussmaul's respirations
   b. ketotonic respirations
   c. Cheyne-Stokes respirations
   d. Christianson's respirations

103. The appropriate treatment for this patient includes
   a. an IV with Ringer's lactate, oxygen, and pitocin
   b. a blood glucose test, an IV with normal saline, insulin subcutaneously
   c. a blood glucose test, limit fluids
   d. hyperventilation, limit fluids, administer sodium bicarbonate

104. The spinal cord ends at the
   a. third cervical vertebra
   b. fifth thoracic vertebra
   c. second lumbar vertebra
   d. first sacral vertebra

105. Asymmetrical movement during respiration suggests the presence of
   a. hypoxemia
   b. flail chest
   c. brain damage
   d. emphysema

106. Your patient suffers a minor head trauma that results in a transient loss of consciousness followed by a complete return of functions. The term for this is
a. contusion
b. epidural hematoma
c. contrecoup injury
d. concussion

107. The procedure for aligning a fractured long bone is to
a. stabilize the entire limb as found
b. immobilize a limb with all joints in the neutral position
c. immobilize the distal portion of the limb first, gently bringing the proximal portion into alignment
d. stabilize the proximal portion as found and then bring the distal portion into alignment

108. You would bandage and splint limb injuries on scene only when you have determined that
a. the patient does not need rapid transport
b. transport time will be longer than one hour
c. other life-threatening injuries are present
d. equipment needed to stabilize the spine is not available

109. If your examination of a limb suggests that it is injured, you should always
a. apply traction to align the ends of long bones and position joints
b. treat it as if a fracture exists
c. check the proximal pulse
d. transport the patient as quickly as possible

110. Which type of wound would most likely require a tourniquet?
a. amputation
b. compound fracture of the femur
c. radiation burn
d. crush injury

111. A patient with hypoglycemia may present with all of the following signs and symptoms EXCEPT
a. bizarre behavior
b. diaphoresis
c. air hunger
d. tachycardia

112. The primary reason that diazepam is given to a seizure patient is to
a. relieve anxiety
b. suppress the spread of electrical activity in the brain and relax muscles
c. prevent hypoglycemia by allowing the brain to use insulin
d. increase blood pressure

113. The correct dosage and route of administration of epinephrine for a patient with severe anaphylaxis is
a. 0.3–0.5 mg epinephrine 1:10,000, administered intravenously
b. 0.1–0.3 mg epinephrine 1:10,000, administered intravenously
c. 0.3–0.5 mg epinephrine 1:1000, administered subcutaneously
d. 0.1–0.3 mg epinephrine 1:1000, administered subcutaneously

114. Beta agonists such as albuterol are used in the treatment of anaphylaxis to
a. relieve anxiety
b. prevent shock
c. raise blood pressure
d. prevent bronchospasm

115. The most common causes of anaphylaxis are injected drugs, foods such as nuts and eggs, and
a. tree and grass pollen
b. tropical fruits
c. bee and wasp stings
d. antiarrhythmics

116. Symptoms of acetaminophen overdose include
a. nausea and vomiting, malaise, diaphoresis, right upper quadrant pain
b. nausea and vomiting, confusion, lethargy, seizures, dysrhythmias
c. altered mental status, hypotension, slurred speech, bradycardia
d. nausea, dilated pupils, rambling speech, headache, dizziness

117. Sodium bicarbonate may be ordered in the field for a patient who has overdosed on
a. acetaminophen
b. benzodiazepines
c. narcotics
d. salicylates

118. Your patient is a 19-year-old female who has been stung by a stingray while swimming. After ensuring the airway, you should
a. apply a tight constricting band between the wound and the heart
b. apply heat or warm water to reduce pain and destabilize the poison
c. use ice to relieve pain and swelling
d. administer morphine sulfate to relieve pain

119. Which drug can cause users to commit dangerous outbursts of violent and aggressive behaviors?
a. Elavil
b. phenobarbital
c. PCP
d. LSD

120. Which of the following patients shows signs and symptoms of heat exhaustion?
a. male, age 34; severe muscle cramps in legs; fatigue and dizziness
b. female, age 45; rapid, shallow respirations; weak pulse; cold, clammy skin; dizziness
c. male, age 42; deep respirations; rapid strong pulse; dry, hot skin; loss of consciousness
d. female, age 70; shallow respirations; weak, rapid pulse; dilated pupils; seizures

121. The correct procedure for thawing a frostbitten body part is to
a. rub it gently with snow or ice
b. immerse it in water of approximately 66° F.
c. immerse it in water of approximately 80° F.
d. immerse it in water of approximately 105° F.

122. Which of the following statements about care of a near-drowning victim is correct?
   a. Use the Heimlich maneuver to clear the respiratory tree.
   b. Ventilation should not be provided until the patient is clear of the water.
   c. The patient should be admitted to the hospital for observation.
   d. Near-drowning victims seldom experience head or neck injury.

123. Which of the following divers is showing signs and symptoms of air embolism?
   a. male, age 23; pruritus; skin pallor and cyanosis; pitting edema
   b. male, age 27; sharp chest pain with sudden onset; neurological deficits
   c. female, age 31; dizziness; auditory and vestibular disturbances; headache
   d. female, age 25; fatigue; pain in chest and lower abdomen; nausea and vomiting

124. You are interviewing Anna, a 43-year-old woman with a long history of schizophrenia. Anna appears to try to cooperate, but there are long periods of silence in your conversation while she listens to her "voices." During these silences, you should
   a. repeat your question
   b. restate Anna's last response
   c. remain attentive
   d. tell an interesting story

125. Which of the following may be a sign of an anxiety disorder?
   a. physical complaints, such as pain
   b. elevated and expansive mood
   c. feelings of depression
   d. hallucinations, delusions, or inappropriate affect

Answer questions 126–128 on the basis of the information below.

You respond on a 12-year-old male patient who is wheezing and having difficulty breathing. The patient has a long history of asthma, and states that he used his inhaler but that it didn't help much. Upon examination you discover that the patient is tachycardic and tachypneic with a nonproductive cough.

126. The primary goal in treating this patient is to
   a. correct hypoxia, reverse bronchospasms, and decrease inflammation
   b. decrease respiratory drive, decrease heart rate, and increase blood pressure
   c. increase heart rate, decrease respiratory rate, and correct carbon dioxide levels
   d. correct carbon dioxide levels, decrease inflammation, and increase heart rate

127. This patient's condition might have been "triggered" by all of the following EXCEPT
   a. warm air
   b. allergens
   c. exercise
   d. medications

128. Treatment for this patient includes which of the following medications?
   a. versed and valium
   b. albuterol and atropine
   c. albuterol, terbutaline, and/or steriods
   d. terbutaline, steriods, and verapamil

129. You are about to start an IV in Cara, age 5. The best thing to say to her is
   a. "There will be some pain as I insert the catheter, but it's necessary for me to begin fluid therapy."
   b. "The needle will hurt for a second. Try to hold still. The medicine will help you get better."
   c. "Hold still, or the pain will be much worse."
   d. "If you don't stop crying, I won't let your mom stay with you any more."

130. Which set of vital signs would be normal in a 3-year-old?
   a. respirations, 16; pulse, 72; systolic BP, 70
   b. respirations, 24; pulse, 92; systolic BP, 96
   c. respirations, 38; pulse, 124; systolic BP, 118
   d. respirations, 34; pulse, 68; systolic BP, 88

131. Your patient is Harry, age 5, who has multiple injuries in various stages of healing, including raccoon eyes and a new suspected broken leg. On questioning, his mother states that Harry fell out of his bunk bed, but his sister, age 9, says that "Daddy beat Harry up." The mother insists that her husband will take Harry to the hospital when he gets home from work. You should
   a. document your findings, convince the mother that it is necessary to transport Harry to the hospital, and report your suspicions of child abuse
   b. make sure Harry's condition is stable, and grant the mother's request for delayed transport
   c. confront the mother with your suspicions, call the police, and have both parents arrested
   d. remove both children from the home immediately and transport Harry to the hospital

132. Until ruled out by a medical doctor, documented fever in an infant less than 3 months old is always considered to result from
   a. epilepsy
   b. Reye's syndrome
   c. epiglottitis
   d. meningitis

133. Management of a child with epiglottitis consists of
   a. visualization of the airway and insertion of an endotracheal tube
   b. administration of epinephrine
   c. airway maintenance and administration of humidified oxygen
   d. administration of bronchodilators and corticosteroids

Answer questions 134–138 on the basis of the information below.

You respond to the residence of a 4-year-old male who was found in his back yard, head down in a 5-gallon bucket of water. The child, according to the mother, had been in the water for approximately 4 minutes. The child is cyanotic, pulseless, and apneic. He is in an asystole on the EKG. The child weighs approximately 40 pounds.

134. According to the current American Heart Association PALS standards, what size endotracheal tube would you want to use on this patient?
   a. 3.5 mm
   b. 4.5 mm
   c. 5.0 mm
   d. 6.5 mm

135. The most reliable method for determining the proper medication dosing for this pediatric patient would be to
   a. give 1/2 the adult dose for all medications
   b. give 1/3 the adult dose for all medications except atropine
   c. use the Broselow Tape or another length/weight measuring system
   d. estimate the patient's weight yourself

136. All of the following medications can be given through the endotracheal tube to pediatric patients EXCEPT
   a. lidocaine
   b. epinephrine
   c. atropine
   d. Valium

137. After endotracheal intubation of a this patient, which of the following steps should be followed?
   a. confirmation of ETT placement via auscultation only
   b. inflation of the cuff to prevent air leakage
   c. dilution of all ETT medication to 10 cc to prevent tissue damage
   d. spinal immobilization to prevent ETT dislodging the tube

138. After your first round of ACLS drugs, the patient converts to a sinus bradycardia at a rate of 40 beats per minute. The drug of choice for managing this patient's bradycardia is
   a. epinephrine
   b. atropine
   c. isoproterenol
   d. dobutamine

139. The correct pediatric dosage of rectal
diazepam is
a. 1.0 mg/kg body weight
b. 0.5 mg/kg body weight
c. 0.2 mg/kg body weight
d. 0.1 mg/kg body weight

140. Which statement about ways to differentiate
bronchiolitis from asthma in children is correct?
a. Bronchiolitis usually occurs in children ages
4 and older.
b. Bronchiolitis is most prevalent in the winter
and early spring.
c. Bronchiolitis usually occurs in patients with
a family history of asthma.
d. Bronchoilitis may be caused by an allergy or
by exercise.

141. Your patient is a 5-year-old girl who presents
with breathing difficulty of rapid onset. She is
sitting upright and drooling. Her temperature
is 104.6° F. You should suspect
a. bronchiolitis
b. asthma
c. croup
d. epiglottitis

142. Approximately how old is a bruise that is dark
blue or purple?
a. less than 24 hours
b. 1–5 days
c. 5–7 days
d. 7–10 days

143. One way to determine the size of the endotracheal tube used in a child is to divide 16 + the
child's age by 4. Another consideration is the
size of the
a. glottic opening
b. pleural space
c. pharynx
d. cricoid ring

144. In order to preserve physical evidence in cases
of suspected sexual assault, you should
a. examine the patient's perineal area carefully
b. bag all soiled articles of clothing together
c. avoid cleaning wounds and handling clothing
d. have the patient change her clothes and
bathe before the medical exam

145. A *nulligravida* is a woman who
a. is not pregnant at the present time
b. has never been pregnant
c. is pregnant at the present time
d. has been pregnant more than once

146. A woman who is about to give birth should be
examined for crowning
a. during a contraction
b. between contractions
c. during an internal pelvic exam
d. only when time permits

147. Your patient is a 32-year-old woman who reports that she is 14 weeks pregnant. She complains of abdominal cramping and vaginal bleeding. You should
   a. perform a vaginal exam
   b. administer high-flow oxygen, monitor fetal heart tones, and transport immediately
   c. treat for signs and symptoms of shock, provide emotional support, and transport
   d. prepare for emergency delivery in the field

148. The cause of the supine-hypotensive syndrome in the pregnant patient is
   a. pressure of the uterus on the inferior vena cava
   b. normal volume depletion during pregnancy
   c. abruptio placentae
   d. abnormal fetal presentation

149. In the multiparous patient, the second stage of labor lasts approximately
   a. 5 hours
   b. 1 hour
   c. 50 minutes
   d. 20 minutes

150. During a normal delivery, you would tell the mother to stop pushing when
   a. crowning begins
   b. the head is delivered
   c. delivery of the infant is complete
   d. the placenta is delivered

151. Treatment for a prolapsed cord is to
   a. attempt to push the cord back into the vagina and deliver normally
   b. place two fingers of a gloved hand on either side of the baby's nose and mouth until the head is delivered
   c. place two fingers of a gloved hand to raise the presenting part of the fetus off the cord and then place the mother in knee-chest position, administer oxygen, and transport
   d. assist and support the mother for a normal delivery

152. Immediately after delivery, you should position the neonate
   a. higher than the mother's vagina, with its head slightly elevated
   b. at the level of the mother's vagina, with its head slightly lower than the body
   c. lower than the mother's vagina, with the head at the same level as the body
   d. at the level of the mother's vagina, with the head slightly elevated

153. A neonate's normal respiratory rate is approximately
   a. 10–20 breaths per minute
   b. 20–40 breaths per minute
   c. 40–60 breaths per minute
   d. 60–80 breaths per minute

154. The first step in resuscitation of a distressed neonate is to
   a. ventilate with 100 percent oxygen for 15–30 seconds
   b. evaluate the heart rate
   c. evaluate the respiratory rate
   d. initiate chest compressions if the heart rate is less than 60 or 60–80 but not increasing

155. Which statement about supplying supplemental oxygen to a neonate is INCORRECT?
   a. Do not withhold oxygen from a neonate in the prehospital setting.
   b. Oxygen toxicity in the prehospital setting is a serious concern.
   c. Administer supplemental oxygen by blowing oxygen across the neonate's face.
   d. Oxygen should be warmed if possible.

156. How much intravenous fluid should you administer to a distressed neonate that weighs 2 kg?
   a. 10 mL
   b. 20 mL
   c. 30 mL
   d. 40 mL

157. The correct procedure for auscultating fetal heart tones in a woman who is approximately 32 weeks pregnant is to
   a. move the high-intensity diaphragm of the stethoscope in a circular pattern around the mother's umbilicus
   b. auscultate using Doppler ultrasound approximately 2 inches below the mother's umbilicus
   c. palpate the mother's abdomen until you feel the fetal chest wall, then auscultate using a regular stethoscope
   d. using a high-intensity stethoscope, begin at the mother's left shoulder and move diagonally downward and to the right

158. Which statement describes a tiered EMS system?
   a. Paramedics are the prehospital team leaders.
   b. Physicians directly supervise all prehospital personnel.
   c. Varying levels of resources are dispatched to calls, depending on the nature of the incident.
   d. After they arrive at the emergency department, patients are assigned a priority for care by a triage nurse.

159. Which event important to the development of EMSD systems occurred in 1966?
   a. Congress passed the National Highway Safety Act
   b. The National Academy of Sciences issued its White Paper
   c. The White House funded a $9 million demonstration project
   d. Congress passed the Emergency Medical Services Systems Act

160. Which activity is an example of indirect medical control?

    a. A licensed physician who does not work in the EMS system assumes control at an accident scene.

    b. A paramedic administers nitroglycerin to a patient with chest pain under standing medical orders.

    c. A mobile intensive care nurse communicates orders to paramedics while en route to the hospital.

    d. An EMS physician provides training to paramedics in advanced airway management techniques.

Answer questions 161–165 on the basis of the information below.

You respond to reports of a bus collision. Upon arrival, you find that you have 35 victims.

161. Your first priority is to

    a. set up the triage area

    b. establish the morgue area

    c. begin rapid treatment

    d. separate the walking wounded from the severely injured

162. Per the START algorithm, the first parameter assessed should be

    a. blood pressure

    b. breathing/airway

    c. circulation

    d. level of consciousness

163. A male patient is found to have a respiratory rate of 38. This would place him in which of the following categories?

    a. delayed

    b. immediate

    c. nonsalvageable

    d. critical

164. Another male patient is found to have a respiratory rate of 28 and a radial pulse of 84. He is confused about the incident. This patient would be placed in which of the following categories?

    a. delayed

    b. immediate

    c. nonsalvageable

    d. critical

165. A female patient is found to have no spontaneous repirations. Your first treatment should be to

    a. use a bag-valve mask and ventilate with 100 percent oxygen

    b. classify the patient as immediate and move her to a treatment area

    c. reposition the airway

    d. start CPR

166. A person with a serious illness can delegate the right to make medical decisions to someone else by enacting a

    a. living will

    b. durable power of attorney for health care

    c. Do Not Resuscitate order

    d. right to die order

167. The legal term for an intentional deviation from the accepted standard of care that results in harm to a patient is
  a. negligence
  b. liability
  c. res ipsa loquitur
  d. proximate cause

168. You are acting under the doctrine of implied consent when you treat a
  a. person who is drunk and refuses treatment
  b. confused elderly man whose adult child is with him
  c. small child whose parent is not present
  d. person who is mentally distraught

169. Your patient is a 28-year-old man who has suffered a seizure. You monitor his condition during the seizure and throughout the postictal period, but when the patient recovers, he refuses transport or further treatment. You should
  a. explain the risks of refusing care and then restrain the patient before you begin treatment
  b. call for police backup to help you transport the patient to the hospital
  c. sedate the patient and transport him to the hospital while he is unconscious
  d. consult with medical control, explain the risks of refusing care, and document the patient's refusal

170. After submitting a patient report, you note an error. You should
  a. obtain the original report and amend it
  b. file an amendment to the original report
  c. do nothing; you can always explain what happened
  d. file a second report on the same incident

171. Which statement about the care of patients who are contaminated by hazardous material is INCORRECT?
  a. Trained personnel should immediately remove nonambulatory patients from the "hot zone."
  b. Decontamination should be carried out in the "warm zone."
  c. Intravenous therapy should begin only under specific physician direction.
  d. Secondary assessment should be done in the "hot zone."

172. Your unit is the first to arrive at the scene of a bombing at a large office building. The purpose of your initial size-up of the incident is to
  a. determine what additional resources will be needed
  b. decide how seriously injured each patient is
  c. assess whether the building can be salvaged
  d. help the police look for clues about who placed the bomb

173. At a major incident response, which of the following would be the responsibility of the staging officer?
   a. establish ambulance triage and treatment areas
   b. evaluate resources needed for treatment, and report to Command
   c. collect and assess patients with minor injuries, and remove them from the treatment areas
   d. maintain a log of units available and an inventory of special equipment

174. Which statement about the triage operation at a mass-casualty incident is correct?
   a. Each patient's initial assessment should take less than 60 seconds.
   b. Secondary assessment of the walking wounded is part of the basic triage operation.
   c. Triage assessment of each individual patient takes approximately 5 minutes.
   d. Triage personnel at a mass-casualty incident should have extensive medical training.

175. Using the START triage method at a multiple-casualty accident scene, you encounter a patient who is making no respiratory effort. You should
   a. tag the patient as nonsalvageable, and move on
   b. request medical backup
   c. attempt to open the patient's airway
   d. move the patient to the care area and intubate

176. Your patient, a 74-year-old male, has died of a massive heart attack. The best thing to tell his family is
   a. "Mr. Evans is no longer with us."
   b. "I'm sorry to tell you that Mr. Evans has died."
   c. "You should be glad that Mr. Evans is sleeping peacefully."
   d. "I think it's possible that Mr. Evans passed in his sleep."

177. Which statement about use of disposable gloves and infection control is INCORRECT?
   a. Gloves should be worn for all patient contacts.
   b. Gloves should be changed for each new patient.
   c. Gloves cannot protect health care workers from needle sticks.
   d. Gloves should be worn while eating or drinking in the ambulance.

178. Which of the following is the lowest-level decontamination procedure that will destroy tuberculosis bacilli?
   a. low-level disinfection
   b. intermediate-level disinfection
   c. high-level disinfection
   d. sterilization

179. Which strain of hepatitis usually occurs as a co-infection with hepatitis B?
   a. hepatitis A
   b. hepatitis C
   c. hepatitis D
   d. hepatitis E

180. The protocols used for triage of trauma patients are based on identifying
   a. significant mechanisms of injury and physical signs of internal injury
   b. patients with the greatest likelihood of CNS damage
   c. potential dangers to rescue workers and others in the vicinity of the accident
   d. injury to the heart, lungs, and brain

ANSWERS

1. **b.** This choice lists the organs that can be palpated in the right upper quadrant.

2. **b.** *Rhin-* means nose, as in rhinoplasty, a surgical procedure.

3. **d.** *Hypo-* means having too little of something, as in a hypoactive thyroid gland.

4. **a.** In the AVPU algorithm, used to assess level of consciousness, the P stands for the patient's response to painful stimuli.

5. **b.** The secondary assessment, undertaken only after immediate threats to life have been corrected, consists of head-to-toe evaluation, vital signs, and patient history.

6. **c.** Pulse pressure refers to the difference between the diastolic and systolic blood pressure readings.

7. **a.** The organs in the left upper quadrant are listed.

8. **c.** The thyroid cartilage forms a prominence that is known as the Adam's apple.

9. **b.** This set of vitals is common in closed head injuries. It is also known as Cushing's triad.

10. **d.** Placing the victim in the sniffing position manipulates the head and neck.

11. **d.** Choices **a, b,** and **c** are all common in closed head injuries; **d** is not.

12. **b.** A patient with a detached retina will often complain of seeing a dark curtain in front of part of the field of vision.

13. **a.** The halo test involves allowing blood to drip on gauze or a towel and looking for a light ring, suggestive of the presence of cerebrospinal fluid, outside the dark red ring.

14. **b.** Traumatic asphyxia occurs when severe rib injury pushes the chest wall in, resulting in severe hypoventilation and backflow of venous blood.

15. **b.** The head and back are each equal to 9 percent of body surface area.

16. **c.** This is often the appearance of a third-degree burn, which is painless because of destruction of nerve cells.

17. **c.** Burns to the entire chest cover a body surface area of approximately 9 percent; this would not in itself require rapid transport unless other problems existed.

18. **c.** Eye opening = 2; verbal response = 2; motor response = 4.

19. **d.** The classic signs and symptoms of appendicitis are given.

20. **b.** A positive tilt test indicates that a patient is relatively hypovolemic and should be evaluated further.

21. **b.** Esophageal varices, or enlarged blood vessels in the esophagus, present as painless vomiting of blood.

22. **a.** Although symptoms of full-blown AIDS include Kaposi's sarcoma and opportunistic infections, initial symptoms of infection with the AIDS virus often consist only of mild fatigue and fever.

23. **d.** Elderly people are more susceptible to shock than young adults because of many age-related anatomical and physiological changes.

24. **a.** The patient is displaying signs and symptoms of bowel obstruction.

25. **c.** There are many atypical signs and symptoms of MI in elderly patients; choices **a, b,** and **d** list three of them.

26. **d.** Kussmaul breathing is characteristic of diabetic ketoacidosis.

27. **c.** The correct description of normal vesicular breath sounds is given.

28. **d.** The PQRST mnemonic is used primarily to define the patient's major complaint.

29. **a.** The pain of stable angina is brought on by exertion and relieved by rest, oxygen, and nitroglycerin.

30. **c.** The goal of the primary assessment of a patient (also referred to as the ABCs) is to find and correct immediate threats to life.

31. **d.** The most common signs and symptoms are given.

32. **c.** The body's physiological mechanisms compensate for the insult that causes shock; therefore, changes in vital signs are ominous late signs in shock patients.

33. **c.** A grain, a unit of measurement used in the apothecary's system, is equal to 60 milligrams.

34. **a.** The release of catecholamines that results from the initial drop in blood pressure causes the feelings of anxiety and restlessness.

35. **d.** This patient is exhibiting the classic signs and symptoms of emphysema.

36. **b.** Epinephrine 1:1000 is not indicated for this patient.

37. **a.** Breathing through pursed lips is a common compensatory reaction exhibited by COPD patients.

38. **b.** Carbon monoxide poisoning can cause a falsely high pulse oximetry reading.

39. **d.** Airway blockage can occur when the patient is in any position.

40. **c.** The modified jaw thrust is used to open the airway of patients with suspected cervical spine injury.

41. **c.** The respiratory syncytial virus, which causes only mild upper-respiratory infections in older persons, causes bronchiolitis, a serious respiratory infection, in infants and young children.

42. **a.** This patient's blood pressure is still compensating for the allergic reaction; therefore, the patient is not in anaphylactic shock.

43. **d.** Dopamine is not indicated for this patient.

44. **c.** This patient needs to be monitored for possible anaphylactic shock.

45. **a.** If breath sounds are stronger on one side than on the other, or absent on one side, this suggests that the tube has been inserted too far and is resting in one bronchus.

46. **c.** Methylprednisolone is a steroid that reduces swelling of the spinal cord and reduces the extent of the injury.

47. b. Nitronox is not given to patients with pneumothorax, since it can move into the air pocket created by the injury.

48. c. Pulsus paradoxus, or a drop in blood pressure with each respiratory cycle, is associated with chronic obstructive pulmonary disease (COPD).

49. d. Tracheal tugging refers to retraction of neck tissues during respiratory effort.

50. c. A dull sound on chest percussion may be associated with pneumonia, hemothorax, or pulmonary edema.

51. a. Once it is attached to the patient's finger, the pulse oximeter will continuously record the pulse rate and oxygen saturation level.

52. b. The patient is showing signs and symptoms of emphysema. Administer low-flow oxygen and medications as indicated.

53. d. Methylprednisolone is an anti-inflammatory drug; the other asthma medications listed are bronchodilators.

54. a. Kussmaul's respirations, which are associated with diabetic ketoacidosis, are characterized by increased rate and depth of respirations.

55. a. Loss of pulmonary surfactant, which can occur in pneumonia and other conditions, increases the tendency of the alveoli to collapse and thus increases the work necessary for respiration.

56. b. Hydrogen ion concentration, or pH, is measured on a scale of 1 (highly acidic) to 14 (highly alkaline), with 7 being neutral. For each unit on the scale, the solution is ten times more acidic or alkaline. These measurements are very important in the consideration of the oxygen diffusing capacity of the blood, where very small changes in pH are highly significant.

57. c. The first step in a conscious child of this age is to perform the Heimlich maneuver, as described. Continue until the obstruction is relieved or the child becomes unconscious.

58. d. To prevent tissue damage, you should attempt to physically remove foreign material only if you can directly visualize the obstruction with a laryngoscope.

59. d. This patient has the symptoms of a pulmonary embolism.

60. b. You would expect to see this patient in tachycardia rather than bradycardia due to the increasing dyspnea and hypoxia resulting from the pulmonary embolism.

61. a. The pulmonary embolism has caused the right side of the heart to have to pump harder against a resistance caused by the partial blockage. This results in the severe shortness of breath and hypoxia.

62. d. This patient should be transported in the position in which it is easiest for her to breathe.

63. c. Myocardial infarction is not a common cause of pulmonary embolism.

64. b. A patient whose fluid status is compromised because of dehydration should receive lactated Ringer's solution or normal saline.

65. a. The shock position is used only if head injury is not suspected.

66. d. Because the PASG corrects a symptom and not the underlying problem, deflation should be attempted only in the hospital after the underlying hypovolemia is corrected.

67. a. This dose may be repeated every 3 to 5 minutes.

68. b. Dopamine is used to treat hypotension associated with cardiogenic shock. It increases both systolic blood pressure and pulse pressure.

69. a. The patient should be supine with the head elevated to enhance venous return. If congestive heart failure is present, the patient should be positioned semi-upright.

70. a. These changes are characteristic of the vital signs of patients with ICP.

71. a. The T wave on the ECG reflects the underlying repolarization of the ventricles.

72. d. Calculate the rate by multiplying the number of complexes in a 6-second interval by 10. The heart rate is 130.

73. b. Normal atrial depolarization is represented in Lead II as a positive, rounded P wave.

74. b. A normal P-R interval is 0.12–0.20 seconds; a normal QRS complex lasts 0.04–0.12 seconds.

75. c. Sinus bradycardia (a slowing of the S-A node resulting in a slow heart rate but normal rhythm) is unlikely to be a problem in a healthy adult.

76. b. The valsalva maneuver (bearing down against a closed glottis) stimulates the vagus nerve, which innervates the heart.

77. a. Atrial fibrillation with a low ventricular rate is suggestive of digitalis toxicity.

78. d. Lidocaine is the first-choice drug for nonperfusing ventricular tachycardia.

79. c. Risk factors for atherosclerosis include diabetes, advanced age, obesity, lack of exercise, hypertension, and smoking.

80. d. The pain of myocardial infarction is not relieved by nitroglycerin; large doses of morphine are usually needed.

81. a. Rales, abnormal breath sounds caused by the presence of fluid in the small airways, suggest the beginning of heart failure.

82. d. Bretylium is most commonly used in the management of life-threatening ventricular dysrhythmias when other agents have failed.

83. b. MI is a common cause of left ventricular failure, which is closely associated with pulmonary edema.

84. c. The primary goal for patients with left ventricular failure and pulmonary edema is to reduce venous return to the heart, or preload, and thus reduce pressure on the pulmonary circulation.

85. b. The patient's history, signs, and symptoms suggest right ventricular failure.

86. a. Signs of cardiogenic shock include a sudden drop in systolic blood pressure and increasing confusion.

87. c. The patient is showing signs and symptoms of abdominal aortic aneurysm. Do not palpate the abdomen unnecessarily; treat for shock and transport.

88. a. The most common signs are given; onset is usually sudden, and there may or may not be chest pain.

89. b. The clinical picture suggests deep venous thrombosis. Do not massage the area or allow the patient to walk, since pulmonary emboli are possible.

90. c. Epinephrine is a sympathomimetic that acts on both alpha and beta adrenergic receptors.

91. b. Initial attempts in an adult patient typically use 200 joules; this is gradually increased to 360 joules.

92. c. Carotid sinus massage can convert PSTs into sinus rhythm by increasing vagal tone and decreasing heart rate.

93. b. External cardiac pacing is used to correct symptomatic bradycardias by taking over the heart's conductive system.

94. c. This is the correct dosage and route when diazepam is used to relax the patient and cause amnesia before defibrillation.

95. a. Dobutamine is used in patients with left heart failure to increase stroke volume and therefore increase cardiac output.

96. b. S1 and S2 are normal sounds; extra sounds are abnormal findings.

97. d. These vital signs are consistent with left ventricular failure with pulmonary edema.

98. a. These are symptoms of diabetic ketoacidosis.

99. b. These are common vitals seen in ketoacidotic patients.

100. b. Ketoacidotic patients have low levels of insulin.

101. c. Most likely this patient has not taken his insulin or he has an infection that upset the glucose-insulin balance.

102. a. Kussmaul's respirations are very deep and rapid and represent the body's attempt to compensate for the metabolic acidosis produced by the ketones and organic acids in the blood.

103. b. The appropriate treatment for this patient would be a blood glucose test, an IV of normal saline, and insulin.

104. c. The spinal cord ends at the second lumbar vertebra.

105. b. Asymmetrical movements during respiration suggest the presence of injury to the chest wall.

106. d. A concussion is a brief loss of consciousness in response to minor head trauma.

107. d. Use gentle traction to bring the distal part of the limb into alignment with the proximal part.

108. a. If the patient's condition is such that rapid transport is necessary, you would care for limb injuries while en route, rather than completing a secondary assessment and bandaging and splinting on scene.

109. b. You cannot harm a patient by immobilizing a limb properly, but you may possibly cause further injury by failing to immobilize a fracture.

110. d. Because a crush wound can tear several different large blood vessels, bleeding may be particularly difficult to control, and a tourniquet may be necessary.

111. c. Changes in behavior are the most common signs of hypoglycemia. Other signs and symptoms include diaphoresis, tachycardia, and headache.

112. b. Although diazepam (Valium) does reduce anxiety, it is given to seizure patients to suppress the spread of electrical activity throughout the brain, as well as to relax the muscles.

113. a. The correct dosage and route of administration is given.

114. d. Beta agonists such as albuterol are most frequently used in the treatment of reactive airway disease (asthma). They are also used to prevent or relieve bronchospasm and laryngeal edema in patients with anaphylaxis.

115. c. Bee and wasp stings are among the most common causes of anaphylaxis.

116. a. The most common symptoms of acetaminophen are listed.

117. d. Sodium bicarbonate is sometimes ordered in the field for overdoses of salicylates.

118. b. Heat will cause the poison to break down and cause less damage to the patient.

119. c. PCP can cause bizarre delusions as well as violent and uncontrollable behavior.

120. b. These are signs and symptoms of heat exhaustion; patients **c** and **d** show signs and symptoms of heat stroke.

121. d. Immerse the frostbitten body part is water of 100–106° F; add warm water frequently to keep the water at the desired temperature.

122. c. Due to the chance of post-event pulmonary edema, all near-drowning victims should be admitted to the hospital for observation.

123. b. All options list signs and symptoms of diving emergencies; only **b** includes signs of air embolism.

124. c. During silences, remain relaxed and attentive and wait to hear what the patient has to say. This will encourage the patient to talk.

125. a. Physical complaints, such as pain, are frequently manifestations of anxiety disorders. Other manifestations include hyperventilation, unrealistic fears, trembling, and sweating.

126. a. The goal with this asthma patient would be to correct hypoxia, reverse bronchospasms, and decrease inflammation.

127. a. Cold air, not warm air, is a common trigger for asthma. Choices **b, c,** and **d** are also triggers.

128. c. These medications are commonly used in the treatment of asthma.

129. b. Tell the child realistically, in language she can understand, what you are doing and why.

130. b. Normal values are: respirations, 20–30; pulse, 80–120; systolic BP, 80–110.

131. a. In cases of suspected child abuse, your responsibility is to report your findings and ensure that the patient receives necessary care immediately.

132. d. Fever in a child less than 3 months old is considered to be meningitis unless proven otherwise; transport all infants with fever promptly.

133. c. Management of epiglottitis consists of airway maintenance, oxygen, and prompt transport.

134. c. The formula for tube size selection is: 16 + patient's age ÷ 4.

135. c. This is the most appropriate way to determine proper medication for a pediatric patient.

136. d. Valium is usually given orally or rectally.

137. d. Spinal immobilization helps to prevent a dislodging of the tube.

138. a. Epinephrine would be indicated for this patient.

139. b. Because absorption is incomplete, the dosage is high for the rectal route.

140. b. This statement is correct; bronchiolitis is a viral disease that is most prevalent in children 6–18 months old with no family history of asthma.

141. d. The signs and symptoms of epiglottitis are given.

142. b. Bruises of this age are dark blue or purple; this information is important in cases of suspected child abuse.

143. d. In addition to the child's age, the size of the endotracheal tube should be based on the size of the cricoid ring, which is the narrowest part of a child's airway.

144. c. To preserve physical evidence, avoid handling clothing and cleaning or bandaging wounds, unless there is hemorrhage. Do not allow the victim to bathe, comb her hair, or change her clothing.

145. b. A *nulligravida* is a woman who has never been pregnant.

146. a. Look for crowning, or the appearance of the baby's head at the opening of the vagina, only during a contraction.

147. c. The patient is most likely suffering a miscarriage. Treat her for signs and symptoms of shock due to blood loss, provide emotional support, retain any clumps of tissue she passes, and transport.

148. a. Supine-hypotensive syndrome, a normal occurrence during late pregnancy, is caused by the pressure of the pregnant uterus on the inferior vena cava when the patient is supine.

149. d. The second stage of labor, the period from complete dilation of cervix until delivery of the infant, typically lasts approximately 20 minutes in multiparous women.

150. b. To avoid a precipitous delivery, tell the mother to stop pushing after the head is delivered.

151. c. A prolapsed cord should be treated by placing two fingers of a gloved hand to raise the presenting part of the fetus off the cord; then place the mother in Trendelenburg or knee-chest position, administer high-flow oxygen, and transport immediately.

152. b. Position the neonate as described to facilitate drainage of secretions.

153. c. A neonate's normal respiratory rate is 40–60 breaths per minute.

154. a. Ventilate with 100 percent oxygen, and then evaluate the heart rate and initiate chest compressions if necessary.

155. b. Oxygen toxicity occurs only if oxygen is administered for several days; do not withhold oxygen in the prehospital setting.

156. b. Fluid therapy for a neonate consists of 10 mL/kg, administered via syringe over a 5- to 10-minute period.

157. a. The correct procedure is given; a fetoscope or Doppler stethoscope may also be used.

158. c. A tiered EMS system is one in which varying levels of resources are dispatched to calls depending upon the nature of the incident as stated by the 911 caller.

159. a. The National Highway Safety Act, passed in 1966, required the states to develop EMS systems or forfeit federal highway construction funds.

160. d. Indirect medical control involves such activities as training, chart review, and quality assurance.

161. d. Using START triage, separating the walking wounded is the first step in triaging large numbers of patients.

162. b. Breathing/airway is the first parameter that should be assessed.

163. b. The START triage algorithm dictates that patients with respiratory rates above 30 be classified as immediate.

164. b. The decreased level of consciousness places the patient in the immediate category.

165. c. Reposition the head and examine for spontaneous respirations. If they are immediately present, categorize the patient as immediate. If they are absent, categorize the patient as dead/unsalvageable and move on to the next patient.

166. b. A durable power of attorney for health care delegates the right to make medical decisions to someone else in the event that the patient becomes disabled or incompetent.

167. a. Negligence refers to an intentional deviation from the accepted standard of care that results in harm to a patient.

168. c. Implied consent covers situations in which the patient is not capable of consenting to treatment but a reasonable person would do so.

169. d. If a competent adult patient refuses treatment and transport, you should consult with medical control, explain to the patient the risks of refusal in detail, document the informed refusal, and, if possible, have the refusal witnessed by someone who is not an EMS employee.

170. b. Never alter a patient report once it is submitted. The proper procedure for changing a report is to file an amendment.

171. d. Only absolutely essential care, such as ABCs and spinal immobilization, should be done in the "hot zone."

172. a. The purpose of the initial scene size-up at a mass-casualty incident is to determine what additional resources will be needed.

173. d. The staging officer is primarily responsible for assembling all available vehicles to make sure they are ready for deployment as needed.

174. a. START and METTAG, systems used at mass-casualty incidents, are designed to be carried out very quickly by minimally trained personnel.

175. c. If a patient is making no respiratory effort, the triage worker would make basic attempts to clear the airway, such as repositioning the head.

176. b. Inform the family that the patient has died in plain, simple language.

177. d. Personnel should not eat or drink inside the ambulance; gloves cannot protect you from food- or airborne-infectious agents.

178. b. Intermediate-level disinfection with a solution of chlorine bleach will destroy *Mycobacterium tuberculosis*.

179. c. Hepatitis D is considered a weak or defective virus that requires a co-infection, usually with hepatitis B, to replicate. The result is a more serious illness than infection with hepatitis B alone.

180. a. Triage at a trauma scene depends on the ability to identify both significant mechanisms of injury and patients with signs of serious internal injury.

C·H·A·P·T·E·R 6

PARAMEDIC PRACTICE EXAM 4

CHAPTER SUMMARY

This is the last of four practice exams in this book based on the National Registry EMT-Paramedic written exam. Using all of your experience and strategy that you gained from the other three, take this exam to see how far you have come since your first one.

This is the last practice exam in this book, but it is not designed to be any harder or trickier than the other three. It is simply another representation of what you might expect for the real test. Just as when you go to take the real test, there shouldn't be anything here to surprise you. In fact, you probably already know what's in a lot of it! That's the idea for the real test, too—that you won't be surprised, so you won't be unprepared.

For this last test, pull together all the tips you've been practicing since the first test. Give yourself the time and the space to work, perhaps in an unfamiliar location such as a library, since you won't be taking the real test in your living room. In addition, draw on what you've learned from reading the answer explanations. Remember the types of questions that tripped you up in the past, and when you are unsure, try to consider how those answers were explained.

Most of all, relax. You have worked hard and have every right to be confident!

1.	(a)	(b)	(c)	(d)		46.	(a)	(b)	(c)	(d)		91.	(a)	(b)	(c)	(d)
2.	(a)	(b)	(c)	(d)		47.	(a)	(b)	(c)	(d)		92.	(a)	(b)	(c)	(d)
3.	(a)	(b)	(c)	(d)		48.	(a)	(b)	(c)	(d)		93.	(a)	(b)	(c)	(d)
4.	(a)	(b)	(c)	(d)		49.	(a)	(b)	(c)	(d)		94.	(a)	(b)	(c)	(d)
5.	(a)	(b)	(c)	(d)		50.	(a)	(b)	(c)	(d)		95.	(a)	(b)	(c)	(d)
6.	(a)	(b)	(c)	(d)		51.	(a)	(b)	(c)	(d)		96.	(a)	(b)	(c)	(d)
7.	(a)	(b)	(c)	(d)		52.	(a)	(b)	(c)	(d)		97.	(a)	(b)	(c)	(d)
8.	(a)	(b)	(c)	(d)		53.	(a)	(b)	(c)	(d)		98.	(a)	(b)	(c)	(d)
9.	(a)	(b)	(c)	(d)		54.	(a)	(b)	(c)	(d)		99.	(a)	(b)	(c)	(d)
10.	(a)	(b)	(c)	(d)		55.	(a)	(b)	(c)	(d)		100.	(a)	(b)	(c)	(d)
11.	(a)	(b)	(c)	(d)		56.	(a)	(b)	(c)	(d)		101.	(a)	(b)	(c)	(d)
12.	(a)	(b)	(c)	(d)		57.	(a)	(b)	(c)	(d)		102.	(a)	(b)	(c)	(d)
13.	(a)	(b)	(c)	(d)		58.	(a)	(b)	(c)	(d)		103.	(a)	(b)	(c)	(d)
14.	(a)	(b)	(c)	(d)		59.	(a)	(b)	(c)	(d)		104.	(a)	(b)	(c)	(d)
15.	(a)	(b)	(c)	(d)		60.	(a)	(b)	(c)	(d)		105.	(a)	(b)	(c)	(d)
16.	(a)	(b)	(c)	(d)		61.	(a)	(b)	(c)	(d)		106.	(a)	(b)	(c)	(d)
17.	(a)	(b)	(c)	(d)		62.	(a)	(b)	(c)	(d)		107.	(a)	(b)	(c)	(d)
18.	(a)	(b)	(c)	(d)		63.	(a)	(b)	(c)	(d)		108.	(a)	(b)	(c)	(d)
19.	(a)	(b)	(c)	(d)		64.	(a)	(b)	(c)	(d)		109.	(a)	(b)	(c)	(d)
20.	(a)	(b)	(c)	(d)		65.	(a)	(b)	(c)	(d)		110.	(a)	(b)	(c)	(d)
21.	(a)	(b)	(c)	(d)		66.	(a)	(b)	(c)	(d)		111.	(a)	(b)	(c)	(d)
22.	(a)	(b)	(c)	(d)		67.	(a)	(b)	(c)	(d)		112.	(a)	(b)	(c)	(d)
23.	(a)	(b)	(c)	(d)		68.	(a)	(b)	(c)	(d)		113.	(a)	(b)	(c)	(d)
24.	(a)	(b)	(c)	(d)		69.	(a)	(b)	(c)	(d)		114.	(a)	(b)	(c)	(d)
25.	(a)	(b)	(c)	(d)		70.	(a)	(b)	(c)	(d)		115.	(a)	(b)	(c)	(d)
26.	(a)	(b)	(c)	(d)		71.	(a)	(b)	(c)	(d)		116.	(a)	(b)	(c)	(d)
27.	(a)	(b)	(c)	(d)		72.	(a)	(b)	(c)	(d)		117.	(a)	(b)	(c)	(d)
28.	(a)	(b)	(c)	(d)		73.	(a)	(b)	(c)	(d)		118.	(a)	(b)	(c)	(d)
29.	(a)	(b)	(c)	(d)		74.	(a)	(b)	(c)	(d)		119.	(a)	(b)	(c)	(d)
30.	(a)	(b)	(c)	(d)		75.	(a)	(b)	(c)	(d)		120.	(a)	(b)	(c)	(d)
31.	(a)	(b)	(c)	(d)		76.	(a)	(b)	(c)	(d)		121.	(a)	(b)	(c)	(d)
32.	(a)	(b)	(c)	(d)		77.	(a)	(b)	(c)	(d)		122.	(a)	(b)	(c)	(d)
33.	(a)	(b)	(c)	(d)		78.	(a)	(b)	(c)	(d)		123.	(a)	(b)	(c)	(d)
34.	(a)	(b)	(c)	(d)		79.	(a)	(b)	(c)	(d)		124.	(a)	(b)	(c)	(d)
35.	(a)	(b)	(c)	(d)		80.	(a)	(b)	(c)	(d)		125.	(a)	(b)	(c)	(d)
36.	(a)	(b)	(c)	(d)		81.	(a)	(b)	(c)	(d)		126.	(a)	(b)	(c)	(d)
37.	(a)	(b)	(c)	(d)		82.	(a)	(b)	(c)	(d)		127.	(a)	(b)	(c)	(d)
38.	(a)	(b)	(c)	(d)		83.	(a)	(b)	(c)	(d)		128.	(a)	(b)	(c)	(d)
39.	(a)	(b)	(c)	(d)		84.	(a)	(b)	(c)	(d)		129.	(a)	(b)	(c)	(d)
40.	(a)	(b)	(c)	(d)		85.	(a)	(b)	(c)	(d)		130.	(a)	(b)	(c)	(d)
41.	(a)	(b)	(c)	(d)		86.	(a)	(b)	(c)	(d)		131.	(a)	(b)	(c)	(d)
42.	(a)	(b)	(c)	(d)		87.	(a)	(b)	(c)	(d)		132.	(a)	(b)	(c)	(d)
43.	(a)	(b)	(c)	(d)		88.	(a)	(b)	(c)	(d)		133.	(a)	(b)	(c)	(d)
44.	(a)	(b)	(c)	(d)		89.	(a)	(b)	(c)	(d)		134.	(a)	(b)	(c)	(d)
45.	(a)	(b)	(c)	(d)		90.	(a)	(b)	(c)	(d)		135.	(a)	(b)	(c)	(d)

136. (a) (b) (c) (d) 151. (a) (b) (c) (d) 166. (a) (b) (c) (d)
137. (a) (b) (c) (d) 152. (a) (b) (c) (d) 167. (a) (b) (c) (d)
138. (a) (b) (c) (d) 153. (a) (b) (c) (d) 168. (a) (b) (c) (d)
139. (a) (b) (c) (d) 154. (a) (b) (c) (d) 169. (a) (b) (c) (d)
140. (a) (b) (c) (d) 155. (a) (b) (c) (d) 170. (a) (b) (c) (d)
141. (a) (b) (c) (d) 156. (a) (b) (c) (d) 171. (a) (b) (c) (d)
142. (a) (b) (c) (d) 157. (a) (b) (c) (d) 172. (a) (b) (c) (d)
143. (a) (b) (c) (d) 158. (a) (b) (c) (d) 173. (a) (b) (c) (d)
144. (a) (b) (c) (d) 159. (a) (b) (c) (d) 174. (a) (b) (c) (d)
145. (a) (b) (c) (d) 160. (a) (b) (c) (d) 175. (a) (b) (c) (d)
146. (a) (b) (c) (d) 161. (a) (b) (c) (d) 176. (a) (b) (c) (d)
147. (a) (b) (c) (d) 162. (a) (b) (c) (d) 177. (a) (b) (c) (d)
148. (a) (b) (c) (d) 163. (a) (b) (c) (d) 178. (a) (b) (c) (d)
149. (a) (b) (c) (d) 164. (a) (b) (c) (d) 179. (a) (b) (c) (d)
150. (a) (b) (c) (d) 165. (a) (b) (c) (d) 180. (a) (b) (c) (d)

PARAMEDIC EXAM 4

1. The prefix *cephalo-* refers to the
   a. neck
   b. arm
   c. heart
   d. head

2. The abbreviation SQ stands for
   a. lower right quadrant
   b. subcutaneous
   c. sublingual
   d. central line

3. Which of the following lists the steps of complete patient assessment in the correct order?
   a. field management procedures, reevaluation, history, primary survey, secondary survey, resuscitation
   b. primary survey, resuscitation, secondary survey, history, field management procedures, reevaluation
   c. primary survey, secondary survey, resuscitation, history, reevaluation, field management procedures
   d. primary survey, history, secondary survey, resuscitation, reevaluation, field management procedures

4. On primary survey, you note that your patient is alert and oriented times three. This means that
   a. the patient is alert to name, location, and date or time
   b. you assessed the patient's mental status three times
   c. the patient was alert on your first three assessments
   d. the patient is alert now, but was unconscious three minutes ago

5. Which patient's vital signs are normal?
   a. male, age 76: P, 88; R, 26; BP, 160/100
   b. female, age 40: P, 72; R, 18; BP, 130/80
   c. male, age 14: P, 62; R, 12; BP, 90/60
   d. female, age 3: P, 130; R, 40; BP, 110/70

6. When using the PQRST mnemonic to assess a patient's pain, you would assess the R portion of the mnemonic by asking
   a. "When did it start?"
   b. "Where does it hurt?"
   c. "What makes it feel better?"
   d. "What does it feel like?"

7. Which set of signs and symptoms is characteristic of a patient in compensated shock?
a. lethargy, confusion; pulse and blood pressure slightly elevated; skin cool; capillary refill delayed
b. coma; pulse and blood pressure very low; skin pale, cold, and clammy
c. confusion lapsing into unconsciousness; pulse and blood pressure moderately elevated; cyanosis of extremities; capillary refill delayed
d. unconsciousness; pulse and blood pressure dropping; extremities cold; capillary refill delayed

8. A driver who follows a down-and-under pathway of injury after a collision is most likely to have which type of injury?
a. fractured ribs
b. ruptured diaphragm
c. fractured femur
d. lacerated liver or spleen

9. The "paper bag effect" occurs when the occupant of a car takes a deep breath just before a collision, resulting in
a. pneumothorax
b. pulmonary embolism
c. shearing of the aorta
d. lung laceration

10. An adult who falls a distance of 20 feet is most likely to land on his or her
a. head
b. hands
c. back
d. feet

11. Your patient, a middle-age female, was a pedestrian struck by a car. She opens her eyes only in response to pain, makes no verbal responses, and her best motor response is withdrawal in response to pain. The Glasgow Coma Scale score is
a. 3
b. 5
c. 7
d. 9

12. Your patient, the victim of assault, is complaining of malocclusion and numbness to the chin. There is also a suspected nasal fracture, as well as significant facial bleeding and bruising. You should
a. secure the airway with a nasopharyngeal tube, control bleeding, and transport
b. secure the cervical spine, control the airway but avoid the use of a nasopharyngeal tube, control bleeding, and transport
c. treat for signs and symptoms of shock, control the airway with a nasopharyngeal tube, and transport
d. secure the cervical spine, attach ECG monitor, apply PASG, control the airway but avoid the use of a nasopharyngeal tube, control bleeding, and observe

13. The presence of marked raccoon eyes on a patient in the prehospital environment should lead you to suspect
a. shock
b. recent cervical spine trauma
c. a significant mechanism of injury
d. significant previous injury

14. The best way to prevent decompensated shock in trauma patients is to routinely
   a. monitor for a drop in blood pressure
   b. search for early signs and symptoms in patients with a significant mechanism of injury
   c. transport rapidly all seriously injured patients without taking time to stabilize on scene
   d. ensure that all external bleeding is stopped as soon as possible

15. Your patient is a middle-age female who has been in a car accident. Because the primary assessment showed no immediate life threats, you are treating her most serious injuries, which include a suspected broken femur and kneecap. After stabilizing the injured leg and checking the distal pulse, you should
   a. repeat the primary assessment
   b. stabilize the cervical spine
   c. check the proximal pulse
   d. apply the PASG

16. Your patient is a 26-year-old construction worker who has fallen approximately 35 feet and received multiple injuries. The Glasgow Coma Scale score is 9; respiratory rate is 32; respiratory expansion is normal; the blood pressure is 100/70; and capillary return is delayed. The patient's Trauma Score is
   a. 19
   b. 15
   c. 11
   d. 7

Answer questions 17–19 on the basis of the information below.

Your unit is dispatched to a single-automobile crash. The patient's car hit a large tree head-on. The patient, a young-adult woman, is found conscious and alert but trapped in the car. The air bag deployed and she denies any head or neck pain, but she complains of hip and left leg pain. After a difficult 20-minute extrication, the patient is finally released from the car. Suddenly, your patient's vital signs begin to collapse.

17. This patient is most likely transitioning from
   a. decompensated shock to hypovolemic shock
   b. cardiogenic shock to hypovolemic shock
   c. compensated shock to decompensated shock
   d. decompensated shock to compensated shock

18. The patient has a closed fracture of the left ankle, and the pelvis is stable. There is no penetrating trauma noted in the chest or abdomen, and the patient denies pregnancy. Which of the following chambers of the PASG should be inflated?
   a. both legs only
   b. both legs and the abdominal compartments
   c. the right leg and the abdominal compartments
   d. the left leg and the abdominal compartments

19. You start a large bore IV of normal saline. Which of the following medications, if any, should you administer next?
  a. procainamide
  b. isoproterenol
  c. verapamil
  d. No other medications should be administered.

20. A patient who complains of pain in the left upper abdominal quadrant may be suffering from
  a. pancreatitis
  b. appendicitis
  c. hepatitis
  d. diverticulitis

21. Signs of uremia resulting from chronic renal failure include
  a. pale skin, diaphoresis, and edematous extremities
  b. pasty, yellow skin and wasting of the extremities
  c. anxiety, delirium, and hallucinations
  d. anorexia, nausea, and vomiting

22. Your patient is Mr. Williams, a 75-year-old man. Mrs. Williams has called EMS because her husband "has a terrible headache and is very confused." Mr. Williams's vital signs are respirations, 26; pulse, 78; blood pressure, 200/120. The primary problem you must address is most likely
  a. hypertensive emergency
  b. senile dementia
  c. cardiac tamponade
  d. elder abuse

23. Which assessment findings are consistent with cardiogenic shock in a patient who is suffering a presumed MI?
  a. respirations, 30; BP, 100/70; cyanosis
  b. respirations, 10; BP, 160/100; diaphoresis
  c. respirations, 36; BP, 90/60; cyanosis
  d. respirations, 18; BP, 140/90; cool, dry skin

24. Your patient is a 67-year-old male who smokes cigarettes and has a history of MI. He complains of severe pain, of sudden onset, in his right leg, as well as numbness and diminished motor function in the right leg. Other assessment findings are diminished pulse, pallor, and lowered skin temperature in the right leg. You should suspect
  a. aortic aneurysm secondary to MI
  b. occlusion of the femoral artery
  c. deep venous thrombosis
  d. hypertensive encephalopathy

Answer questions 25–28 on the basis of the information below.

You respond on a 41-year-old male who has been injured in an explosion at a possible illegal chemistry laboratory. During your assessment you notice a spinal deformity and a possible closed head injury. Your patient also has ruptured tympanic membranes and sinus injuries.

25. Which of the following is NOT a blast phase of injury?
  a. alpha
  b. primary
  c. secondary
  d. tertiary

26. This patient's sinus injuries most likely occurred during which blast phase?
    a. alpha
    b. primary
    c. secondary
    d. tertiary

27. Your victim has first- and second-degree burns to his face. These are flash burns from the explosion. Witnesses denied that the patient's clothes were on fire. You should suspect
    a. extensive lung tissue burns
    b. extensive airway burns
    c. pneumonia
    d. pneumothorax

28. During your assessment you notice a rigid, very tender abdomen. This may be blunt force trauma from flying debris or
    a. thermal burns to the stomach
    b. deceleration injuries from being thrown by the blast
    c. tertiary injuries
    d. compression of air-containing organs

29. Your patient is a 27-year-old male who is found unconscious on a bathroom floor. He is not breathing, has pinpoint pupils, and has a fresh puncture wound to his right forearm. He has multiple scars that form a bluish streak over the veins of the backs of both hands. This patient is most likely suffering from
    a. a seizure disorder
    b. multiple spider bites
    c. a narcotic overdose
    d. a rodent bite that led to anaphylactic shock

30. Your patient is an 84-year-old man with extreme difficulty breathing, apprehension, cyanosis, and diaphoresis. Assessment findings include elevated pulse and blood pressure and rales and rhonchi on auscultation. There is no chest pain. You should treat this patient for
    a. right ventricular failure
    b. cardiogenic shock secondary to MI
    c. dissecting aortic aneurysm
    d. left ventricular failure secondary to MI

31. Which condition is likely to cause a patient's respiratory rate to increase?
    a. pain and anxiety
    b. metabolic alkalosis
    c. narcotic overdose
    d. CNS lesion

32. Normal vesicular breath sounds are described as
    a. rapid, deep, shorter on expiration than on inspiration
    b. rapid, deep, longer on expiration than on inspiration
    c. low-pitched, soft, longer on expiration than on inspiration
    d. low-pitched, soft, shorter on expiration than on inspiration

33. A patient with a partial airway obstruction but adequate air exchange should be
    a. treated as though a complete airway obstruction exists
    b. intubated and given low-flow oxygen
    c. allowed to continue her spontaneous efforts to clear the airway, with monitoring
    d. intubated, given high-flow oxygen, and transported to the hospital immediately

34. Common causes of aspiration are reduced level of consciousness and
   a. myocardial infarction
   b. attempts to control the airway
   c. trauma
   d. diabetic coma and insulin shock

35. An important disadvantage of both nasal and oral airways is that they
   a. are unable to protect the lower airway from aspiration
   b. may become obstructed by aspirated material
   c. can be used only in patients whose gag reflex is intact
   d. are not made in a wide enough range of sizes to fit all patients

36. After inserting an EOA tube, what step should you take before inflating the balloon to ensure that the tube is properly positioned?
   a. measure the distance between the angle of the patient's jaw and the tip of the ear
   b. hyperventilate the patient with 100 percent oxygen
   c. look for chest rise and auscultate the lungs and abdomen
   d. auscultate in the midaxillary line only for bilateral breath sounds

37. An endotracheal tube that has been advanced too far is most likely to enter the
   a. esophagus
   b. trachea
   c. left main bronchus
   d. right main bronchus

Answer questions 38–43 on the basis of the information below.

Your are called to a nursing home and find a bedridden 78-year-old male patient who is in acute respiratory distress. The staff reports that the patient has been generally ill for the last few days and has had a persistent productive cough with a thick yellow sputum. His blood pressure is 168/72 and his respiratory rate is 40, labored with a coarse rhonchi upon auscultation of lung sounds. Lung sounds are absent in about the lower third of his lung fields. The patient is also febrile with hot, dry flushed skins.

38. This patient is most likely suffering from
   a. chronic bronchitis
   b. right-side heart failure
   c. emphysema
   d. pneumonia

39. Treatment of this patient should include
   a. albuterol
   b. methylprednisolone
   c. oxygen
   d. epinephrine 1:1000

40. All of the following would distinguish this patient's condition from congestive heart failure EXCEPT
   a. fever
   b. productive cough with yellow sputum
   c. hot, dry flushed skins
   d. dyspnea

41. All of the following are risk factors for this patient's disease or condition EXCEPT
   a. being elderly
   b. having a low level of activity
   c. suffering from immunosuppression (HIV, AIDS)
   d. having a medical history of diabetes

42. Were this patient to require tracheal suctioning, which of the following steps should NOT be followed?
   a. suction upon withdrawal of the suction catheter
   b. sterile technique
   c. protective eye wear, mask, and gown
   d. hyperventilation of the patient prior to suctioning

43. How should this patient be positioned for transport?
   a. high Fowler's position
   b. supine
   c. left lateral recumbent
   d. prone

44. Which drug is administered only by inhalation?
   a. albuterol
   b. terbutaline
   c. aminophylline
   d. epinephrine 1:1000

45. Prehospital care of an open pneumothorax includes
   a. high-flow oxygen, monitoring for signs of tension pneumothorax, assisted ventilation if needed
   b. needle decompression, creation of a one-way valve to relieve tension, rapid transport
   c. chest wound dressing, high-flow oxygen, IV fluids, rapid transport
   d. airway maintenance, ventilatory support, rapid transport

46. Diphenhydramine HCL is
   a. a beta agonist
   b. a sympathomimetic
   c. a diuretic
   d. an antihistamine

47. A whistling sound heard on expiration is referred to as
   a. snoring
   b. wheezing
   c. stridor
   d. friction rub

48. Your patient is an adult female who is unconscious as a result of an upper-airway obstruction. You use the jaw-thrust/chin-lift to open the airway and then attempt to give two ventilations, which are unsuccessful. The next thing you should do is to
   a. give five abdominal thrusts
   b. give five chest thrusts
   c. attempt the tongue lift and finger sweeps
   d. attempt two more ventilations

49. Your patient is a 67-year-old male who reports a history of 45 pack-years of cigarette smoking and frequent respiratory infections. He reports a chronic cough, which has recently become much worse. He is overweight and displays peripheral cyanosis. Auscultation of the chest reveals rhonchi. There is also noticeable jugular vein distention. You should suspect
a. emphysema
b. status asthmaticus
c. chronic bronchitis
d. lung cancer

50. When using a Wright meter to measure peak expiratory flow, the correct procedure is to tell the patient to inhale and exhale
a. once only, taking a normal breath
b. twice, taking normal breaths; the lowest reading is recorded
c. once only, as hard as possible
d. twice, as hard as possible; the highest reading is recorded

51. The correct dosage of methylprednisolone for a patient who is experiencing a severe asthma attack is
a. 0.3–0.5 mg, given subcutaneously
b. 125–250 mg, given via IV or intramuscularly
c. 0.25 mg, given subcutaneously
d. 0.2–0.3 mg, diluted in 2–3 mL normal saline, via nebulizer

52. Hyperventilation syndrome most often occurs in a patient who is
a. anxious
b. having an asthma attack
c. in shock
d. a heavy smoker

53. Your patient is a 51-year-old male with a history of COPD. He states that he has called EMS because he "can hardly breathe at all today." On primary survey, you determine that the patient is in obvious respiratory distress but not too hypoxic. You should
a. administer high-flow oxygen and prepare to intubate
b. withhold oxygen to avoid decreasing the hypoxic drive
c. administer high-flow oxygen at a rate of 30 L/min via bag-valve-mask
d. administer low-flow oxygen at a rate of 2 L/min via nasal cannula

54. Your patient is an obese 77-year-old woman who has called EMS complaining of dyspnea, cough, hemoptysis, and diaphoresis. On examination, you note tachypnea and tachycardia, crackles and localized wheezing, distended neck veins and varicose veins. You should suspect
a. myocardial infarction
b. pulmonary embolism
c. aortic aneurysm
d. status asthmaticus

55. When transporting a patient suspected of having tuberculosis, you should maintain respiratory isolation by having
a. the patient ride alone in the back of the ambulance
b. the patient wear a mask
c. all personnel wear masks
d. both patient and personnel wear masks

Answer questions 56–61 on the basis of the information below.

You are called to the home of a 26-year-old male who is having difficulty breathing. Your assessment reveals a pulse rate of 100 strong and regular radially, a blood pressure of 132/78, and a respiratory rate of 36, labored with audible wheezes. The patient's skins are pale, moist, and normal to temperature. He is having difficulty getting air out and says that he has experienced this before. This event rates approximately a 9 on a 1–10 severity scale. The patient states that the event was unprovoked and that he has been having dyspnea for approximately 20–30 minutes.

56. This patient is most likely suffering from
   a. pulmonary edema
   b. upper airway obstruction
   c. asthma
   d. pneumonia

57. Treating this patient with nebulized steroids would
   a. provide no immediate relief of the bronchospasm
   b. reverse the effects of the bronchospasm
   c. actually increase the severity of the bronchospasm
   d. be potentially dangerous as there can be a significant increase in blood pressure

58. Medications used for the treatment of this patient may include all of the following EXCEPT
   a. oxygen
   b. epinephrine 1:1000
   c. albuterol
   d. methylprednisolone

59. This patient's respiratory distress is due to
   a. increased cardiac preload
   b. decreased cardiac preload
   c. increased cardiac afterload
   d. constriction of the smaller airways

60. This patient's disease is regarded as
   a. a chronic obstructive pulmonary disease
   b. an acute obstructive pulmonary disease
   c. a chronic inflammatory disease
   d. an acute inflammatory disease

61. This patient's respiratory distress may have been caused by one of several triggers; these precipitating factors include all of the following EXCEPT
   a. allergens
   b. too much sleep
   c. exercise
   d. irritants such as cigarette smoke, smog, or dust

62. Blood enters the right atrium of the heart through the
   a. aorta
   b. right ventricle
   c. left pulmonary arteries
   d. superior and inferior vena cava

63. If a patient's carotid pulse is palpable but the radial pulse is not, the systolic blood pressure is estimated to be
   a. 20–40 mm Hg
   b. 40–60 mm Hg
   c. 60–80 mm Hg
   d. 80–100 mm Hg

64. Simultaneous palpation of the apical impulse and the carotid pulse allows you to compare the relationship between the
   a. heart and the lungs
   b. central and peripheral circulation
   c. pulse and blood pressure
   d. ventricular contractions and pulse

65. Which catheter size would you most likely use to administer fluids at a "to keep open" rate?
   a. 12 gauge
   b. 14 gauge
   c. 16 gauge
   d. 18 gauge

66. You are starting an IV, and your first puncture attempt is unsuccessful. The second attempt should be made
   a. distal to the first
   b. proximal to the first
   c. on a different limb
   d. in a central vein

67. Medical control has ordered you to administer 300 mg of bretylium. You have a 10 mL vial that contains 500 mg of bretylium. How many milliliters should you administer to the patient?
   a. 5 mL
   b. 6 mL
   c. 7 mL
   d. 8 mL

68. The vasopressor drug that is most commonly used in cardiogenic shock is
   a. norepinephrine
   b. epinephrine
   c. dopamine
   d. dobutamine

69. Your patient has received penetrating trauma to the neck and is bleeding profusely from several large vessels. You should
   a. apply constant direct pressure
   b. apply a tourniquet
   c. clamp the injured vessels
   d. tamponade the vessels with gauze

70. Signs and symptoms of cerebral hemorrhage include
   a. disorientation and confusion, decreased pulse and blood pressure, cyanosis
   b. transient loss of consciousness, headache, drowsiness, nausea and vomiting
   c. leakage of cerebrospinal fluid, headache, bleeding
   d. headache, Battle's sign, confusion, lethargy

71. Infusing 3 L of crystalloid solution into a patient expands the vascular volume by
   a. 4 L
   b. 3 L
   c. 2 L
   d. 1 L

72. Which statement about hypoglycemia is INCORRECT?
   a. Hypoglycemia may occur in nondiabetic patients, especially in chronic alcoholics.
   b. In diabetics, hypoglycemia usually results from too much insulin, too little food, or too much activity.
   c. Signs and symptoms of hypoglycemia are slow in onset and usually develop over several hours.
   d. In early stages of hypoglycemia, the patient may complain of extreme hunger.

73. Predisposing factors for development of hyperosmolar hyperglycemic nonketotic coma (HHNK) are
   a. old age, Type II diabetes, coexisting cardiac or renal disease, increased insulin requirements
   b. young age, Type I diabetes, coexisting cardiac or respiratory disease, decreased insulin requirements
   c. obesity, Type II diabetes, chronic alcoholism
   d. coexisting kidney disease, Type I diabetes, narcotics use

74. Myocardial infarction may go unrecognized in elderly patients because they
   a. tend to have abnormal ECGs
   b. take prescription nitroglycerin to relieve symptoms
   c. are not able to describe their symptoms clearly
   d. lack typical symptoms such as chest pain

75. From the pulmonary veins, blood flows into the
   a. left atrium
   b. right atrium
   c. lungs
   d. right ventricle

76. Stroke volume is equal to the amount of blood that is
   a. ejected from the ventricles during systole
   b. left in the ventricles after systole
   c. forced into the atria during diastole
   d. forced into the ventricles during systole

77. The effect of parasympathetic stimulation on the heart is to
   a. increase the heart rate and increase stroke volume
   b. decrease the heart rate and increase stroke volume
   c. increase the heart rate and decrease stroke volume
   d. decrease the heart rate and decrease stroke volume

78. The order in which electrical excitation spreads through the pacemaker sites within the heart is
   a. bundle branches and Purkinje fibers, AV node, SA node
   b. bundle branches and Purkinje fibers, SA node, AV node
   c. SA node, AV node, bundle branches and Purkinje fibers
   d. SA node, bundle branches and Purkinje fibers, AV node

79. A normal PR interval on an ECG recording indicates that the
   a. interventricular septum has been depolarized
   b. right and left ventricles have begun to depolarize
   c. ventricular myocardial cells have repolarized during the last part of ventricular systole
   d. electrical impulse has been conducted through atria and AV node

80. A QRS complex that is longer than 0.12 seconds or bizarre in shape indicates
    a. an artifact on the ECG tracing
    b. a conduction abnormality in the ventricles
    c. a pacemaker abnormality in the AV node
    d. a conduction abnormality in the atria

81. Which statement about care of a patient with a cardiac problem is INCORRECT?
    a. The paramedic should always treat the patient, not the dysrhythmia.
    b. Most intravenous medications are administered by rapid IV bolus.
    c. Administration of medications always takes precedence over basic and advanced life-support measures.
    d. Epinephrine, lidocaine, and atropine can all be administered via the endotracheal tube.

82. On the ECG tracing, dysrhythmias that originate in the SA node share which of the following features in Lead II?
    a. All P waves are upright and similar in appearance.
    b. All QRS complexes are elongated.
    c. All P-R intervals are shortened and irregular.
    d. The rhythm is highly irregular and is usually regularly irregular.

83. The treatment of choice for a patient with atrial fibrillation with a ventricular rate greater than 150 is
    a. vagal maneuvers
    b. cardioversion
    c. administration of adenosine
    d. administration of lidocaine

84. Which statement about ventricular fibrillation is correct?
    a. Fine ventricular fibrillation indicates a more recent onset of dysrhythmia and is more likely to be reversed by defibrillation than coarse ventricular fibrillation.
    b. Always try a single precordial thump before beginning BLS or defibrillation.
    c. Ventricular fibrillation and nonperfusing ventricular tachycardia are treated alike, with life support and defibrillation.
    d. Patients can commonly tolerate ventricular fibrillation for up to 15 minutes before ominous signs and symptoms appear.

85. The presence of the fourth heart sound (S4) often indicates that the patient is suffering from
    a. myocardial infarction
    b. congestive heart failure
    c. ventricular tachycardia
    d. angina pectoris

86. S-T segment elevation on at least two ECG leads indicates that the patient
    a. has suffered a myocardial infarction
    b. is in ventricular fibrillation
    c. is suffering from unstable angina
    d. has a Mobitz Type II heart block

87. A patient with a suspected MI but without respiratory compromise should receive oxygen at a flow rate of
    a. 3–4 L/min
    b. 5–10 L/min
    c. 10–15 L/min
    d. 15–20 L/min

88. Which of the following factors would EXCLUDE a patient from receiving thrombolytic therapy after an MI?
   a. less than 75 years old
   b. chest pain that persists after administration of nitroglycerin
   c. chest pain for longer than 30 minutes but less than 6 hours
   d. ulcer or gastrointestinal bleeding

89. If it is not treated, left ventricular failure culminates in
   a. ischemic heart disease
   b. pulmonary edema
   c. chronic hypertension
   d. cor pulmonale

90. Which of the following features distinguishes dissecting aortic aneurysm from MI?
   a. The pain of dissecting aortic aneurysm is severe from the outset.
   b. The pain of dissecting aortic aneurysm does not migrate.
   c. Patients with dissecting aortic aneurysm have equal peripheral pulses.
   d. Patients with dissecting aortic aneurysm do not show signs of pericardial tamponade.

91. Prehospital treatment for patients with suspected deep venous thrombosis consists of
   a. treatment for shock, including oxygen and PASG
   b. administration of nitroglycerin
   c. initiation of thrombolytic therapy
   d. immobilization and elevation of the extremity

92. The presence of delta waves on an ECG is indicative of
   a. myocardial infarction
   b. bundle branch block
   c. Wolff-Parkinson-White syndrome
   d. paroxysmal junctional tachycardia

93. Your patient is a 47-year-old male who is experiencing paroxysmal junctional tachycardia. He called EMS because of a sensation of palpitations and lightheadedness. There is no previous history of heart disease. The ventricular rate is approximately 130 per minute; the BP is 100/70 and falling; respirations are 32 and shallow. You should
   a. do nothing; this dysrhythmia is usually well-tolerated
   b. attempt vagal maneuvers to slow the heart rate
   c. administer 6 mg adenosine by rapid IV bolus
   d. attempt synchronized cardioversion

94. Which of the following features is common to all dysrhythmias that originate in the AV junction?
   a. inverted P waves, shortened P-R interval, normal duration of QRS complex
   b. absent P waves, prolonged QRS complex
   c. upright P waves, normal P-R interval, normal duration of QRS complex
   d. P waves change from beat to beat or disappear entirely, normal duration of QRS complex

95. The initial dose of lidocaine for a patient with ventricular tachycardia is
   a. 0.5–0.75 mg/kg
   b. 0.75–1.0 mg/kg
   c. 1.0–1.5 mg/kg
   d. 3.0 mg/kg

96. A transmural myocardial infarction is associated with what kinds of changes on the ECG?
   a. Q wave changes
   b. rate changes
   c. rhythm changes
   d. P wave changes

97. Which statement about radiation exposure is INCORRECT?
   a. Alpha particles can be stopped by paper or clothing.
   b. Alpha particles can cause severe damage if they enter the body through inhalation or absorption.
   c. Lead shielding is required to stop beta particles.
   d. Gamma rays and X rays are the most dangerous forms of radiation.

98. The purpose of the body's physiological response to a stressor is to
   a. signal the brain that danger is present
   b. decrease normal physiological functions
   c. shut down the autonomic nervous system
   d. prepare for the most efficient reaction

99. Anxiety may be best defined as
   a. a general feeling of uneasiness
   b. an unconscious reaction to a stressful situation
   c. a factor or event that causes stress
   d. regulation of involuntary movement

Answer questions 100–102 on the basis of the information below.

You respond on a 17-year-old female found unconscious in her back yard by her parents. She has a skin rash on her right arm, previously unnoticed by her parents, and is having difficulty breathing. You note that she is wheezing. Her parents state that she has no history of respiratory problems or other medical disorders.

100. Which of the following is a possible cause of her condition?
   a. anaphylaxis
   b. febrile seizures
   c. status asthmaticus
   d. epiglottitis

101. The first step in managing this patient is to
   a. administer IV diphenhydramine
   b. administer 2 liters of oxygen per minute via nasal cannula
   c. aggressively manage the airway
   d. administer morphine sulfate

102. The next step in treating this patient is to start a normal saline or Ringer's lactate IV and to give which of the following medications?
   a. epinephrine
   b. diphenhydramine
   c. atropine sulfate
   d. morphine sulfate

103. A puncture wound located proximal to the knee and on the anterior surface of the leg would be on the
   a. calf
   b. shin
   c. front of the thigh
   d. back of the thigh

104. The *visceral peritoneum* refers to the
   a. serous membrane that covers the abdominal organs
   b. serous membrane that covers the wall of the body cavity
   c. connective tissue that holds the peritoneal organs in place
   d. peritoneal cavity

105. Rotating the forearm so that the anterior surface is downward is called
   a. rotation
   b. supination
   c. pronation
   d. extension

106. Before using nitrous oxide (Nitronox) for a chest-injury patient, you should exclude the possibility that the patient has
   a. cervical spine injury
   b. flail chest
   c. pericardial tamponade or cardiac contusion
   d. head injury or pneumothorax

107. Your patient is a 26-year-old male with one suspected femur fracture and no other apparent injuries. The patient is alert and oriented, and all vital signs are normal. The best way to immobilize this fracture is to use
   a. the PASG
   b. a long spine board
   c. a traction splint
   d. a softly padded board

108. In a patient with a thermal burn to the airway, it is most important to watch for signs and symptoms of
   a. laryngeal edema
   b. shock
   c. respiratory arrest
   d. bronchiolitis

109. An adult with burns over the front of both arms and the chest is burned over what percentage of her body surface area?
   a. 9 percent
   b. 13 1/2 percent
   c. 18 percent
   d. 27 percent

110. The skin over a second-degree burn will appear
   a. bright red
   b. mottled red
   c. pearly white
   d. charred

111. Which patient is likely to be transported to a burn center for definitive care?
   a. female, age 34, second-degree burn over 10 percent of BSA, mostly involving the legs
   b. male, age 46, third-degree burn over a small area of the back
   c. female, age 52, second-degree burns to face and right hand
   d. male, age 27, second-degree burn over entire left arm excluding hand

112. Prehospital care for a patient who has moderate to severe burns includes
   a. wet dressings, one IV line held at a TKO rate, IV antibiotics
   b. wet dressings, two IV lines with large-bore catheters
   c. dry sterile dressings, one IV line held at a TKO rate, epinephrine 1:1,000
   d. dry sterile dressings, two IV lines with large-bore catheters held at a TKO rate

113. In the acronym AEIOU Tips, used for remembering causes of coma, the E stands for
   a. emphysema
   b. epistaxis
   c. epilepsy
   d. encephalitis

114. A patient who experienced a seizure, rather than a period of syncope, usually reports that the episode
   a. started when she was standing up
   b. happened without any warning
   c. was associated with bradycardia
   d. lasted only 2 or 3 minutes

115. Management of a patient in a postictal state includes
   a. having the patient sit up, administering high-flow oxygen, and transporting immediately
   b. placing the patient in shock position and treating for signs and symptoms of shock
   c. moving obstacles away from the patient or moving him or her to a safe place
   d. placing the patient in lateral-recumbent position and administering supplemental oxygen

116. What is the correct dosage of epinephrine 1:1000 for a patient who is experiencing mild or moderate signs of anaphylaxis and who is alert?
   a. 0.1–0.3 mg
   b. 0.3–0.5 mg
   c. 0.5–0.7 mg
   d. 0.7–0.9 mg

117. The two most common causes of severe anaphylaxis are
   a. shellfish and peanuts
   b. aspirin and opiates
   c. egg whites and sesame seeds
   d. penicillin and insect stings

118. The correct dosage of ipecac for an adult is
   a. 15 mL, followed by 2–3 glasses of water; do not repeat
   b. 15 mL, followed by 2–3 glasses of water; repeat in 20 minutes if necessary
   c. 30 mL, followed by 2–3 glasses of water; do not repeat
   d. 30 mL, followed by 2–3 glasses of water; repeat in 20 minutes if necessary

119. If activated charcoal is administered along with ipecac, the charcoal should be given
- a. before the ipecac to increase absorption
- b. after gastric emptying is complete
- c. at the same time as the ipecac
- d. immediately after the ipecac but before the patient has started to vomit

120. In addition to supportive care and gastric lavage, prehospital care for a patient who has ingested methanol includes
- a. inhalation of amyl nitrite
- b. activated charcoal
- c. ethanol and sodium bicarbonate
- d. neutralization with lemon juice or vinegar

121. Which finding is helpful in distinguishing poisoning by spider venom from an acute abdominal condition?
- a. abdominal rigidity with no palpable tenderness
- b. right-lower-quadrant pain in the absence of fever
- c. diaphoresis accompanied by chills
- d. the presence of multiple bite marks

122. Early symptoms of overdose of tricyclic antidepressants include
- a. tachycardia accompanied by a wide QRS complex
- b. anorexia, nausea, and vomiting
- c. psychosis
- d. CNS symptoms, such as altered mental status and slurred speech

123. A typical victim of classic heat stroke would be
- a. a healthy young adult who has been exercising in hot weather
- b. a worker who sweats profusely and drinks large amounts of water without salt intake
- c. an elderly person with chronic illnesses who is confined to a hot room
- d. an infant who is exposed to too-high ambient temperatures before thermal control is established

124. Your patient is a hypothermia victim whose body temperature has fallen to 94° F. This patient's most severe symptom is likely to be
- a. shivering
- b. impaired judgment
- c. respiratory depression
- d. fixed and dilated pupils

125. Which statement about suicide is correct?
- a. People who talk about suicide rarely act on it.
- b. All suicidal people are mentally ill.
- c. The suicide rate is lowest during holiday seasons, such as December.
- d. There is a high correlation between suicide attempts and alcohol.

Answer questions 126–128 on the basis of the information below.

You respond on a 4-year-old female who has taken an unknown amount of children's aspirin. On arrival, you find the patient conscious and crying but lethargic. Her mother states that she found the child playing in the bathroom. A flavored children's aspirin bottle was found nearby with only a few tablets in it.

126. In this situation you should make the assumption that
  a. the aspirin bottle was full
  b. the child couldn't possibly have taken all the aspirin tablets
  c. there is a reason to suspect child abuse
  d. because of the flavorings, the child is not in danger of overdosing.

127. Children's aspirin is in which of the following classes of common medications?
  a. tricyclics
  b. acetaminophen
  c. salicylates
  d. benzodiazepines

128. Treatment for this patient may include
  a. IV, oxygen, and naloxone
  b. IV, oxygen, ECG, ipecac, and activated charcoal
  c. IV, ECG, and naloxone
  d. IV, naloxone, and activated charcoal

129. Your patient is Tyler, age 5, who has signs and symptoms of severe croup. Tyler is frightened of the oxygen mask that you want to put over his face. The best thing to say to Tyler is
  a. "You are oxygen-deprived and you need supplemental O_2."
  b. "The air you breathe in through this special mask will help you feel better."
  c. "You play with the mask for a while, and then put it on all by yourself."
  d. "We are going to hold you down if you won't let us put the oxygen equipment on you."

130. Children of which age group are in the greatest danger from airway obstruction caused by aspirated foreign objects?
  a. 1–12 months
  b. 1–3 years
  c. 3–5 years
  d. 6–12 years

131. The usual pediatric dose of methylprednisolone is
  a. 1–2 mg/kg via IV bolus
  b. 2–3 mg/kg via IV bolus
  c. 3–4 mg/kg via IV bolus
  d. 4–5 mg/kg via IV bolus

132. A child would be considered severely dehydrated if he or she had a minimum body weight loss of
  a. 5 percent
  b. 10 percent
  c. 12 percent
  d. 15 percent

133. You would perform chest compressions on an infant if, after oxygenation and ventilation, the heart rate was less than
  a. 60/min
  b. 80/min
  c. 100/min
  d. 120/min

134. Your patient is Zack, age 7, who has a suspected broken arm, in addition to numerous bruises. The mother states that Zack was hurt when he fell off his bike this morning. What finding would lead you to suspect that the mother's account of the injuries may not be true?
  a. multiple bruises on the child's limbs
  b. the child cries from pain
  c. the child clings to the parent
  d. both purple and yellow or green bruises

Answer questions 135–137 on the basis of the information below.

You respond on a 25-year-old female who is complaining of vaginal bleeding and abdominal pain. The patient states that she is 33 weeks pregnant, and this is her first pregnancy. Upon further questioning, she says that the pain felt like "something was tearing." She denies vaginal bleeding during the pregnancy prior to this event. Upon assessment you notice what appears to be approximately 500 cc of dark, almost black, blood.

135. This patient is most likely suffering from
  a. abruptio placentae
  b. placenta previa
  c. preeclampsia
  d. eclampsia

136. This event is dangerous to
  a. the mother only
  b. the baby only
  c. neither the mother nor the baby
  d. both the mother and the baby

137. In addition to high-flow oxygen, continuous monitoring of both the mother's vital signs and the baby's fetal heart tones, you should treat this patient with
  a. 1 or 2 large bore IVs of normal saline or Ringer's lactate and PASG without inflating the abdominal compartment
  b. 1 minidrip IV of normal saline and pitocin and PASG with all compartments inflated
  c. 1 minidrip IV of normal saline and PASG with all compartments inflated
  d. basic life support treatments only

138. Patients with pelvic inflammatory disease often complain of
  a. diffuse lower abdominal pain
  b. severe vaginal bleeding
  c. ripping, tearing pain in the uterus
  d. difficulty breathing, diaphoresis, and agitation

139. The two primary goals of prehospital care of a sexual assault victim are to preserve the victim's privacy and dignity and to
  a. obtain a complete description of the assault
  b. clean and bandage all wounds
  c. preserve all physical evidence
  d. help the victim bathe and change her clothing

140. The function of the ductus arteriosus is to
  a. allow blood to bypass the fetus's lungs before birth
  b. allow the neonate to take his or her first breath
  c. provide a way for fetal waste products to exit the material circulation
  d. decrease ambient pressure in the lungs before birth

141. A *multipara* is a woman who
  a. is pregnant and obese
  b. has delivered more than one baby
  c. has never delivered a viable infant
  d. is over 45 and pregnant

142. Your patient is a 32-year-old woman who reports that she is 9 weeks pregnant. She is complaining of severe abdominal pain, slight vaginal bleeding, and shoulder pain. Abdominal examination reveals significant tenderness in the lower right quadrant. The patient is somewhat agitated and tachycardic. You should suspect developing shock resulting from
  a. ruptured appendix
  b. abruptio placentae
  c. placenta previa
  d. ectopic pregnancy

143. The usual presentation of placenta previa is
  a. tearing pain and dark red bleeding
  b. diffuse abdominal pain and slight bleeding
  c. painless bright red bleeding
  d. elevated blood pressure, edema, and diffuse abdominal pain

144. Which of the following factors would make you opt for immediate transport of a pregnant woman rather than for delivery in the field?
  a. the mother's urge to push
  b. the presence of crowning
  c. meconium staining
  d. multiparity

145. During a normal delivery, you would suction the infant's mouth and nose just after
  a. the head is born
  b. the placenta is delivered
  c. you massage the uterus
  d. you clamp the cord

146. An Apgar score of 5 means that a neonate
  a. is nonviable
  b. requires vigorous resuscitation
  c. requires oxygenation and stimulation
  d. requires only routine care

147. The correct way to stimulate a neonate is to
  a. hold it by the feet while you slap the buttocks
  b. slap the soles of the feet and rub the back
  c. uncover it completely
  d. rub the head

148. With which of the following conditions would you LEAST likely need to begin positive-pressure ventilations on a neonate?
  a. an Apgar score of 5
  b. a heart rate less than 100
  c. apnea
  d. central cyanosis after supplemental oxygen is given

149. The correct dosage of sodium bicarbonate for a neonate is
a. 1 mEq/kg via IV
b. 2 mEq/kg via IV
c. 3 mEq/kg via IV
d. 4 mEq/kg via IV

150. How many blood vessels are there in the umbilical cord?
a. one artery and one vein
b. two arteries and two veins
c. one artery and two veins
d. two arteries and one vein

Answer questions 151–154 on the basis of the information below.

You respond on a 19-year-old female who is 25 weeks pregnant and is complaining of a severe headache and blurred vision. Upon initial assessment you notice that she has substantial edema especially in her feet and hands. She states that she has not been under the regular care of a physician during this pregnancy.

151. With regard to this patient's vital signs, you would expect to see that she is
a. tachycardic
b. tachypneic
c. hypertensive
d. hypotensive

152. This patient is most likely suffering from the condition known as
a. abruptio placentae
b. placenta previa
c. preeclampsia
d. supine-hypotensive disorder

153. Treatment for this patient includes rapid transport without lights and sirens and an IV of normal saline or Ringer's lactate. It may also call for the administration of
a. magnesium sulfate
b. pitocin
c. dopamine
d. atropine sulfate

154. If left untreated, this patient's condition may worsen and she may begin to
a. experience angina pectoris
b. experience necrosis of peripheral tissues
c. develop grand mal seizures
d. develop a migraine headache

155. The role of the First Responder in the EMS system is to
a. call EMS for help
b. dispatch help to the scene
c. stabilize the patient until EMS arrives
d. coordinate care among different EMS units

156. You are caring for a 69-year-old MI victim under on-line medical control. A bystander, who identifies herself as a physician, looks at the ECG, sees you beginning to administer epinephrine and requests you to substitute atropine. You should
a. have the on-line physician consult directly with the on-scene physician
b. follow the directions of the on-scene physician
c. follow the directions of the on-line physician
d. request another medical opinion from the emergency department

157. The purpose of medical protocols is to
   a. provide a standardized approach to common patient problems
   b. give ultimate responsibility to the medical control physician
   c. remove the possibility of malpractice
   d. allow the paramedic to train less-experienced EMS workers

158. The advantage of enhanced 911 service (E-911) is that it gives the dispatcher automatic
   a. information about the chief complaint
   b. location of the nearest responding unit
   c. location of the caller and instant callback
   d. name, address, and telephone number of the caller

159. The initial impetus for the development of the EMS system in the United States was the
   a. Trauma Care Systems Planning and Development Act of 1990
   b. Emergency Medical Services Act of 1973
   c. founding of the National Registry of Emergency Medical Technicians in 1970
   d. Highway Safety Act of 1966

160. Which of the following situations constitutes abandonment?
   a. A paramedic yields control of a patient's care to a physician who arrives on the scene.
   b. A paramedic yields control of a patient's care to an EMT.
   c. An EMT yields control of a patient's care to a paramedic.
   d. A patient refuses transport, and the paramedic leaves, after explaining the situation clearly to the patient and obtaining a signature on a refusal of treatment form.

161. In most states, you are required to report all of the following to law enforcement EXCEPT
   a. rape
   b. trauma
   c. child abuse
   d. animal bites

162. Which patient may be legally placed in protective custody by the police if he or she refuses treatment?
   a. a competent 85-year-old man who has signed a DNR order
   b. a patient who is drunk and disorderly and who refuses treatment for a head wound
   c. an epileptic patient who has just recovered from a seizure but refuses transport
   d. a competent adult who understands the consequences of refusing treatment

163. You are dispatched to the home of a dying patient who has signed a Do Not Resuscitate order. You should
   a. contact medical control before providing any care
   b. give emotional support to the patient and family members only
   c. carry out all necessary care, since such orders apply only to hospital care
   d. leave immediately without providing any care

164. The two basic components of patient packaging are
   a. primary and secondary survey
   b. securing the airway and stabilizing the cervical spine
   c. oxygen and bleeding control
   d. stabilization and preparation for transport

165. Which of the following situations is most likely to be declared a major incident?
a. an accident in which a school bus that contained no passengers hit a highway median
b. a fire at a chemical plant during working hours
c. a water accident involving a single diver
d. a fire involving an isolated, single-family residence

166. The major responsibility of the support sector at a major incident is to
a. coordinate the medical supply needs of other sectors
b. coordinate with police to create a vehicle staging area
c. determine patient transportation needs
d. determine where triage and treatment will be accomplished

167. You are conducting triage using the START system at a major incident. You encounter a patient who is not breathing. After you position the airway, the patient begins to breathe. This patient would be categorized as
a. nonsalvageable
b. immediate
c. delayed
d. critically injured

168. In the international classification system for hazardous materials, Class 3 materials are
a. explosives
b. gases
c. flammable liquids
d. poisonous and infectious materials

169. Which of the following is an example of the defense mechanism of reaction formation?
a. A paramedic fails to discover a serious injury in a patient, and explains this by saying that the accident scene was stressful.
b. A paramedic dislikes inserting IVs, so he practices this technique repeatedly until he excels at it.
c. A woman whose husband is critically injured insists that the doctors will be able to fix her husband right up.
d. A paramedic who has a 5-year-old son cares for an injured boy of the same age.

170. For which of the following procedures is it necessary to wear gloves, gown, mask, *and* protective eyewear?
a. starting an IV
b. oral or nasal suctioning
c. assisting with childbirth
d. administering an intramuscular injection

171. Which form of hepatitis does NOT lead to a chronic carrier state?
a. hepatitis A
b. hepatitis B
c. hepatitis C
d. hepatitis D

172. Hot-water disinfection (high-level disinfection) can kill all forms of microbial life EXCEPT
a. Mycobacterium tuberculosis bacilli
b. varicella viruses
c. the HIV virus
d. large numbers of bacterial spores

173. When you are caring for more than one trauma patient at a time, you should change your gloves
a. whenever time permits
b. for each new patient
c. for each new procedure
d. whenever they become soiled

174. You are interviewing Mrs. Rodriguez, age 87, who called EMS but seems reluctant to state her primary problem. Mrs. Rodriguez speaks English but is answering your questions slowly and haltingly. Her 20-year-old grandson is also present. In an attempt to obtain the necessary information, you should
a. direct your questions to the grandson only, since Mrs. Rodriguez is probably senile
b. ask the grandson to translate for Mrs. Rodriguez
c. ask questions slowly, clearly, and respectfully, giving Mrs. Rodriguez time to respond
d. stop the interview; Mrs. Rodriguez is probably not ill

175. Which of the following is NOT a characteristic of the typical abused elderly person?
a. wealthy but refuses to give financial assistance to relatives
b. has multiple physical and mental impairments, such as dementia and cancer
c. female
d. over age 75

176. Which of the following is an example of acknowledging and labeling the patient's feelings.
a. "Stop threatening me. I've never hurt you."
b. "You seem angry. Do you want to tell me about it?"
c. "I get angry myself sometimes."
d. "Anger is a hostile emotion. Let's be more positive."

Answer questions 177–180 on the basis of the information below.

You arrive first in ambulance to a suspected radiation emergency. Dispatch has stated that a box containing radioactive material was found left unattended and open in a park. No patients have been identified yet, but the police department is sealing off the area.

177. When you approach the park, the three principles of safety to keep in mind are
a. time, distance, and shielding
b. distance, crowd control, and decontamination
c. decontamination, clothing, and eye protection
d. gloves, eye protection, and distance

178. If you were asked to set up a staging area for further rescue crews, which of the following would be the best?
a. upwind, close visual range, in an open area
b. downwind, in an open area
c. upwind, in a building
d. downwind, in a building

179. In the above situation, decontamination of patients would be the responsibility of the

a. first in ambulance

b. first in fire agency

c. hazardous materials team

d. police department

180. Which type of radiation is the most serious?

a. alpha particles

b. beta particles

c. gamma rays

d. delta rays

ANSWERS

1. **d.** *Cephalo-* refers to the head, as in encephalitis.

2. **b.** SQ is the abbreviation for subcutaneous.

3. **b.** The basic steps are listed in order; not all steps are carried out for all patients, however.

4. **a.** "Alert and oriented times three" means alert to person, place, and date or time.

5. **b.** Only this patient's vital signs are within normal limits for her age.

6. **b.** In the PQRST mnemonic, R stands for region: "Where does it hurt?"

7. **a.** The signs and symptoms given are characteristic of early, or compensated, shock.

8. **c.** The down-and-under pathway results in injury to the pelvis and legs rather than to the abdominal and thoracic organs.

9. **a.** The "paper bag effect" is thought to be responsible for most pneumothoraces that result from car crashes.

10. **d.** Adults who fall more than 15 feet tend to land on their feet; this tends to cause bilateral calcaneus fractures, hip dislocations, and compression fractures of the spinal column.

11. **c.** The score is composed of 2 points for pain, 1 point for verbal response, and 4 points for motor response.

12. **b.** Patients with facial fractures also have suspected spinal trauma; avoid the use of a nasopharyngeal tube in a patient with facial fractures.

13. **d.** Raccoon eyes (bruises circling the eyes) seen in the prehospital environment suggest significant previous injury because this condition takes time to develop after injury.

14. **b.** The best way to prevent shock is to actively look for early signs and symptoms rather than to wait for late signs, such as a drop in blood pressure.

15. **a.** Repeat the primary assessment after every significant intervention.

16. **c.** The score on the Glasgow Coma Scale translates into 4 points on the Trauma Score; the patient receives 3 points for respiratory rate, 1 point for respiratory expansion, 2 points for blood pressure, and 1 point for delayed capillary refill.

17. **c.** This patient's body is showing signs that it can no longer compensate for the damage done by the traumatic event.

18. **b.** PASG can help with both support of the pelvis and ankle and assist in shock management.

19. **d.** This patient is most likely hemorrhaging from a pelvic fracture resulting in hypovolemic shock. Medications are rarely used in the prehospital management of hypovolemic shock. Treatment centers around improving oxygenation.

20. **a.** Pain in the left upper quadrant is most often due to pancreatitis, gastritis, or disease of the left kidney.

21. **b.** Signs of uremia are pasty, yellow skin and thin extremities; urea frost is a late sign.

22. a. Although reason for the call to EMS was head-ache and confusion (the chief complaint), it is likely that the primary problem for health-care workers to address is hypertensive crisis.

23. c. In a patient with acute MI, signs of cardiogenic shock include low blood pressure; cyanosis or cool, clammy skin; and rapid breathing.

24. b. The patient is displaying signs and symptoms of acute occlusion of the femoral artery.

25. a. The three blast phases are primary, secondary, and tertiary. The primary phase occurs during the initial air blast and pressure wave. The secondary phase occurs when the patient is hit by debris and propelled by the overpressure of the blast wave. The tertiary phase occurs when the victim is thrown from the blast and into the ground or hard objects.

26. b. The pressure wave and initial air blast result in compression of air-containing organs such as the sinuses, auditory canals, stomach, and intestines.

27. d. Flash burns rarely result in extensive airway or lung tissue burns. The pneumothorax is due not to thermal conditions but rather the overpressure resulting from the explosion.

28. d. Compression of air-containing organs is common in the primary blast phase.

29. c. Common signs of a narcotic overdose are described.

30. d. The patient is displaying signs and symptoms of left ventricular failure, which most often occurs secondary to MI.

31. a. Pain and anxiety are likely to cause a patient's respiratory rate to be higher than normal.

32. d. This is the typical description of normal vesicular sounds, which are heard throughout both lungs.

33. c. If a patient has a partial airway obstruction but adequate air exchange, allow her to continue her spontaneous efforts to clear the airway (coughing), but monitor her carefully. If air exchange becomes inadequate, treat her as if the obstruction is total.

34. b. Attempts to control the upper airway by insertion of tubes are common causes of aspiration, which carries a high mortality rate.

35. a. Neither the nasal airway nor the oral airway is long enough to protect the lower airway from aspirated material.

36. c. Before inflating the cuff in the esophagus, make sure that the tube is properly inserted by looking for chest rise and fall and listening for breath sounds in the chest and abdomen.

37. d. Because of anatomical structure, it is most common for an ET tube that has been inserted too far to enter the right main bronchus, resulting in atelectasis and insufficiency of the left lung.

38. d. This patient shows signs and symptoms for pneumonia. The fever is the symptom that provides the differential diagnosis.

39. c. In addition to oxygen, this patient needs antibiotics.

40. d. Dyspnea is common to both CHF and pneumonia.

41. d. Pneumonia is not a common problem with diabetic patients.

42. b. Sterile technique is not necessary because there is an infection present already.

43. a. The best position for this patient would be high Fowler's position.

44. a. Albuterol (Ventolin) is administered only by inhalation.

45. c. The steps involved in management of this injury are given.

46. d. Diphenhydramine is an antihistamine.

47. b. Wheezing, a whistling sound heard on expiration, is associated with asthma.

48. a. For an unconscious adult patient, the next step after unsuccessful attempts at ventilations is abdominal thrusts.

49. c. The patient's history, signs, and symptoms are consistent with chronic bronchitis.

50. d. The correct procedure is to have the patient inhale and exhale twice, as hard as possible, and to record the highest reading.

51. b. The correct dosage and route is given.

52. a. Hyperventilation syndrome, which is characterized by rapid breathing, is most often caused by anxiety, but it is also associated with many organic diseases.

53. d. Administer low-flow oxygen to patients with exacerbation of COPD; do not withhold oxygen.

54. b. This patient displays many of the risk factors for pulmonary embolism; her signs and symptoms also fit.

55. d. Both the patient and all personnel who come in contact with him or her should wear masks in order to maintain respiratory isolation.

56. c. This patient shows the clinical symptoms of asthma.

57. a. Nebulized steriods would provide no immediate relief of this patient's bronchospasm.

58. d. Methylprednisolone is not indicated for this patient.

59. d. Constriction of the smaller airways is causing air to be trapped in the alveoli.

60. c. Asthma is regarded as a chronic inflammatory disease.

61. b. Allergens, exercise, and irritants are common triggers of asthmatic attacks.

62. d. Blood enters the right atrium through the superior and inferior vena cava and is pumped into the right ventricle. From there it passes through the pulmonary arteries into the lungs.

63. c. If, on primary survey, the carotid pulse is palpable but the radial pulse is not, the patient's systolic blood pressure is approximately 60–80 mm Hg.

64. d. Determining the relationship between the apical impulse and the carotid pulse may give you the first indication of a cardiac irregularity, such as a dysrhythmia.

65. d. To run fluids at a TKO rate, you would most likely use a small-bore (18–20 gauge) catheter.

66. b. A second puncture attempt should be made proximal to the first.

67. b. 300 mg divided by 500 mg equals 0.6; 0.6 times 10 (the volume on hand) equals 6 mL.

68. c. Dopamine is the preferred drug for raising blood pressure in patients in cardiogenic shock.

69. a. Attempt to stop the bleeding with constant, direct pressure; do not clamp neck vessels. Medical control may also direct tamponade with a gloved finger.

70. b. The common signs and symptoms of cerebral hemorrhage are given.

71. d. Infusing 3 L of crystalloid solution increases the patient's vascular volume by only 1 L because a great deal of fluid leaks out of the capillaries into the interstitial space.

72. c. Signs and symptoms of hypoglycemia develop rapidly, often within minutes.

73. a. The most significant predisposing factors are listed here.

74. d. More than half of all elderly patients who suffer MI do not complain of chest pain; therefore, their MIs often go unrecognized.

75. a. Oxygenated blood flows from the lungs, via the pulmonary veins, into the left atrium.

76. a. Stroke volume is the amount of blood ejected from each ventricle during one contraction.

77. b. Parasympathetic stimulation through the vagus nerve acts to decrease the heart rate; this paradoxically increases stroke volume because the longer time interval between contractions allows the ventricles to fill more efficiently.

78. c. Electrical excitation begins at the SA node and spreads through the AV node to the left and right bundle branches and Purkinje fibers.

79. d. The PR interval represents the conduction of the electrical impulse through the atria and AV node, up to the instant of ventricular depolarization.

80. b. Abnormally long or oddly shaped QRS complexes indicate a conduction abnormality in the ventricles.

81. c. Life support measures (airway, ventilation, oxygen, chest compression, and defibrillation) always take precedence over administration of medications or starting IV lines.

82. a. In dysrhythmias originating in the SA node, the QRS complex is usually of normal duration, the P waves are upright and similar, and the P-R interval is of normal duration.

83. b. Cardioversion is the recommended treatment for atrial fibrillation when the ventricular rate is greater than 150.

84. c. Ventricular fibrillation and nonperfusing ventricular tachycardia, both life threatening dysrhythmias, are treated alike; defibrillation is the key to treatment.

85. b. S4, an extra sound late in diastole, is often heard in patients with congestive heart failure.

86. a. An elevated S-T segment indicates an acute MI.

87. a. Patients with no respiratory compromise benefit from low-flow oxygen to increase comfort and limit the size of the infarct.

88. d. Any condition that would present a significant bleeding hazard excludes a patient from receiving thrombolytic therapy.

89. b. Because the left ventricle fails to function as an effective forward pump, left ventricular failure, if untreated, results in pulmonary edema.

90. a. Patients with dissecting aortic aneurysm describe their pain as extremely severe from the outset, whereas the pain of MI tends to build slowly.

91. d. Prehospital treatment is limited to elevation and immobilization of the extremity, and transport.

92. c. Delta waves are characteristic of preexcitation syndromes, of which Wolff-Parkinson-White is the most common.

93. b. Because the patient does not seem to be tolerating the rapid heart rate well, vagal maneuvers should be attempted first, followed by pharmacological therapy if necessary.

94. a. These features are characteristic of all dysrhythmias that originate in the AV node.

95. c. The initial dose is 1.0–1.5 mg/kg IV, followed by additional doses of 0.5–0.75 mg/kg until a total dose of 3.0 mg/kg is reached.

96. a. A transmural infarction is also referred to as a Q-wave infarction because it is associated with Q wave changes.

97. c. Lead shielding is necessary only for external exposure to gamma and X rays.

98. d. All the components of the stress reaction—release of ACTH, relaxation of the bronchial tree, slowdown of digestion, release of adrenalin—prepare the body to react to the stressor as efficiently as possible.

99. a. Anxiety is a general feeling of uneasiness or apprehension that results from continued stress.

100. a. The previously unseen rash, wheezing, and difficulty breathing are keys to this being a case of possible anaphylactic shock.

101. c. You should aggressively manage the airway. It may be necessary to carefully intubate this patient, and you may get only one attempt. Once the tube contacts the larynx, the vocal chords can spasm and completely shut off the airway.

102. a. Epinephrine reverses the many effects of histamine overload.

103. c. Proximal means in the direction of the center of the body, and anterior means toward the front.

104. a. The *visceral peritoneum* is the membrane that covers the organs located in the peritoneum.

105. c. Pronation refers to rotating the forearm so that the anterior surface is facing down.

106. d. Nitronox should not be used with patients with head injury because it can increase intracranial pressure; it should not be used with patients who have pneumothorax because the drug can move by diffusion to air spaces in the body.

107. c. In a patient who is stable, the PASG is unnecessary and the traction splint is a better choice.

108. a. A burn to the highly vascularized tissue of the airway can lead to laryngeal edema and a blocked airway.

109. c. Using the rule of nines, the front of each arm equals 4 1/2 percent of BSA, and the chest equals 9 percent; the total burn covers 18 percent of the BSA.

110. b. The skin over a second-degree burn will most frequently appear mottled red.

111. c. Burns to the face, hands, feet, and perineum often warrant burn center care, even if they are not extensive.

112. d. Cover the burns with dry sterile dressings and be ready to institute aggressive fluid therapy as ordered.

113. c. The E in the AEIOU Tips acronym stands for epilepsy.

114. b. Seizures, unlike syncope, do not usually have warning signs, such as a period of lightheadedness.

115. d. Place the patient in the lateral-recumbent position to prevent aspiration and administer supplemental oxygen as needed; provide privacy and transport.

116. b. The correct dosage is 0.3–0.5 mg, given subcutaneously.

117. d. Injected antigens are likely to cause the most severe reactions; penicillin and insect stings are the two most common causes of severe anaphylaxis.

118. d. This is the correct dosage for adults; repeat in 20 minutes if vomiting has not occurred.

119. b. Activated charcoal may be administered once gastric emptying is complete.

120. c. Ethanol is given because it binds with the toxic byproducts of methanol consumption; sodium bicarbonate is given to correct metabolic acidosis.

121. a. This finding is helpful in ruling out acute abdomen; spiders rarely bite more than once, ruling out option **d.**

122. a. Tachycardia with wide QRS complex is an important early sign.

123. c. This is the typical profile of a victim of classic heat stroke.

124. b. This patient is experiencing mild hypothermia and is likely to manifest both impaired judgment and slurred speech.

125. d. Alcoholics are prone to commit suicide, and people who do not normally drink often do so before killing themselves.

126. a. Unless you know otherwise, always assume a medication bottle was full.

127. c. Salicylates is the correct class of drugs for children's aspirin.

128. b. The appropriate treatment is given. Be prepared to treat dysrhythmias and to provide a fluid challenge if ordered. Sodium bicarbonate may also be ordered by medical direction.

129. b. With children of this age, explain what you are going to do clearly and simply and emphasize that it will make the child feel better.

130. b. Children between 1 and 3, who tend to put everything into their mouths, are of greatest danger from aspiration of foreign objects.

131. a. The pediatric dosage is 1–2 mg/kg body weight, given by IV bolus.

132. d. A body weight loss of 15 percent is considered severe dehydration in a child.

133. b. The threshold for bradycardia in an infant is 80 beats per minute.

134. d. The presence of bruises in various stages of healing would lead you to suspect that Zack had been injured more than once.

135. a. The tearing feeling and the dark-colored blood are classics signs and symptoms of abruptio placentae.

136. d. Both lives are at stake. Oxygen is passed from the mother to the baby via the placenta. A separation greatly decreases the blood supply.

137. a. This treatment is appropriate when combined with rapid transport.

138. a. The most common presentation of PID is diffuse, moderate to severe, lower abdominal pain.

139. c. In order to preserve physical evidence of the assault, avoid cleaning wounds and do not allow the victim to bathe or change her clothing.

140. a. The ductus arteriosus is an opening in the fetal heart that allows blood to bypass the lungs before birth. It normally closes soon after birth.

141. b. A *multipara* is a woman who has delivered more than one baby.

142. d. Signs and symptoms of ectopic pregnancy include lower abdominal pain that is often referred to the shoulder, abdominal tenderness, and rapidly developing shock.

143. c. Placenta previa usually presents as painless bright red bleeding that occurs in the third trimester of pregnancy.

144. c. Because meconium staining in the amniotic fluid can indicate fetal distress, it may indicate the need for immediate transport.

145. a. Suction the infant's mouth and nose immediately after the head is born.

146. c. An Apgar score of 4–6 indicates a neonate that requires oxygenation and stimulation.

147. b. Stimulate a neonate by slapping the soles of the feet and rubbing the back.

148. a. You would begin positive pressure ventilations if any of the other conditions—**b, c,** or **d**—were present.

149. b. The correct dosage is 2 mEq/kg, given slowly via IV.

150. d. The umbilical cord contains two arteries and one vein; only the umbilical vein is used for vascular access.

151. c. This is a hypertensive disorder of pregnancy.

152. c. This patient is most likely suffering from preeclampsia.

153. a. Magnesium sulfate is the appropriate medication for a patient with preeclampsia.

154. c. Seizures indicate that the patient's condition has worsened. This is called ecampsia.

155. c. The First Responder, who may be a police officer, firefighter, or layperson, stabilizes the patient until EMS arrives.

156. c. If there is an on-line medical control physician, he or she is ultimately responsible for the care the patient receives.

157. a. Medical protocols provide health-care workers with a standardized approach to common patient problems.

158. c. E-911 automatically gives the dispatcher the location of the caller, routing to the correct response unit, and call back capability.

159. d. This act directed the states to develop effective EMS programs or lose up to 10 percent of their federal highway construction funds.

160. b. Abandonment means either that a health-care worker terminates treatment inappropriately or turns care over to less-qualified personnel.

161. b. Most states require the reporting of abuse or neglect of children or older adults, rape, gunshot and stab wounds, animal bites, and certain communicable diseases.

162. b. Protective custody is used legally in cases of patients who are drunk, high on drugs, or a danger to themselves and others.

163. a. Contact medical control about the specific situation before providing care; this will allow you to provide the type of care that is palliative only.

164. d. Although all the items mentioned in options **a, b,** and **c** may be part of patient packaging, the two overriding goals are stabilization and preparation for transport.

165. b. This situation involves both multiple casualties and dangerous materials; the other situations described are unlikely to meet either of these criteria for a major incident.

166. a. The major responsibility of the support sector is to coordinate the supply and equipment needs of all other sectors.

167. b. This patient would be categorized as in need of immediate care using the START system.

168. c. Class 3 materials are flammable liquids, which are further categorized by their flashpoint.

169. b. Reaction formation involves masking an unpleasant feeling with a more appropriate reaction.

170. c. Because of the great possibility of coming into contact with blood and other body fluids, all protective gear should be worn while assisting with childbirth.

171. a. Hepatitis A is the only form of hepatitis that does not lead to a chronic carrier state.

172. d. High-level disinfection is effective against all forms of microbial contamination except large numbers of bacterial spores.

173. b. Changing gloves for each new patient contact prevents cross-contamination.

174. c. Give Mrs. Rodriguez plenty of time to respond, plenty of encouragement, and treat her respectfully.

175. a. The typical abused elder is poor and dependent on the abuser.

176. b. This is one way to acknowledge what a patient is feeling and to encourage him or her to express those feelings.

177. a. Limit your time of exposure, stay a good distance from the source, and place shielding between you and the source.

178. c. Upwind in a building helps to provide further shielding from the radioactive source.

179. c. Decontamination should be performed by specially trained hazardous materials personnel.

180. c. Gamma rays are the most serious type of ionizing radiation.

C·H·A·P·T·E·R 7
EMT-PARAMEDIC PRACTICAL EXAM

CHAPTER SUMMARY
The text of this chapter is part of the manual on the practical skills examination produced by the National Registry of EMTs and is used with NR-EMT's permission. If your state uses the NR-EMT practical exam, this chapter shows exactly what your practical exam will be like. If your state has its own practical exam, you'll still learn a lot by reading this chapter, since you're likely to be tested on many of the same skills.

The practical section of the examination process consists of six (6) separate stations presented in a scenario-type format to approximate the abilities of the EMT-Paramedic to function in the prehospital setting. All stations have been developed in accordance with the National Standard EMT-Basic Curriculum, the behavioral and skill objectives of the National Standard EMT-Paramedic Training Curriculum, and current A.H.A. standards. The process is a formal verification of the candidate's "hands-on" abilities and knowledge, rather than a teaching, coaching or remedial training session. Candidates are permitted to bring their own equipment for the examination, provided it is approved for testing by the National Registry Representative in attendance at the examination. **All candidates are urged to review all practical examination criteria in the supplemental brochure "Performance Standards for Advanced Level Practical Examination Candidates" before attempting the examination.**

The candidate must demonstrate an acceptable level of competency in each of the following stations:

1. PATIENT ASSESSMENT/MANAGEMENT

Candidates will be required to perform a "hands-on," head-to-toe, physical assessment and voice treatment of a moulaged victim for a given scenario. This station includes:

a. Primary Survey/Resuscitation
b. Secondary Survey

2. VENTILATORY MANAGEMENT

Given a scenario of having just found an apneic patient with a palpable pulse, the candidate must demonstrate immediate, aggressive management of the patient using simple airway adjuncts, bag-valve-mask device, supplemental oxygen, and successful placement of an endotracheal tube (ET).

3. CARDIAC ARREST SKILLS

The candidate's ability to manage cardiac arrests and interpret ECGs will be verified in two portions:

a. Dynamic Cardiology
Candidates will be evaluated in their ability to manage codes, including actual delivery of electrical therapy, and "voicing" all interpretations and other treatments given a scenario. The presentation of this portion will be similar to the American Heart Association's "megacode."
b. Static Cardiology
Given four (4) prepared ECG tracings with associated vital patient information, the candidate must verbalize the interpretation of the dysrhythmia and all associated treatments.

4. IV AND MEDICATION SKILLS

This station consists of three interrelated parts:

a. Intravenous Therapy
Candidates will be required to establish a patent IV in a manikin arm given a scenario.
b. Intravenous Bolus Medications
c. Intravenous Piggyback Medications
Candidates will then be required to actually administer an IV bolus of medication and mix, hang, and administer an IV piggyback drip of medication given a scenario.

5. SPINAL IMMOBILIZATION (SEATED PATIENT)

Using any type of half-spine immobilization device (wooden board, commercial vest-type), each candidate must demonstrate appropriate application and spinal immobilization given a scenario.

6. RANDOM BASIC SKILLS

Each candidate will need to demonstrate acceptable performance of two (2) of the following skills tested at random. The skills will be paired to balance performance time. All instruments in this station must adhere to the National Registry EMT-Basic Practical Examination Guide.

a. Bleeding-Wounds-Shock
b. Long Bone Splinting
c. Traction Splinting
d. Spinal Immobilization (Lying Patient)

EMT-Paramedic candidates who have successfully completed the entire National Registry EMT-Intermediate practical examination within the preceding twelve (12) months of their first attempt on the National Registry EMT-Paramedic practical examination may apply their passed EMT-I results to the EMT-P examination. **Passed EMT-Intermediate practical examination results may only be applied to the first full attempt of the EMT-P examination for the following two (2) stations:**

1. SPINAL IMMOBLIZATION (SEATED PATIENT)
2. RANDOM BASIC SKILLS

Candidates applying passed EMT-I results should note that outright failure of the first full attempt or failure of the second retest opportunity of the first attempt on the EMT-Paramedic practical examination will require the candidate to officially document remedial training over all skills before starting the next full attempt of the practical examination and re-examining over the entire EMT-Paramedic practical examination (all six [6] stations) on another date.

Grading of the practical examination is on a Pass/Fail basis. Failure of three (3) or less stations (when taking the entire practical) entitles the candidate to two (2) retesting opportunities. If a same-day retest is offered at the examination site, only one (1) of these retest opportunities may be completed at that test. Failure of any portion of the second retest attempt constitutes failure of the entire practical examination. The candidate is then required to officially document remedial training over all skills before starting the next full attempt of the practical examination by re-examining over all six (6) stations on another date.

Example: A candidate fails stations #1, #3, and #4 on the first attempt of the entire practical examination. The candidate retests these three stations at the site on a same day retest and fails station #3 again. The candidate must go to another test and complete only station #3 on their second retest attempt. If the candidate fails station #3 on the second retest attempt, they must officially document remedial training over all skills before starting their second full attempt of the practical examination.

Failure of four (4) or more stations constitutes failure of the entire practical examination. The candidate is then required to officially document remedial training over all skills before starting the next full attempt of the practical examination by re-examining over all six (6) stations on another date.

In the Patient Assessment/Management Station, primary survey/resuscitation and secondary survey represent portions of one skill. They are reported to assist the candidate with remedial training if any errors are identified. Failure of any of these portions will require the candidate to complete the entire Patient Assessment/Management Station. In a similar fashion, failure of any portion of the Cardiac Arrest Skills (Dynamic or Static), the IV and Medications Skills (IV Therapy, IV Bolus Medications, or IV Piggyback Medications), and the Random Basic Skills station will require the candidate to complete the entire Random Basic Skills station by retesting over two (2) skills which must include the skill or skills failed.

The passed portion of the examination, either the written or practical, will remain valid for a 12-month period from the date of the examination. Candidates not completing the failed portion of the examination within that 12-month period will be required to repeat the invalid portion.

Candidates are allowed three full attempts to pass the practical examination (one "full attempt" is defined as completing all six [6] stations and two retests if so entitled). Candidates who fail a full attempt or any portion of a second retest must submit official documentation of remedial training over all skills before starting the next full attempt of the practical examination and re-examining over all six (6) stations. This official documentation must be signed by the EMT-Paramedic Training Program Director or medical director of training/operations which verifies remedial training over all skills has occurred since the last unsuccessful attempt and the candidate has demonstrated competence in all skills. Should a candidate fail the third full and final attempt of the practical examination, the candidate must complete a new, entire, state-approved EMT-Paramedic Training Program.

INSTRUCTIONS TO THE CANDIDATE FOR PATIENT ASSESSMENT/MANAGEMENT

This station is the Patient Assessment and Management station. In this station, you will have ten (10) minutes to perform your assessment and "voice" treat all conditions and injuries discovered. You must conduct your assessment as you would in the field, including communicating with your patient. As you approach the patient, you should assume the scene is clear of safety hazards. You may remove the patient's clothing down to his/her shorts or swimsuit if you feel it is necessary. As you conduct your survey, you should state everything you are assessing. Specific clinical information not obtainable by visual or physical inspection, for example blood pressure, will be given to you only when you ask following demonstration of how you would normally obtain that information in the field. You may assume you have two (2) partners working with you who are trained to your level of care. They will correctly perform the verbal treatments you indicate necessary. I will acknowledge your treatments and may ask you for additional information if clarification is needed. Do you have any questions?

National Registry of Emergency Medical Technicians
Advanced Level Practical Examination
PATIENT ASSESSMENT/MANAGEMENT

Candidate:_____ Examiner:_____

Date:_____ Signature:_____

Scenario #_____ Time Start:_____ Time End:_____

PRIMARY SURVEY/RESUSCITATION

		Possible Points	Points Awarded
Takes or verbalizes infection control precautions		1	
Airway with C-Spine Control	Takes or directs manual in-line immobilization of head (1 point) Opens and assesses airway (1 point) Inserts adjunct (1 point)	3	
Breathing	Assesses breathing (1 point) Initiates appropriate oxygen therapy (1 point) Assures adequate ventilation of patient (1 point) Manages any injury which may compromise breathing/ventilation (1 point)	4	

Circulation	Checks pulse (1 point)
	Assesses peripheral perfusion (1 point)
	  [checks either skin color, temperature, or capillary refill]
	Assesses for and controls major bleeding if present (1 point)
	Takes vital signs (1 point)
	Verbalizes application of or consideration for PASG (1 point)
	  [candidate must assess body parts to be enclosed prior to application]
		5	

	Volume replacement [usually deferred until patient loaded]
	  - Initiates first IV line (1 point)
	  - Initiates second IV line (1 point)
	  - Selects appropriate catheters (1 point)
	  - Selects appropriate IV solutions and administration sets (1 point)
	  - Infuses at appropriate rate (1 point)
		5	

Disability	Performs mini-neuro assessment: AVPU (1 point) Applies cervical collar (1 point)	2	
Expose	Removes clothing	1	
Status	Calls for immediate transport of the patient when indicated	1	
PRIMARY SURVEY/RESUSCITATION SUB-TOTAL		**22**	

SECONDARY SURVEY

NOTE: Areas denoted by "**" may be integrated within sequence of Primary Survey

		Possible Points	Points Awarded
Head	Inspects mouth**, nose**, and assesses facial area (1 point) Inspects and palpates scalp and ears (1 point) Checks eyes: PEARRL** (1 point)	3	
Neck**	Checks position of trachea (1 point) Checks jugular veins (1 point) Palpates cervical spine (1 point)	3	
Chest**	Inspects chest (1 point) Palpates chest (1 point) Auscultates chest (1 point)	3	
Abdomen/Pelvis**	Inspects and palpates abdomen (1 point) Assesses pelvis (1 point)	2	
Lower Extremities**	Inspects and palpates left leg (1 point) Inspects and palpates right leg (1 point) Checks motor, sensory, and distal circulation (1 point/leg)	4	
Upper Extremities	Inspects and palpates left arm (1 point) Inspects and palpates right arm (1 point) Checks motor, sensory, and distal circulation (1 point/arm)	4	
Posterior Thorax/Lumbar** and Buttocks	Inspects and palpates posterior thorax (1 point) Inspects and palpates lumbar and buttocks area (1 point)	2	
Identifies and treats minor wounds/fractures appropriately (1 point each)		2	
SECONDARY SURVEY SUB-TOTAL		**23**	

CRITICAL CRITERIA
____ Failure to initiate or call for transport of the patient within 10 minute time limit
____ Failure to take or verbalize infection control precautions
____ Failure to immediately establish and maintain spinal protection
____ Failure to provide high concentration of oxygen
____ Failure to evaluate and find all presented conditions of airway, breathing, and circulation (shock)
____ Failure to appropriately manage/provide airway, breathing, hemorrhage control or treatment for shock
____ Failure to differentiate patient's needing transportation versus continued on-scene survey
____ Does other detailed physical examination before assessing & treating threats to airway, breathing & circulation

You must factually document your rationale for checking any of the above critical items on the reverse side of this form.

P-201/11-93

INSTRUCTIONS TO THE CANDIDATE FOR VENTILATORY MANAGEMENT (ET)

This progressive station is designed to test your ability to provide immediate and aggressive ventilator assistance to an apneic patient who has no other associated injuries. This is a non-trauma situation and cervical precautions are not necessary. You are required to sequentially demonstrate all procedures you would perform from simple maneuvers and adjuncts to endotracheal intubation. You will have three (3) attempts to successfully incubate the manikin. You are only permitted to use the devices present in this station even though other acceptable airway adjuncts exist. You must actually ventilate the manikin for at least thirty (30) seconds with each adjunct and procedure utilized. I will serve as your trained assistant and will be interacting with you throughout this station. I will correctly carry out your orders upon your direction. Do you have any questions?

At this time, please take two (2) minutes to check your equipment and prepare whatever you feel is necessary.

[After two (2) minutes or sooner if the candidate states "I'm prepared," examiner continues reading the following:]

Upon your arrival to the scene, you observe the patient as he/she goes into respiratory arrest. Bystander ventilations have **not** been initiated. The scene is safe and no hemorrhage or other immediate problem is found. A palpable carotid pulse is still present.

National Registry of Emergency Medical Technicians
Advanced Level Practical Examination

VENTILATORY MANAGEMENT (ET)

Candidate:_____   Examiner:_____

Date:_____   Signature:_____

NOTE: If canditate elects to initially ventilate with BVM attached to reservoir and oxygen, full credit must be awarded for steps denoted by "****" so long as first ventilation is delivered within initial 30 seconds.

	Possible Points	Points Awarded
Takes or verbalizes infection control precautions	1	
Opens the airway manually	1	
Elevates tongue, inserts simple adjunct [either oropharyngeal or nasopharyngeal airway]	1	
NOTE: Examiner now informs candidate no gag reflex is present and patient accepts adjunct		
**Ventilates patient immediately with bag-valve-mask device unattached to oxygen	1	
**Hyperventilates patient with room air	1	
NOTE: Examiner now informs candidate that ventilation is being performed without difficulty		
Attaches oxygen reservoir to bag-valve-mask device and connects to high flow oxygen regulator [12-15 liters/min.]	1	
Ventilates patient at a rate of 10-20/min. and volumes of at least 800ml	1	
NOTE: After 30 seconds, examiner auscultates and reports breath sounds are present and equal bilaterally and medical control has ordered intubation. The examiner must now take over ventilation.		
Directs assistant to hyperventilate patient	1	
Identifies/selects proper equipment for intubation	1	
Checks equipment for: - Cuff leaks (1 point) - Laryngoscope operational and bulb tight (1 point)	2	
NOTE: Examiner to remove OPA and move out of way when candidate is prepared to intubate		
Positions head properly	1	
Inserts blade while displacing tongue	1	
Elevates mandible with laryngoscope	1	
Introduces ET tube and advances to proper depth	1	
Inflates cuff to proper pressure and disconnects syringe	1	
Directs ventilation of patient	1	
Confirms proper placement by auscultation bilaterally and over epigastrium	1	
NOTE: Examiner to ask "If you had proper placement, what would you expect to hear?"		
Secures ET tube [may be verbalized]	1	

CRITICAL CRITERIA

TOTAL 19

___ Failure to initiate ventilations within 30 seconds after applying gloves or interrupts ventilations for greater than 30 seconds at any time

___ Failure to take or verbalize infection control precautions

___ Failure to voice and ultimately provide high oxygen concentrations [at least 85%]

___ Failure to ventilate patient at rate of at least 10/minute

___ Failure to provide adequate volumes per breath [maximum 2 errors/minute permissable]

___ Failure to hyperventilate patient prior to intubation

___ Failure to successfully intubate within 3 attempts

___ Using teeth as a fulcrum

___ Failure to assure proper tube placement by auscultation bilaterally **and** over the epigastrium

___ If used, stylette extends beyond end of ET tube

___ Inserts any adjunct in a manner dangerous to patient

You must factually document your rationale for checking any of the above critical items on the reverse side of this form.

P202A

INSTRUCTIONS TO THE CANDIDATE FOR CARDIAC ARREST SKILLS

A. Dynamic Cardiology

This two-part station is designed to test your ability to recognize and treat cardiac dysrhythmias in accordance with current American Heart Association guidelines and algorithms. In the first part, you will be evaluated utilizing the defibrillation manikin and ECG monitor/defibrillator. Four (4) separate dysrhythmias will be presented in which you must act as the team leader and voice your interpretation of each dysrhythmia as well as basic life support and pharmacologic interventions you wish to administer. You must physically demonstrate and actually perform all electrical interventions necessary throughout this station. Please leave the defibrillator turned down to its lowest energy setting and verbally state the energy level you would be delivering to the patient prior to shocking the manikin. **JUST AS IT SOMETIMES OCCURS IN THE FIELD, SOME PATIENTS DO NOT RESPOND FAVORABLY DESPITE APPROPRIATE INTERPRETATION AND TREATMENT. THE PATIENT'S RESPONSE IN THESE PREPARED SCENARIOS IS NOT MEANT TO GIVE ANY INDICATION WHATSOEVER AS TO YOUR PERFORMANCE IN THIS STATION.** Please take a few moments to familiarize yourself with the equipment before we begin and I will be happy to explain any of the specific operational features of the monitor/defibrillator.

[After an appropriate time period or when the candidate informs you he/she is familiar with the equipment, the examiner continues reading the following:]

You will have eight (8) minutes to complete this portion of the station once we begin. I may ask questions for clarification and will acknowledge the verbal treatments you indicate are necessary. Do you have any questions?

You respond to a "man down" call and find this patient who is unconscious and unresponsive.

National Registry of Emergency Medical Technicians
Paramedic Practical Examination
CARDIAC ARREST SKILLS STATION
DYNAMIC CARDIOLOGY

Candidate:_____   Examiner:_____

Date:_____   Signature:_____

Set #_____   Time Start:_____Time End:_____

	Possible Points	Points Awarded
Takes or verbalizes infection control precautions	1	
Checks level of responsiveness	1	
Checks ABC's	1	
Initiates CPR if appropriate [verbally]	1	
Performs "Quick Look" with paddles	1	
Correctly interprets initial rhythm	1	
Appropriately manages initial rhythm	2	
Notes change in rhythm	1	
Checks patient condition to include pulse and, if appropriate, BP	1	
Correctly interprets second rhythm	1	
Appropriately manages second rhythm	2	
Notes change in rhythm	1	
Checks patient condition to include pulse and, if appropriate, BP	1	
Correctly interprets third rhythm	1	
Appropriately manages third rhythm	2	
Notes change in rhythm	1	
Checks patient condition to include pulse and, if appropriate, BP	1	
Correctly interprets fourth rhythm	1	
Appropriately manages fourth rhythm	2	
Orders high percentages of supplemental oxygen at proper times	1	

CRITICAL CRITERIA   TOTAL 24 [ ]

___ Failure to deliver first shock in a timely manner due to operator delay in machine use or providing treatments other than CPR with simple adjuncts

___ Failure to deliver second or third shocks without delay other than the time required to reassess and recharge paddles

___ Failure to verify rhythm before delivering each shock

___ Failure to ensure the safety of self and others [verbalizes"All clear" and observes]

___ Inability to deliver DC shock [does not use machine properly]

___ Failure to demonstrate acceptable shock sequence

___ Failure to order initiation or resumption of CPR when appropriate

___ Failure to order correct management of airway [ET when appropriate]

___ Failure to order administration of appropriate oxygen at proper time

___ Failure to diagnose or treat 2 or more rhythms correctly

___ Orders administration of an inappropriate drug or lethal dosage

___ Failure to correctly diagnose or adequately treat v-fib, v-tach, or asystole

You must factually document your rationale for checking any of the above critical items on the reverse side of this form.

P203A

INSTRUCTIONS TO THE CANDIDATE FOR CARDIAC ARREST SKILLS

B. Static Cardiology

The final portion of this station is designed to evaluate your ability to recognize and verbally treat cardiac dysrhythmias in accordance with current American Heart Association guidelines and algorithms. Four (4) static ECG recordings will be presented and you must verbally inform me of your interpretation and voice all treatments and interventions you would provide this patient in the field. Vital patient information is provided on each card, and I am not permitted to supply any additional information not contained on the cards. You will have six (6) minutes to complete this portion. Do you have any questions?

National Registry of Emergency Medical Technicians
Paramedic Practical Examination
CARDIAC ARREST SKILLS STATION
STATIC CARDIOLOGY

Candidate:_____   Examiner:_____

Date:_____   Signature:_____

Set #_____

NOTE: No points for treatment may be awarded if the diagnosis is incorrect.
Only document incorrect responses in spaces provided.

	Possible Points	Points Awarded
STRIP #1		
Diagnosis:	1	
Treatment:	2	
STRIP #2		
Diagnosis:	1	
Treatment:	2	
STRIP #3		
Diagnosis:	1	
Treatment:	2	
STRIP #4		
Diagnosis:	1	
Treatment:	2	
TOTAL	12	

INSTRUCTIONS TO THE CANDIDATE FOR IV AND MEDICATION SKILLS

This station is designed to test your ability to establish an IV and administer medications by the IV bolus (push) and piggyback methods just as you would in the field. You will be required to establish the IV within three (3) attempts. If you do not successfully establish the IV, you will not be able to administer IV bolus and piggyback medications to the patient. Although we are using the manikin arm, you should conduct yourself as if this were a real patient. You should assume that I am the actual patient and may ask me any questions you would normally ask a patient in this situation. You have six (6) minutes to establish the IV, three (3) minutes to begin blousing the patient, and five (5) minutes to begin piggyback medication administration. Do you have any questions?

National Registry of Emergency Medical Technicians
Advanced Level Practical Examination
INTRAVENOUS THERAPY

Candidate:_____ Examiner:_____

Date:_____ Signature:_____

Time Start:_____ Time End:_____

	Possible Points	Points Awarded

Checks selected IV fluid for:
    - Proper fluid (1 point)
    - Clarity (1 point)
	2	

Selects appropriate catheter	1	
Selects proper administration set	1	
Connects IV tubing to the IV bag	1	
Prepares administration set [fills drip chamber and flushes tubing]	1	
Cuts or tears tape [at any time before venipuncture]	1	
Takes/verbalizes infection control precautions [prior to venipuncture]	1	
Applies tourniquet	1	
Palpates suitable vein	1	
Cleanses site appropriately	1	

Performs venipuncture
 	
    - Inserts stylette (1 point)
    - Notes or verbalizes flashback (1 point)
    - Occludes vein proximal to catheter (1 point)
    - Removes stylette (1 point)
    - Connects IV tubing to catheter (1 point)
	5	

Releases tourniquet	1	
Runs IV for a brief period to assure patent line	1	
Secures catheter [tapes securely or verbalizes]	1	
Adjusts flow rate as appropriate	1	
Disposes/verbalizes disposal of needle in proper container	1	
TOTAL	**21**	

CRITICAL CRITERIA

____ Exceeded the 6 minute time limit in establishing a patent and properly adjusted IV

____ Failure to take or verbalize infection control precautions prior to performing venipuncture

____ Contaminates equipment or site without appropriately correcting situation

____ Any improper technique resulting in the potential for catheter shear or air embolism

____ Failure to successfully establish IV within 3 attempts during 6 minute time limit

____ Failure to dispose/verbalize disposal of needle in proper container

You must factually document your rationale for checking any of the above critical items on the reverse side of this form.

P-204A   9-19-94

National Registry of Emergency Medical Technicians
Paramedic Practical Examination
INTRAVENOUS BOLUS MEDICATIONS

Candidate:_____

Date:_____

Examiner:_____

Signature:_____

Time Start:_____ Time End:_____

NOTE: Check here (____) if candidate did not establish
a patent IV and do not evaluate these skills.

	Possible Points	Points Awarded
Asks patient for known allergies	1	
Selects correct medication	1	
Assures correct concentration of drug	1	
Assembles prefilled syringe correctly and dispels air	1	
Continues infection control precautions	1	
Cleanses injection site (Y-port or hub)	1	
Reaffirms medication	1	
Stops IV flow (pinches tubing)	1	
Administers correct dose at proper push rate	1	
Flushes tubing (runs wide open for a brief period)	1	
Adjusts drip rate to TKO (KVO)	1	
Voices proper disposal of syringe and needle	1	
Verbalizes need to observe patient for desired effect/adverse side effects	1	

CRITICAL CRITERIA

IV BOLUS SUB-TOTAL 13 [   ]

____Failure to begin administration of medication within 3 minute time limit

____Contaminates equipment or site without appropriately correcting situation

____Failure to adequately dispel air resulting in potential for air embolism

____Injects improper drug or dosage (wrong drug, incorrect amount, or pushes at inappropriate rate)

____Failure to flush IV tubing after injecting medication

____Recaps needle or failure to dispose/verbalize disposal of syringe and needle in proper container

INTRAVENOUS PIGGYBACK MEDICATIONS

	Possible Points	Points Awarded
Has confirmed allergies by now (award point if previously confirmed)	1	
Checks selected IV fluid for: - Proper fluid (1 point) - Clarity (1 point)	2	
Checks selected medication for: - Clarity (1 point) - Concentration of medication (1 point)	2	
Injects correct amount of medication into IV solution given scenario	1	
Connects appropriate administration set to medication solution	1	
Prepares administration set (fills drip chamber and flushes tubing)	1	
Attaches appropriate needle to administration set	1	
Continues infection control precautions	1	
Cleanses port of primary line	1	
Inserts needle into port without contamination	1	
Adjusts flow rate of secondary line as required	1	
Stops flow of primary line	1	
Securely tapes needle	1	
Verbalizes need to observe patient for desired effect/adverse side effects	1	
Labels medication/fluid bag	1	

CRITICAL CRITERIA

IV PIGGYBACK SUB-TOTAL 17 [   ]

____ Failure to begin administration of medication within 5 minute time limit

____ Contaminates equipment or site without appropriately correcting situation

____ Administers improper drug or dosage (wrong drug, incorrect amount, or infuses at inappropriate rate)

____ Failure to flush IV tubing of secondary line resulting in potential for air embolism

____ Failure to shut-off flow of primary line

You must factually document your rationale for checking any of the above critical items on the reverse side of this form.

P-204B 3/93

INSTRUCTIONS TO THE CANDIDATE FOR SPINAL IMMOBILIZATION (SEATED PATIENT)

This station is designed to test your ability to provide spinal immobilization to a sitting patient using a half-spine immobilization device. You arrive on the scene of an auto accident with an EMT assistant. The scene is safe and there is only one (1) patient. The assistant EMT has completed the primary survey, and no critical condition was found in the primary survey requiring any intervention. For the purposes of this testing station, the patient's vital signs remain stable. You are required to treat the specific, isolated problem of an unstable spine using a half-spine immobilization device. You are responsible for the direction and subsequent actions of the EMT assistant. Transferring and immobilizing the patient to the long backboard should be accomplished verbally. You have ten (10) minutes to complete this station. Do you have any questions?

National Registry of Emergency Medical Technicians
Advanced Level Practical Examination
SPINAL IMMOBILIZATION
(SEATED PATIENT)

Candidate:_____   Examiner:_____

Date:_____   Signature:_____

Time Start:_____Time End:_____

	Possible Points	Points Awarded
Takes or verbalizes infection control precautions	1	
Directs assistant to place/maintain head in neutral, in-line position	1	
Directs assistant to maintain manual immobilization of head	1	
Assesses motor, sensory, and distal circulation in extremities	1	
Applies appropriately sized extrication collar	1	
Positions the immobilization device behind the patient	1	
Secures device to the patient's torso	1	
Evaluates torso fixation and adjusts as necessary	1	
Evaluates and pads behind the patient's head as necessary	1	
Secures patient's head to the device	1	
Reassesses motor, sensory, and distal circulation in extremities	1	
Verbalizes moving the patient to a long board properly	1	

TOTAL   12   [ ]

CRITICAL CRITERIA

___ Did not immediately direct or take manual immobilization of head

___ Releases or orders release of manual immobilization before it was maintained mechanically

___ Patient manipulated or moved excessively causing potential spinal compromise

___ Did not complete immobilization of the torso prior to immobilizing the head

___ Device moves excessively up, down, left, or right on patient's torso

___ Torso fixation inhibits chest rise resulting in respiratory compromise

___ Head immobilization allows for excessive movement

___ Upon completion of immobilization, head is not in neutral, in-line position

You must factually document your rationale for checking any of the above critical items on the reverse side of this form.

INSTRUCTIONS TO THE CANDIDATE FOR BLEEDING-WOUNDS-SHOCK

This station is designed to test your ability to treat progressive shock due to a profound arterial hemorrhage. This is a scenario-based testing station. As you progress through the scenario, you will be offered various signs and symptoms appropriate for the patient's condition. You will be required to manage the patient based on these signs and symptoms. A scenario will be read aloud to you and you will be given an opportunity to ask clarifying questions about the scenario. However, you will not receive answers to any questions about the actual steps of the procedures to be performed. You may use any of the supplies and equipment available in this room. You have ten (10) minutes to complete this skill station. Do you have any questions?

National Registry of Emergency Medical Technicians
Advanced Level Practical Examination
RANDOM BASIC SKILLS
BLEEDING - WOUNDS - SHOCK

Candidate:_____ Examiner:_____

Date:_____ Signature:_____

Time Start:_____ Time End:_____

	Possible Points	Points Awarded
Takes or verbalizes infection control precautions	1	
Applies direct pressure to the wound	1	
Elevates the extremity	1	
Applies pressure dressing to the wound	1	
Bandages wound	1	
NOTE: The examiner must now inform the candidate that the wound is still continuing to bleed. The second dressing does not control the bleeding.		
Locates and applies pressure to appropriate arterial pressure point	1	
NOTE: The examiner must indicate that the victim is in compensatory shock.		
Applies high concentration oxygen	1	
Properly positions patient (supine with legs elevated)	1	
Prevents heat loss (covers patient as appropriate)	1	
NOTE: The examiner must indicate that the victim is in profound shock. Medical control has ordered application and inflation of the Pneumatic Anti-shock Garment.		
Removes clothing or checks for sharp objects	1	
Quickly assesses areas that will be under the PASG	1	
Positions PASG with top of abdominal section at or below last set of ribs	1	
Secures PASG around patient	1	
Attaches hoses	1	
Begins inflation sequence (examiner to stop inflation at 15mm Hg)	1	
Checks blood pressure	1	
Verbalizes when to stop inflation sequence	1	
Operates PASG to maintain air pressure in device	1	
Reassesses vital signs	1	

TOTAL 19 [ ]

CRITICAL CRITERIA

___ Failure to take or verbalize infection control precautions

___ Did not apply high concentration of oxygen

___ Applies tourniquet before attempting other methods of hemorrhage control

___ Did not control hemorrhage or attempt to control hemorrhage in a timely manner

___ Inflates abdominal section of PASG before the legs

___ Did not reassess patient's vital signs after PASG inflation

___ Places PASG on inside-out

___ Allows deflation of PASG after inflation

___ Positions PASG above level of lowest rib

You must factually document your rationale for checking any of the above critical items on the reverse side of this form.

INSTRUCTIONS TO THE CANDIDATE FOR LONG BONE SPLINTING

This station is designed to test your ability to properly immobilize a closed non-angulated long bone fracture. You are required to treat only the specific, isolated injury. The primary assessment has been completed, and during the secondary survey a closed, non-angulated fracture of the _____(humerus, radius, ulna, tibia, fibula) is detected. Continued assessment of the patient's airway, breathing, and central circulation is not necessary. You may use any equipment available in this room. You have five (5) minutes to complete this procedure. Do you have any questions?

National Registry of Emergency Medical Technicians
Advanced Level Practical Examination
RANDOM BASIC SKILLS
LONG BONE IMMOBILIZATION

Candidate_____   Examiner:_____

Date_____   Signature:_____

Time Start:_____Time End:_____

	Possible Points	Points Awarded
Takes or verbalizes infection control precautions	1	
Directs application of manual stabilization	1	
Assesses motor, sensory, and distal circulation	1	
NOTE: Examiner acknowledges present and normal		
Measures splint	1	
Applies splint	1	
Immobilizes joint above fracture	1	
Immobilizes joint below fracture	1	
Secures entire injured extremity	1	
Immobilizes hand/foot in position of function	1	
Reassesses motor, sensory, and distal circulation	1	
NOTE: Examiner acknowledges present and normal		

TOTAL 10 [ ]

CRITICAL CRITERIA

____ Grossly moves injured extremity

____ Did not immobilize adjacent joints, injury, or limb

____ Did not reassess motor, sensory, and distal circulation after splinting

You must factually document your rationale for checking any of the above critical items on the reverse side of this form.

INSTRUCTIONS TO THE CANDIDATE FOR TRACTION SPLINTING

This station is designed to test your ability to properly immobilize a mid-shaft femur fracture with a traction splint. You will have an EMT assistant to help you in the application of the device by applying manual traction when directed to do so. You are required to treat only the specific, isolated injury. The primary assessment has been accomplished on the victim, and during the secondary survey you detect a mid-shaft femur fracture. Continued assessment of the patient's airway, breathing, and central circulation is not necessary. You may use any equipment available in this room. You have ten (10) minutes to complete this procedure. Do you have any questions?

National Registry of Emergency Medical Technicians
Advanced Level Practical Examination
RANDOM BASIC SKILLS
TRACTION SPLINTING

Candidate:_____   Examiner:_____

Date:_____   Signature:_____

Time Start:_____   Time End:_____

	Possible Points	Points Awarded
Takes or verbalizes infection control precautions	1	
Directs manual stabilization of injured leg	1	
Directs application of manual traction	1	
Assesses motor, sensory, and distal circulation	1	
NOTE: Examiner acknowledges present and normal		
Prepares/adjusts splint to proper length	1	
Positions splint at injured leg	1	
Applies proximal securing device (e.g. ischial strap)	1	
Applies distal securing device (e.g. ankle hitch)	1	
Applies mechanical traction	1	
Positions/secures support straps	1	
Re-evaluates proximal/distal securing devices	1	
Reassesses motor, sensory, and distal circulation	1	
NOTE: Examiner acknowledges present and normal		
NOTE: Examiner must ask candidate how he/she would prepare for transport		
Verbalizes securing torso to long board to immobilize hip	1	
Verbalizes securing splint to long board to prevent movement of splint	1	

TOTAL 14 [ ]

CRITICAL CRITERIA

____ Loss of traction at any point after it is assumed

____ Did not reassess motor, sensory, and distal circulation **after** splinting

____ The foot is excessively rotated or extended after splinting

____ Did not secure ischial strap **before** taking traction

____ Final immobilization failed to support femur or prevent rotation of injured leg

NOTE: If Sagar is used without elevating the leg, application of manual traction is not necessary. Candidate will be awarded 1 point as if manual traction were applied.

NOTE: If the leg is elevated at all, manual traction must be applied before elevating the leg. The ankle hitch may be applied before elevating the leg and used to pull manual traction.

You must factually document your rationale for checking any of the above critical items on the reverse side of this form.

P-206C/4-93

INSTRUCTIONS TO THE CANDIDATE FOR SPINAL IMMOBILIZATION (LYING PATIENT)

This station is designed to test your ability to provide spinal immobilization on a patient using a long spine immobilization device. You arrive on the scene with an EMT assistant. The assistant EMT has completed the primary survey, and no critical condition was found in the primary survey requiring any intervention. For the purposes of this testing station, the patient's vital signs remain stable. You are required to treat the specific, isolated problem of an unstable spine using a long spine immobilization device. When moving the patient to the device, you should use the help of the assistant EMT and me. The assistant EMT should control the head and cervical spine of the patient while you and I move the patient to the immobilization device. You are responsible for the direction and subsequent actions of the EMT assistant. You have the (10) minutes to complete this procedure. Do you have any questions?

National Registry of Emergency Medical Technicians
Advanced Level Practical Examination
RANDOM BASIC SKILLS
SPINAL IMMOBILIZATION
(LYING PATIENT)

Candidate:_____

Examiner:_____

Date:_____

Signature:_____

Time Start:_____Time End:_____

	Possible Points	Points Awarded
Takes or verbalizes infection control procedures	1	
Directs assistant to move patient's head to the neutral in-line position	1	
Directs assistant to maintain manual immobilization of head	1	
Evaluates motor, sensory, and distal circulation in extremities	1	
Applies cervical collar	1	
Positions immobilization device appropriately	1	
Moves patient onto device without compromising the integrity of the spine	1	
Applies padding to voids between the torso and the board as necessary	1	
Immobilizes torso to the device	1	
Evaluates and pads under the patient's head as necessary	1	
Immobilizes the patient's head to the device	1	
Secures legs to the device	1	
Secures patient's arms to the board	1	
Reassesses motor, sensory, and distal circulation	1	

TOTAL 14

CRITICAL CRITERIA

___ Did not immediately direct manual immobilization of head

___ Orders release of manual immobilization before it was maintained mechanically

___ Did not complete immobilization of the torso prior to immobilizing the head

___ Device excessively moves up, down, left, or right on patient's torso

___ Head immobilization allows for excessive movement

___ Head is not immobilized in the neutral in-line position

___ Patient moved excessively causing potential spinal compromise

___ Did not reassess motor, sensory, and distal circulation **after** immobilization

You must factually document your rationale for checking any of the above critical items on the reverse side of this form.

P-206 D/11-93

C·H·A·P·T·E·R

STATE CERTIFICATION REQUIREMENTS

CHAPTER SUMMARY

This chapter outlines EMT-Paramedic certification requirements for all 50 states and the District of Columbia. It also lists state EMT agencies you can contact for more information about certification requirements.

The table on pages 3–4 shows some of the minimum requirements you must meet to be certified as a paramedic in all 50 states and the District of Columbia. The next few paragraphs explain the entries on the table. After the table is a state-by-state list of EMT agencies, which you can contact for more specific information.

You should know that some minimum requirements are pretty standard and so are not listed on the table. For instance, you must be physically, mentally, and emotionally able to perform all the tasks of an EMT. Usually you are required to have a high school diploma or GED before you begin training. You must have a clean criminal record. And, of course, you must successfully complete an EMT-Paramedic training program that meets the standards set by the U.S. Department of Transportation.

The first entry, **Time to Become Certified,** means the amount of time you have between completing your training program and meeting the certification requirements. If you allow too much time to pass between taking the course and taking the exam, you could end up taking the whole course over again! In some states, the exam comes immediately at the end of training. If this is the case, you will see "Immediate" in this column.

States use their own written and practical skills exams, exams from the National Registry of EMTs, or a combination of both. The entry under **Exam** will be "State," meaning the state has its own exam, "NR-EMT" for National Registry, or an entry indicating a combination of both exams. Even when the state has its own exam, you'll find it's pretty similar to the National Registry exam, and therefore to the exams in this book. After all, the federal government mandates the curriculum of paramedic courses nationwide. So you could expect exams based on similar curricula to be similar.

See the next column to find out if a state with its own exam also accepts the National Registry exam. Under **Accepts National Registry,** the possible entries are "no," meaning the state requires you to go through *its* certification process; "yes," meaning you can be certified in this state if you are already certified by the National Registry, or "with state," meaning that if you are certified by the National Registry, you can be certified in this state by taking that state's written and skills exam. Obviously, if the entry under **Exam** in the previous column was "NR-EMT," that state accepts the National Registry exam.

The same idea follows under **Accepts Out-of-State Certification**—the state does accept certification by another state, doesn't accept it, or accepts it if you take their exam. Some states require that you be certified through the National Registry if you're transferring in from out-of-state. For these states you will see "With NR-EMT" in this column. In most cases, a state that accepts out-of-state certification will insist that your training program and your exam have met or exceeded its standards, so sometimes it will come down to whether or not the state you're coming from is deemed to have done so. Some states have additional certification requirements for transferring paramedics, such as background investigations, being a state resident, being employed with an EMS agency in that state, or taking a refresher course. If you are certified in another state, you will need to show proof of certification when applying in a different state.

Some states have what is known as "legal recognition," which means they will recognize and accept your training for a limited time period, often one year. This is similar to a temporary certification. During this period of legal recognition, you apply for official certification and fulfill the necessary requirements. Once this process is complete, your certification will be good for as long as that state allows. Check with the appropriate state's EMS office for more details.

Recertification indicates the number of years from your initial certification to the time when you will have to be recertified. Recertification usually requires a given number of hours of continuing education, demonstration of your continuing ability to perform the necessary skills, or both—but you'll find out all about that once you're certified in the first place.

State	Time to Become Certified	Exam	Accepts Nat'l Registry	Accepts Out-of-State	Recertification
Alabama	2 years	NR-EMT	Yes	With NR-EMT	2 years
Alaska	1 year	NR-EMT	Yes	With state exam	2 years
Arizona	1 year	NR-EMT	Yes	With NR-EMT	2 years
Arkansas	1 year	State Practical, NR Written	Yes	With state exam or NR-EMT	2 years
California	1 year	NR-EMT	Yes	With NR-EMT	2 years
Colorado	6 months	NR-EMT	Yes	Legal Recognition	3 years
Connecticut	Immediate	State	Yes	Yes	1 year
Delaware	Immediate	State or NR-EMT	Yes	With state exam	1 year
District of Columbia	Immediate	NR-EMT	Yes	With NR-EMT	2 years
Florida	1 year	State	Yes	With state exam	2 years
Georgia	2 years	NR-EMT	Yes	With NR-EMT	2 years
Hawaii	Immediate	NR-EMT	Yes	With NR-EMT	2 years
Idaho	2 years	NR-EMT	Yes	With NR-EMT	3 years
Illinois	1 year	State or NR-EMT	Yes	Yes	4 years
Indiana	1 year	NR-EMT	Yes	With NR-EMT	1 year
Iowa	1 year	NR-EMT	Yes	With NR-EMT	2 years
Kansas	1 year	NR-EMT or state	Yes	With NR-EMT	1 year
Kentucky	2 years	State Practical, NR Written	Yes	With NR-EMT or state	2 years
Louisiana	2 years	NR-EMT or state	Yes	With NR-EMT	2 years
Maine	3 years	State	Yes	With NR-EMT	3 years
Maryland	Immediate	NR-EMT and state	With state	With NR-EMT and state	2 years
Massachusetts	2 years	NR-EMT	Yes	With NR-EMT or state	2 years
Michigan	1 year	State	No	With state exam	3 years
Minnesota	2 years	State Practical, NR Written	Yes	Yes	2 years
Missouri	3 years	State	Yes	Yes	3 years

State	Time to Become Certified	Exam	Accepts Nat'l Registry	Accepts Out-of-State	Recertification
Mississippi	2 years	NR-EMT	Yes	With NR-EMT	2 years
Montana	2 years	NR-EMT	Yes	With NR-EMT	2 years
Nebraska	Immediate	NR-EMT	Yes	With NR-EMT	2 years
New Hampshire	1 year	NR-EMT	Yes	With NR-EMT	2 years
New Jersey	Immediate	NR-EMT	Yes	Yes	2 years
New York	1 year	State	No	Yes	3 years
North Carolina	1 year	State	Yes	With state exam	4 years
North Dakota	2 years	NR-EMT	Yes	With NR-EMT	2 years
Ohio	2 years	NR-EMT	Yes	With NR-EMT	3 years
Oklahoma	1 year	NR-EMT	Yes	With NR-EMT	2 years
Oregon	1 year	NR-EMT	Yes	Yes	2 years
Pennsylvania	1 year	State	Yes	With NR-EMT	None
Rhode Island	2 years	NR-EMT	Yes	With NR-EMT	2 years
South Carolina	2 years	NR-EMT	Yes	With NR-EMT or state	3 years
South Dakota	2 years	NR-EMT	Yes	With NR-EMT	2 years
Tennessee	6 months	State, then NR-EMT	Yes	Yes	2 years
Texas	Immediate	State	No	Yes, for 1 year	4 years
Utah	Immediate	State	No	With state exam	4 years
Vermont	2 years	NR-EMT	Yes	With NR-EMT	2 years
Virginia	2 years	NR-EMT	Yes	With NR-EMT	4 years
Washington	1 year	State and NR-EMT	Yes	With state exam	3 years
West Virginia	2 years	NR-EMT	Yes	With NR-EMT	2 or 4 years
Wisconsin	2 years	State	Yes	With NR-EMT	2 years
Wyoming	None*	NR-EMT	Yes	With NR-EMT	2 years

* Wyoming does not have its own paramedic training program; it requires paramedics to go out-of-state to complete paramedic training.

STATE EMT AGENCIES

The following is a list of the agencies that control EMT certification in each state, with their addresses and phone numbers and, in some cases, World Wide Web sites. You can contact those offices for more information on their certification requirements.

ALABAMA

Emergency Medical Services Division
Alabama Department of Health
The RSA Tower, 201 Monroe Street, Suite 750
Montgomery, AL 36130-3017
Telephone: 334-206-5383

ALASKA

Community Health and Emergency Medical
 Services Section
Department of Health and Human Services/
 Public Health
P.O. Box 110616
Juneau, AK 99811-0616
Telephone: 907-465-2541
Web site: *health.state.ak.us*

ARIZONA

Bureau of Emergency Medical Services
Arizona Department of Health Services
1651 E. Morten, Suite 120
Phoenix, AZ 85020
Telephone: 602-255-1170
Web site: *hs.state.az.us*

ARKANSAS

Division of Emergency Medical Services and
 Trauma Systems
Arkansas Department of Health
4815 W. Markham Street, Slot 38
Little Rock, AR 72205-3867
Telephone: 501-661-2178
Web site: *doh.state.ar.us*

CALIFORNIA

Emergency Medical Services Authority
1930 9th Street, Suite 100
Sacramento, CA 95814
Telephone: 916-322-4336
Web site: *emsa.cahwnet.gov*

COLORADO

Colorado Department of Health
Emergency Medical Services Division
4300 Cherry Creek Drive South
Denver, CO 80222
Telephone: 303-692-2980
Web site:*state.co.us/gov_dir/cdphe_dir/*
 em/emhom.htm

CONNECTICUT
Office of Emergency Medical Services
Department of Public Health
410 Capital Avenue, MS#12EMS
P.O. Box 340308
Hartford, CT 06134-0308
Telephone: 860-509-7574

DELAWARE
Emergency Medical Services
Blue Hen Corporate Center
655 South Bay Road, Suite 4-H
Dover, DE 19901
Telephone: 302-739-6637

DISTRICT OF COLUMBIA
Emergency Health and Medical Services
800 9th Street, SW, 3rd Floor
Washington, DC 20024
Telephone: 202-645-5628

FLORIDA
Bureau of Emergency Medical Services
Florida Department of Health
2002-D Old St. Augustine Road
Tallahassee, FL 32301-4881
Telephone: 850-487-1911
Web site: *state.fl.us/health/ems*

GEORGIA
Georgia Medical Board
166 Pryor Street, SW
Alanta, GA 30303
Telephone: 404-656-3923
Web site: *dhr.state.ga.us*

HAWAII
Emergency Medical Services System
State Department of Health
3627 Kilauea Avenue, Room 102
Honolulu, HI 96816
Telephone: 808-733-9210

IDAHO
Emergency Medical Services Bureau
Department of Health and Welfare
3092 Elder Street
Boise, ID 83705
Telephone: 208-334-4000

ILLINOIS
Division of Emergency Medical Services
Illinois Department of Public Health
525 W. Jefferson Street
Springfield, IL 62761
Telephone: 217-785-2080

INDIANA

Indiana Emergency Medical Services Commission
302 W. Washington, Room E208 IGCS
Indianapolis, IN 46204-2258
Telephone: 800-666-7784

IOWA

Emergency Medical Services
Iowa Department of Public Health
Lucas State Office Building
Des Moines, IA 50319-0075
Telephone: 515-281-3239

KANSAS

Board of Emergency Medical Services
109 SW 6th Avenue
Topeka, KS 66603-3826
Telephone: 913-296-7296

KENTUCKY

Emergency Medical Services Branch
Department for Health Services
275 E. Main Street
Frankfort, KY 40621
Telephone: 502-564-8963

LOUISIANA

Bureau of Emergency Medical Services
P.O. Box 94215
Baton Rouge, LA 70804
Telephone: 504-342-4881

MAINE

Maine Emergency Medical Services
16 Edison Drive
Augusta, ME 04330
Telephone: 207-287-3953
Web site: *state.me.us/bms/bmshome.html*

MARYLAND

Maryland Department of Emergency
  Medical Services
636 W. Lombard Street
Baltimore, MD 21201-1528
Telephone: 800-762-7157
Web site: *134.192.108.12/home.html*

MASSACHUSETTS

Office of Emergency Medical Services
Department of Public Health
470 Atlantic Avenue, 2nd Floor
Boston, MA 02201-2208
Telephone: 617-753-8300

MICHIGAN

Division of Emergency Medical Services
Michigan Department of Consumer and
  Industry Affairs
P.O. Box 30664
Lansing, MI 48909
Telephone: 517-241-3018

MINNESOTA

Minnesota Emergency Medical Services
  Regulatory Board
2829 University Avenue SE, Suite 310
Minneapolis, MN 55414-3222
Telephone: 612-627-6000
Web site: *emsrb.state.mn.us*

MISSISSIPPI

Emergency Medical Services
State Department of Health
P.O. Box 1700
Jackson, MS 39215-1700
Telephone: 601-987-3880

MISSOURI

Bureau of Emergency Medical Services
Missouri Department of Health
P.O. Box 570
Jefferson City, MO 65101
Telephone: 573-751-6356

MONTANA

Emergency Medical Services and
  Injury Prevention Section
Department of Public Health and
  Human Services
Cogswell Building
P.O. Box 202951
Helena, MT 59620-2951
Telephone: 406-444-4458

NEBRASKA

Division of Emergency Medical Services
301 Centennial Mall South, 3rd Floor
P.O. Box 95007
Lincoln, NE 68509-5007
Telephone: 402-471-0124

NEVADA

Emergency Medical Services Office
Nevada State Health Division
1550 E. College Parkway, #158
Carson City, NV 89710
Telephone: 702-687-3065

NEW HAMPSHIRE

Bureau of Emergency Medical Services
Health and Welfare Building
6 Hazen Drive
Concord, NH 03301-6527
Telephone: 603-271-4568

NEW JERSEY

New Jersey Department of Health and
    Senior Services
Office of Emergency Medical Services
CN-360; 50 East State Street, 6th Floor
Trenton, NJ 08625-0360
Telephone: 609-633-7777
Web site: *state.nj.us/health/ems/hlthems.html*

NEW MEXICO

Emergency Medical Services Bureau
Department of Health
P.O. Box 26110
Santa Fe, NM 87502-6110
Telephone: 505-476-7000

NEW YORK

Bureau of Emergency Medical Services
New York State Health Department
433 River Street, Suite 303
Troy, NY 12180-2299
Telephone: 518-402-0996
Web site: *health.state.ny.us/nysdoh/ems*

NORTH CAROLINA

Office of Emergency Medical Services
701 Barbour Drive
P.O. Box 29530
Raleigh, NC 27603
Telephone: 919-733-2285

NORTH DAKOTA

Division of Emergency Health Services
North Dakota Department of Health
600 E. Boulevard Avenue
Bismarck, ND 58505-0200
Telephone: 701-328-2388

OHIO

Ohio Department of Public Safety
Emergency Medical Services
P.O. Box 7167
Columbus, OH 43266-0563
Telephone: 614-466-9447

OKLAHOMA

Emergency Medical Services Division
State Department of Health
1000 NE 10th Street, Room 1104
Oklahoma City, OK 73117-1299
Telephone: 405-271-4027

OREGON

Emergency Medical Services and Systems
Oregon Health Division
800 NE Oregon, Suite 607
Portland, OR 97232
Telephone: 503-731-4011

PENNSYLVANIA

Division of Emergency Medical Services Systems
Pennsylvania Department of Health
P.O. Box 90
Harrisburg, PA 17108
Telephone: 717-787-8741

RHODE ISLAND

Emergency Medical Services Division
Department of Health, Room 404
3 Capitol Hill
Providence, RI 02908-5097
Telephone: 401-222-2401

SOUTH CAROLINA

South Carolina Division of Emergency
  Medical Services
2600 Bull Street
Columbia, SC 29201
Telephone: 803-737-7204
Web site: *state.sc.us/dhec/hrems.html*

SOUTH DAKOTA

Emergency Medical Services Program
Department of Health
445 East Capitol
Pierre, SD 57501
Telephone: 605-773-3361

TENNESSEE

Division of Emergency Medical Services
Department of Health
426 Fifth Avenue, North, 1st Floor, Room 88
Nashville, TN 37247-0701
Telephone: 615-741-2584

TEXAS

Bureau of Emergency Management
Texas Department of Health
1100 49th Street
Austin, TX 78756-3199
Telephone: 512-834-6740
Web site: *tdh.state.tx.us*

UTAH

Bureau of Emergency Medical Services
Department of Health
288 N. 1460 West
Box 142852
Salt Lake City, UT 84114-2852
Telephone: 801-538-6435

VERMONT

Emergency Medical Services Division
Department of Health
108 Cherry Street
Box 70
Burlington, VT 05402
Telephone: 802-863-7310

VIRGINIA

Office of Emergency Medical Services
Virginia Department of Health
1538 E. Parham Road
Richmond, VA 23228
Telephone: 804-371-3500
Web site: *vdh.state.va.us/oems/index.html*

WASHINGTON

Department of Health
Office of Emergency Medical and
    Trauma Prevention
P.O. Box 47853
Olympia, WA 98504-7853
Telephone: 360-705-6745
Web site: *doh.wa.gov/hsqa/emtp*

WEST VIRGINIA

West Virginia Office of Emergency
    Medical Services
1411 Virginia Street, East
Charleston, WV 25301
Telephone: 304-558-3956

WISCONSIN
Emergency Medical Services
Division of Health
P.O. Box 309
Madison, WI 53701-0309
Telephone: 608-266-9781 or 800-793-6820

WYOMING
Emergency Medical Services Program
State of Wyoming
Hathaway Building, Room 527
Cheyenne, WY 82002
Telephone: 307-777-6018

FIVE WAYS TO MASTER THE BASICS!

IT ISN'T LUCK!

Anyone who wants to get good grades in school, pass entry-level or other job-related exams, or perform well on the job, must master basic skills: Reading Comprehension, Math, Vocabulary and Spelling, Writing, and basic Reasoning Skills.

What's the best way to master these skills?

With LearningExpress **SKILL BUILDERS**! Each book is designed to help you learn the important skills you need in the least amount of time.

Arranged in 20 quick and easy lessons, each guide:

- Pinpoints the areas where you need the most help
- Gives you hundreds of exercises with full answer explanations
- Provides you with tips on scoring your best on school and job-related tests

Skill Builders also feature:

- Specially designed "Before and After" tests to quickly pinpoint strengths, weaknesses *and* chart your progress
- "Skill Building Until Next Time": inventive ways to continue learning on the go

GIVE YOURSELF THE EXCLUSIVE LEARNINGEXPRESS ADVANTAGE!

1. ___	READING COMPREHENSION SUCCESS IN 20 MINUTES A DAY	Item #126-5
2. ___	WRITING SKILLS SUCCESS IN 20 MINUTES A DAY	Item #128-1
3. ___	VOCABULARY/SPELLING SUCCESS IN 20 MINUTES A DAY	Item #127-3
4. ___	PRACTICAL MATH SUCCESS IN 20 MINUTES A DAY	Item #129-X
5. ___	REASONING SKILLS SUCCESS IN 20 MINUTES A DAY	Item #116-8

SPECIFICATIONS: 8 1/2 x 11 • 192-240 PAGES • $16.00 EACH (PAPERBACK)

ORDER THE LEARNINGEXPRESS SKILL BUILDERS YOU NEED TODAY:

Fill in the quantities beside each book and mail your check/money order*
for the amount indicated (please include $6.95 postage/handling
for the first book and $1.00 for each additional book) to:

LearningExpress, Dept. A040, 20 Academy Street, Norwalk, CT 06850

Or call, TOLL-FREE: **1-888-551-JOBS, Dept. A040,** to place a credit card order.

Also available in your local bookstores

Please allow at least 2-4 weeks for delivery. Prices subject to change without notice   *NY, CT, & MD residents add appropriate sales tax

Order Form

CALIFORNIA EXAMS

___ @ $35.00   CA Allied Health
___ @ $35.00   CA Corrections Officer
___ @ $35.00   CA Firefighter
___ @ $20.00   CA Law Enforcement Career Guide
___ @ $35.00   CA Police Officer
___ @ $30.00   CA Postal Worker
___ @ $35.00   CA State Police
___ @ $17.95   CBEST (California Basic Educational Skills Test)

NEW JERSEY EXAMS

___ @ $35.00   NJ Allied Health
___ @ $35.00   NJ Corrections Officer
___ @ $35.00   NJ Firefighter
___ @ $20.00   NJ Law Enforcement Career Guide
___ @ $35.00   NJ Police Officer
___ @ $30.00   NJ Postal Worker
___ @ $35.00   NJ State Police

TEXAS EXAMS

___ @ $17.95   TASP (Texas Academic Skills Program)
___ @ $32.50   TX Allied Health
___ @ $35.00   TX Corrections Officer
___ @ $35.00   TX Firefighter
___ @ $20.00   TX Law Enforcement Career Guide
___ @ $35.00   TX Police Officer
___ @ $30.00   TX Postal Worker
___ @ $29.95   TX Real Estate Exam
___ @ $30.00   TX State Police

NEW YORK EXAMS

___ @ $30.00   New York City Firefighter
___ @ $25.00   NYC Police Officer
___ @ $35.00   NY Allied Health
___ @ $35.00   NY Corrections Officer
___ @ $35.00   NY Firefighter
___ @ $20.00   NY Law Enforcement Career Guide
___ @ $30.00   NY Postal Worker
___ @ $35.00   NY State Police
___ @ $30.00   Suffolk County Police Officer

MASSACHUSETTS EXAMS

___ @ $30.00   MA Allied Health
___ @ $30.00   MA Police Officer
___ @ $30.00   MA State Police Exam

ILLINOIS EXAMS

___ @ $25.00   Chicago Police Officer
___ @ $25.00   Illinois Allied Health

FLORIDA EXAMS

___ @ $32.50   FL Allied Health
___ @ $35.00   FL Corrections Officer
___ @ $20.00   FL Law Enforcement Career Guide
___ @ $35.00   FL Police Officer
___ @ $30.00   FL Postal Worker

REGIONAL EXAMS

___ @ $29.95   AMP Real Estate Sales Exam
___ @ $29.95   ASI Real Estate Sales Exam
___ @ $30.00   Midwest Police Officer Exam
___ @ $30.00   Midwest Firefighter Exam
___ @ $17.95   PPST (Praxis I)
___ @ $29.95   PSI Real Estate Sales Exam
___ @ $25.00   The South Police Officer Exam
___ @ $25.00   The South Firefighter Exam

NATIONAL EDITIONS

___ @ $20.00   Allied Health Entrance Exams
___ @ $14.95   ASVAB (Armed Services Vocational Aptitude Battery): Complete Preparation Guide
___ @ $12.95   ASVAB Core Review
___ @ $17.95   Border Patrol Exam
___ @ $12.95   Bus Operator Exam
___ @ $15.00   Federal Clerical Exam
___ @ $12.95   Postal Worker Exam
___ @ $12.95   Sanitation Worker Exam
___ @ $17.95   Treasury Enforcement Agent Exam

NATIONAL CERTIFICATION & LICENSING EXAMS

___ @ $20.00   Cosmetology Licensing Exam
___ @ $20.00   EMT-Basic Certification Exam
___ @ $20.00   Home Health Aide Certification Exam
___ @ $20.00   Nursing Assistant Certification Exam
___ @ $20.00   Paramedic Licensing Exam

CAREER STARTERS

___ @ $14.95   Administrative Assistant/Secretary
___ @ $14.00   Civil Service
___ @ $14.95   Computer Technician
___ @ $14.95   Cosmetology
___ @ $14.95   EMT
___ @ $14.95   Firefighter
___ @ $14.95   Health Care
___ @ $14.95   Law Enforcement
___ @ $14.95   Paralegal
___ @ $14.95   Real Estate
___ @ $14.95   Retailing
___ @ $14.95   Teacher

To Order, Call TOLL-FREE: 1-888-551-JOBS, Dept. A040

Or, mail this order form with your check or money order* to:

LearningExpress, Dept. A040, 20 Academy Street, Norwalk, CT 06850

Please allow at least 2-4 weeks for delivery. Prices subject to change without notice

*NY, CT, & MD residents add appropriate sales tax

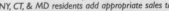

LEARNINGEXPRESS
An Affiliate Company of Random House, Inc.